TEACHINGS OF PRESIDENTS OF THE CHURCH

JOHN TAYLOR

Published by
The Church of Jesus Christ of Latter-day Saints
Salt Lake City, Utah

Your comments and suggestions about this book would be appreciated. Please submit them to Curriculum Planning, 50 East North Temple Street, Floor 24, Salt Lake City, UT 84150-3200 USA.

E-mail: cur-development@ldschurch.org

Please list your name, address, ward, and stake. Be sure to give the title of the book. Then offer your comments and suggestions about the book's strengths and areas of potential improvement.

Printed in the United States of America

English approval: 1/00

Contents

John Taylor was ordained an Apostle in 1838 and sustained as the third President of the Church in 1880.

Introduction

Each chapter in this book includes four sections: (1) an opening quotation that briefly introduces the focus of the chapter; (2) "From the Life of John Taylor," which illustrates the messages of the chapter with a story or counsel from President Taylor; (3) "Teachings of John Taylor," which presents important doctrines from his many messages and sermons; and (4) "Suggestions for Study and Discussion," which encourages personal review and inquiry, further discussion, and application to our lives today through questions.

How to Use This Book

For personal or family study. This book is intended to enhance each member's understanding of gospel principles taught by President John Taylor. Through prayerful reading and thoughtful study, each member may receive a personal witness of these truths. This volume will also add to each member's gospel library and will serve as an important resource for family instruction and for study in the home.

For discussion in Sunday meetings. This book is the text for Melchizedek Priesthood quorum and Relief Society Sunday meetings. Elder Dallin H. Oaks taught that the books in the series *Teachings of Presidents of the Church* "contain doctrine and principles. They are rich and relevant to the needs of our day, and they are superb for teaching and discussion."[1] Teachers should focus on the content of the text and related scriptures and should apply these teachings to circumstances with which class members will be familiar.

Teachers should draw from the questions at the end of the chapter to encourage class discussion. Reviewing the questions before studying President Taylor's words may give additional insight into his teachings.

The Sunday meetings should concentrate on gospel principles, personal examples that teach these principles, and testimonies of the truth. When teachers humbly seek the Spirit in preparing and directing the lesson, all who participate will be strengthened in their knowledge of the truth. Leaders and teachers should encourage class members to read the chapters before they are discussed in Sunday meetings. They should remind class members to bring their books to their meetings and should honor class members' preparation by teaching from President John Taylor's words. When class members have read the chapter in advance, they will be prepared to teach and edify each other.

It is not necessary or recommended that members purchase additional commentaries or reference texts to support the material in the text. Members are encouraged to turn to the scriptures that have been suggested for further study of the doctrine.

Since this text is designed for personal study and gospel reference, many chapters contain more material than can be fully addressed in Sunday meetings. Therefore, study at home becomes essential to more thoroughly benefit from President Taylor's teachings.

Sources Quoted in This Book

The teachings of President Taylor in this book are direct quotations from a variety of sources. Unless editorial changes were necessary to improve readability, the quotations have retained the punctuation, spelling, and capitalization of the original sources. For this reason, readers may notice minor inconsistencies in the text.

Notes

1. In Conference Report, Oct. 1999, 102; or *Ensign,* Nov. 1999, 80.

Historical Summary

This book is not a history, but rather a compilation of gospel principles as taught by President John Taylor. However, in order to put his teachings in a historical framework, the following chronology is provided. This summary omits many important events of his life, including his marriages and the births and deaths of his children, to whom he was devoted.

1808, November 1	Born in Milnthorpe, Westmoreland, England, the second of James and Agnes Taylor's 10 children.
1819	Moves with his family to Hale (near Milnthorpe), where he helps work on a small farm left to his father by an uncle (11; numbers in parentheses show John Taylor's age).
1822	Apprenticed as a cooper (barrel maker) in Liverpool. Within a year his master's business fails and he returns home (14).
1824	Leaves the Church of England and becomes a Methodist. Spends most of his free time studying the Bible, reading theological works, and praying (16).
1825	Becomes a Methodist "exhorter," or lay preacher. Receives a strong impression that he will go to America to preach the gospel (17).
1830	Parents and remainder of family emigrate to Toronto, Canada, leaving him in England to settle family business (21 or 22).

1832	Leaves England for New York City. Commences preaching in Canada (23 or 24).
1833–36	Serves as a preacher in the Methodist Church in Toronto. Continues studying and searching the scriptures (24–27).
1836, spring	Elder Parley P. Pratt arrives in Toronto to preach the restored gospel (27). Elder Pratt had been called to the Quorum of the Twelve Apostles in 1835.
1836, May 9	Baptized by Parley P. Pratt (27).
1836–37	Serves as the Church's presiding officer in Canada (27–28).
1837, March	Goes to Kirtland to meet the Prophet Joseph (28).
1838	Ordained an Apostle at Far West, Missouri, on 19 December, by Brigham Young and Heber C. Kimball, under the direction of Joseph Smith, who was in Liberty Jail (30).
1840	Arrives in Great Britain as a missionary. Is the first missionary to preach the restored gospel in Ireland and on the Isle of Man. Oversees the preparation and printing of the first edition of the Book of Mormon published outside the United States; also assists in preparing a hymnbook and publishes several missionary pamphlets (31).
1841	Returns to the United States with several of the other Apostles (32).
1842	Appointed by Joseph Smith to edit the *Times and Seasons,* a Church publication. Also edits the *Wasp* (1842–43) and then its successor, the *Nauvoo Neighbor* (1843–45), both Nauvoo newspapers.

1842	Chosen to be a member of the Nauvoo City Council, a regent of the University of Nauvoo, and Judge-Advocate in the Nauvoo Legion (33).
1844, June 27	Witnesses the martyrdom of Joseph and Hyrum Smith in Carthage Jail and is seriously wounded during the attack (35).
1846	Helps organize the Mormon Battalion at Council Bluffs. Goes to Great Britain on a second mission with Parley P. Pratt and Orson Hyde (37).
1847	Returns to Winter Quarters from England. Leads a large company of Saints to Utah, arriving in October (38).
1850–51	Serves in France as a missionary. Near Boulogne offers a prayer dedicating the country for the preaching of the gospel. Establishes and edits the first Church periodical in France, *Étoile du Déseret* (Star of Deseret). Helps translate the Book of Mormon into French. Publishes the first Church periodical in Germany, a monthly newspaper named *Zion's Panier* (Zion's Banner). Under his direction the Book of Mormon is first published in German. Writes *The Government of God* (41–42).
1854	Elected as a legislator for the Territory of Utah (45).
1854–56	Serves a mission in New York, where he superintends the affairs of the Church in the eastern states. Publishes a newspaper titled *The Mormon* (46–48).
1857	Returns to Utah. Is elected Speaker of the House of the Utah Territorial Legislature, a

	responsibility he fulfills for several years—in addition to his duties in the Church (49).
1868–70	Serves as Probate Judge of Utah County (59–61).
1877, August 29	Brigham Young dies. For the next three years, John Taylor leads the Church as President of the Quorum of the Twelve (68–71).
1878	Primary organization established (69).
1880, October	Sustained as President of the Church, with George Q. Cannon and Joseph F. Smith as counselors (71).
1882	United States Congress passes the Edmunds bill, making plural marriage a felony and prohibiting polygamists from voting, holding public office, or performing jury duty (73).
1882	Publishes *The Mediation and Atonement* (73).
1884, May	Dedicates the Logan Utah Temple (75).
1885	Receives word during a visit to California that federal officials have ordered his arrest for practicing polygamy. Returns to Salt Lake City on 27 January. On 1 February, preaches his last public sermon and, in hopes of limiting the persecution against the Church by federal authorities, goes into hiding (76).
1887, July 25	At age 78, dies in the Thomas Roueché home in Kaysville, Utah. During his administration, Church membership reached over 150,000.

The Life and Ministry of John Taylor

When Brigham Young died on 29 August 1877, John Taylor was 68 years old. For the next three years, President Taylor led the Church as President of the Quorum of the Twelve Apostles. At a general conference on 10 October 1880, he was sustained as prophet, seer, and revelator, and President of The Church of Jesus Christ of Latter-day Saints, a position he occupied until his death on 25 July 1887. During his time as President and throughout his previous decades of service as an Apostle, John Taylor was always ready to teach and defend the truth. Through one of the most trying periods in Church history, he was a source of great strength and direction for the Saints.

Description of President Taylor

President Taylor was described as being a man of fine appearance, standing about six feet tall and having a heavenly countenance. His hair was snow white, and his complexion was dark. Possessing a noble and dignified manner, "he was not a man whom a friend, however intimate, would slap familiarly on the back or turn and twist about when shaking hands; such proceedings with him would have been as much out of place as with the proudest crowned monarch."[1] Yet there was no haughtiness in his character; he was gracious, polite, and friendly to all. "Whosoever went into his presence, either in private or in public, felt intuitively that he was in the presence of a great man, a man of honor and merit."[2]

Sir Richard Burton, a British author and world traveler who met President Taylor, described him as a "stout, good-looking, somewhat elderly personage, with a kindly gray eye, pleasant expression, and a forehead of the superior order."[3] Another historian wrote, "When I was introduced to him in 1884, Mr. Taylor being then in his seventy-seventh year, there stepped forward . . . a white-haired, benevolent-looking man of medium height and well-knit figure, long, oval face, gray, deep-set, penetrating eye, square, broad forehead, and firmly clasped lips, displaying a fixed determination, slightly tinged with melancholy, such as might be expected from one who had passed through many trying scenes."[4]

His Early Life

Born in 1808 in the Westmoreland region of northwestern England, John Taylor was blessed with humble, kind, and loving parents who taught him to read and believe the Bible, to trust in God, and to have hope in Christ. His parents, James and Agnes Taylor, had him baptized in the Church of England shortly after his birth. His upbringing in the Church of England planted in him a great appreciation for sacred lyrics and music, formal biblical teaching, and private and public prayer. A deep and abiding devotion to and love for God were qualities that John Taylor developed as a child. "At [an] early period of my life I learned to approach God," he told Latter-day Saints after he became President of the Church. "Many a time I have gone into the fields and concealing myself behind some bush, would bow before the Lord and call upon Him to guide and direct me. And He heard my prayer. . . . That was the spirit that I had when a little boy. . . . My spirit was drawn out after God then; and I feel the same yet."[5]

As a small boy he had seen "in vision, an angel in the heavens, holding a trumpet to his mouth, sounding a message to the nations." Though he did not understand the prophetic nature of that vision until later in his life, he continued to feel close to God throughout his teenage years. "Often when alone," he wrote, "and sometimes in company, I heard sweet, soft, melodious music, as if performed by angelic or supernatural beings."[6]

At about 16 years of age he left the Church of England and became a Methodist. The following year he was appointed to be an exhorter, or lay preacher, in that church—a rare responsibility for such a young man. A boldness based on certain conviction characterized his life even then—conviction based on his own experience. During this same period of his life he received a strong impression that God had called him to one day preach the gospel in the United States of America.

His Search for the Kingdom of God

In 1830 John Taylor's parents and other family members emigrated to Toronto, Canada, leaving him behind in England to sell the family farm and settle other family business. When finished, he left England on a ship bound for New York City. During the voyage, the ship encountered a severe storm that had already damaged several ships in the area. The captain and officers of the ship expected that they would sink, but the voice of the Spirit testified to John Taylor, "You must yet go to America and preach the gospel." President Taylor recalled: "So confident was I of my destiny, that I went on deck at midnight, and amidst the raging elements felt as calm as though I was sitting in a parlor at home. I believed I should reach America and perform my work."[7] He arrived safely in New York, and after a few months rejoined his parents in Toronto, where he continued in the Methodist faith and began preaching. During this time, he met Leonora Cannon, herself a devout Methodist who had recently immigrated to Canada from England. Sharing a deep religious conviction and a love for learning, culture, and each other, they married on 28 January 1833 in Toronto.

While in Canada, he joined with a group of friends in a serious effort to study the Bible and increase his understanding of the truth. It was during this time of intense searching that Elder Parley P. Pratt, a member of the Quorum of the Twelve Apostles, was sent on a mission to Toronto.

Upon arriving in Toronto, Elder Pratt petitioned many ministers and city officials for a place to preach. However, his requests were rejected. Even John Taylor, who had heard many rumors about the Church, was at first unreceptive to Elder Pratt. With no apparent hope of success, Elder Pratt decided to leave Toronto and stopped at the Taylor home to say farewell. Feeling impressed that Elder Pratt was a man of God, John Taylor's neighbor offered to feed and house Elder Pratt and allow him to hold meetings. Elder Pratt accepted the offer and was soon introduced to John Taylor's friends who had been meeting together to search for the truth.

John Taylor commenced a thorough investigation of the doctrines of the Church. "I made a regular business of it for three weeks," he said, "and followed Brother Parley from place to place." He wrote down and studied Elder Pratt's sermons and compared them with the scriptures. At length, the Holy Spirit bore witness of the truthfulness of Elder Pratt's message, and John and Leonora Taylor were baptized on 9 May 1836. He later testified that he had "never doubted any principle of Mormonism since."[8]

A Faithful New Member and Leader

Shortly after joining the Church, John Taylor was called to serve as the Church's presiding officer in Canada, a position he held for a little over a year. His duties required a significant amount of travel, but he tirelessly preached the gospel and oversaw many spiritual and temporal matters relating to the Church there. During this time one of his greatest desires was to meet the Prophet Joseph Smith. In March 1837 he traveled to Kirtland, Ohio, where he was received at the home of the Prophet. He described feeling "a charge like an electrical shock" when he took the Prophet by the hand in greeting.[9] At the Smith home, the Prophet taught him many more truths related to the latter-day work. The two men quickly formed a bond of friendship and trust that would never be broken.

While in Kirtland, John Taylor encountered much criticism of the Prophet Joseph Smith. Frequently, outspoken apostates held meetings in which they would criticize the Prophet. Toward the end of one such meeting in the Kirtland Temple, Elder Taylor requested permission to speak, and he fearlessly defended the

Prophet. "It was Joseph Smith, under the Almighty, who developed the first principles," he said, "and to him we must look for further instructions. If the spirit which he manifests does not bring blessings, I am very much afraid that the one manifested by those who have spoken, will not be very likely to secure them. The children of Israel, formerly, after seeing the power of God manifested in their midst, fell into rebellion and idolatry, and there is certainly very great danger of us doing the same thing."[10] While many of the apostates continued their same course, the faithful Saints were strengthened by Elder Taylor's loyalty and conviction.

His Calling and Service as an Apostle

In the fall of 1837, John Taylor received word from Joseph Smith to move to Far West, Missouri, to fill a vacancy in the Quorum of the Twelve Apostles (he was formally ordained in December 1838). Referring to the prospect of serving as an Apostle, John Taylor stated: "The work seemed great, the duties arduous and responsible. I felt my own weakness and littleness; but I felt determined, the Lord being my helper, to endeavor to magnify it."[11] Humility before God and a commitment to seek His guidance would become hallmarks of Elder Taylor's service. After he became President of the Church, he told the Saints: "I have no ideas only as God gives them to me; neither should you. Some people are very persistent in having their own way and carrying out their own peculiar theories. I have no thoughts of that kind, but I have a desire, when anything comes along, to learn the will of God, and then to do it."[12]

A Witness to the Martyrdom

As an Apostle, Elder Taylor was a loyal and trusted associate of the Prophet Joseph Smith. Referring to Elder Taylor's friendship with the Prophet, Elder Franklin D. Richards of the Twelve said, "There were but very few men that attained the warm, personal relation that he attained to and maintained most successfully with the Prophet Joseph Smith till he died, and the story of that personal affection was consummated by the bullets he received in Carthage jail with the Prophet."[13]

One of the most trying events of Elder Taylor's life was the martyrdom of the Prophet Joseph Smith. Elder Taylor voluntarily went to Carthage Jail, where the Prophet and his brother Hyrum were illegally imprisoned on 25 June 1844. It soon became apparent that the Carthage mob had no intention of releasing them and that they were in danger. On 27 June, other Church members who had come to Carthage from Nauvoo went on various errands to help obtain justice. By that afternoon, only Elder Taylor and fellow Apostle Willard Richards remained in the jail with Joseph and Hyrum. With a plan to rally the brethren in Nauvoo to rescue the Prophet Joseph, Elder Taylor said, "Brother Joseph, if you will permit it, and say the word, I will have you out of this prison in five hours, if the jail has to come down to do it."[14] Joseph refused this course of action.

As the afternoon of 27 June wore on, a feeling of great sadness settled upon the four men. Being gifted with a wonderful tenor voice, Elder Taylor was twice asked to sing "A Poor, Wayfaring Man of Grief" to help lift their spirits. Shortly after he finished singing the hymn for the second time, a mob with blackened faces stormed up the stairs of the jail. Hyrum Smith and Willard Richards immediately braced themselves against the door to try to prevent it from opening. As the first shots came through the door, Hyrum was hit and killed. The mob continued firing and quickly began forcing their rifles through the partially open doorway. Using a heavy walking stick, Elder Taylor stood next to the doorway and tried to deflect the rifle barrels that were pointed into the room. "It certainly was a terrible scene," Elder Taylor recorded. "Streams of fire as thick as my arm passed by me as these men fired, and, . . . it looked like certain death. I remember feeling as though my time had come, but I do not know when, in any critical position, I was more calm, unruffled, energetic, and acted with more promptness and decision."[15]

In the midst of this scene, the Prophet Joseph, who had also been trying to fend off the mob, said to Elder Taylor, "That's right, Brother Taylor, parry them off as well as you can."[16] These would be the last words he would hear the Prophet speak on earth.[17] Aware that their position behind the door could not be main-

President Taylor taught that in spite of the martyrdom of the Prophet Joseph, the Church would continue to grow. "This church has the seeds of immortality in its midst. It is not of man, nor by man—it is the offspring of Deity."

tained for long, Elder Taylor sprang to the window. As he was going to leap out, a shot from inside the jail struck him in the left thigh. For a moment he lay helpless on the window sill and would have fallen out, but a shot from outside the jail struck the watch in his breast pocket, sending him back into the room. In this condition, Elder Taylor tried to crawl under a bed in the room. As he did he was shot three more times. One ball entered a little below his left knee, never to be extracted. Another lodged in the palm of his left hand. A third ball struck the fleshy part of his left hip and tore away several inches of flesh. Though badly wounded and in a great deal of pain, Elder Taylor survived the attack and was later taken home to Nauvoo by several of the Saints.

Within moments after Elder Taylor was shot, the Prophet Joseph also attempted to leap from the jail window but was immediately shot and fell to the ground outside. Elder Taylor later recorded that when he learned of the Prophet's fate, he felt "a dull, lonely, sickening sensation."[18]

Doctrine and Covenants section 135 contains an account of the Martyrdom written by Elder Taylor. The section does not provide many details of the event, but it serves as a powerful testimony of the Prophet Joseph: "Joseph Smith, the Prophet and Seer of the Lord, has done more, save Jesus only, for the salvation of men in this world, than any other man that ever lived in it. . . . He lived great, and he died great in the eyes of God and his people; and like most of the Lord's anointed in ancient times, has sealed his mission and his works with his own blood."[19]

Defender of the Faith

As a member of the Quorum of the Twelve, Elder Taylor dedicated his time and talents to proclaiming and defending the gospel. Using his gift for writing, he served as the editor for the *Times and Seasons,* the *Wasp,* and the *Nauvoo Neighbor,* all Nauvoo periodicals. Later, while presiding over the Church in the eastern United States, he edited and published *The Mormon,* a weekly New York–based paper that presented the doctrines of the Church. His book-length writings included two doctrinal expositions, *The Government of God* and *An Examination into and an Elucidation of the Great Principle of the Mediation and Atonement of Our Lord and Savior Jesus Christ* (published while he was President of the Church). Elder Taylor's skill in writing and editing earned him the titles of "Defender of the Faith" and "Champion of Truth" among Church members. President Brigham Young said of Elder Taylor: "I will say that he has one of the strongest intellects of any man that can be found; he is a powerful man, he is a mighty man. . . . He is one of the strongest editors that ever wrote."[20]

In addition to proclaiming the gospel through the written word, Elder Taylor served four full-time missions: two in Great Britain, one in France and Germany, and one in New York. In all, his full-time missionary service totaled over seven years. Although these prolonged absences from his loved ones required great sacrifice, Elder Taylor's conviction of the Lord's work never wavered. In a letter to his family during one of his missions, he wrote: "I am engaged in my Master's business; I am a minister of Jehovah to proclaim His will to the nations. I go to unlock the door of life to a mighty nation, to publish to millions the principles of life, light and truth, intelligence and salvation, to burst their fetters, liberate the oppressed, reclaim the wandering, correct their views, improve their morals, save them from degradation, ruin and misery, and lead them to light, life, truth and celestial glory. Do not your spirits co-operate with mine? I know they do."[21]

Husband and Father

Even with the substantial time commitment required by his Church service, John Taylor was an attentive and loving husband and father. He cherished the time he could spend with his family and frequently took advantage of opportunities to both enjoy their company and to teach them. As a result, he was dearly loved by his family. In later years, his son Moses W. Taylor wrote, "He was held in such high esteem by his children that to please him seemed to be their greatest desire."[22]

In his interaction with his children, John Taylor exemplified warmth, kindness, and good humor. His son Ezra Oakley Taylor recalled the following experience:

"As I was growing up, it was the custom to hold Sunday afternoon meetings in the Tabernacle. All of us were expected to be there, and at a later time be able to report as to who gave the sermon, what it was about, who gave the prayers, and what hymns were sung. This particular Sunday, some of us decided to skip just this once and to get one of our friends to give us the necessary information. Then came the [family] council and sure enough Father asked me about the sermon, and who gave it. All prepared, my friend said he couldn't remember very well, I repeated his words, 'Oh, it was some old windbag, and I can't remember his name, but it was surely uninteresting.' With a twinkle in his eye, Father said, 'That old windbag was your father' and continued with the council meeting."[23]

As an Apostle, and later as President of the Church, President Taylor consistently exhorted the Saints to love and strengthen their families. He encouraged Church members to set aside an evening each week for family gospel study and entertainment, and he promised them "a peace and love, a purity and joy, that would make [their] home life ideal" if they faithfully instituted that practice.[24]

Presiding over the Church

During the years President Taylor led the Church as President of the Quorum of the Twelve and then as President of the Church, he continued to serve with energy and devotion in his efforts to edify the Saints.

Order and Righteousness in the Priesthood

One of his most significant labors as President involved setting in order the quorums of the priesthood and exhorting them to fulfill their duties. He instructed bishops to hold weekly priesthood meetings in their wards and counseled stake presidents to hold monthly stake priesthood meetings. Elder B. H. Roberts recorded, "Who does not remember with what earnestness and power in conferences and other public meetings, he was wont [or accustomed] to admonish Presidents of Stakes and bishops of wards to set in order the priesthood and institutions under their supervision?"[25]

In a revelation given through President Taylor in October 1882, the Lord instructed the Saints, particularly the brethren of the priesthood, to organize themselves and walk in holiness before Him. The following paragraphs are excerpts from that revelation:

"And let the Presidents of Stakes also purify themselves, and the priesthood and people of the Stakes over which they preside, and organize the priesthood in their various Stakes according to my law, in all the various departments thereof, in the High Councils, in the Elders' quorums, and in the Bishops and their councils, and in the quorums of Priests, Teachers and Deacons, that every quorum may be fully organized according to the order of my Church. . . .

"And let my priesthood humble themselves before me, and seek not their own will but my will; for if my priesthood, whom I have chosen, and called, and endowed with the spirit and gifts of their several callings, and with the powers thereof, do not acknowledge me I will not acknowledge them, saith the Lord; for I will be honored and obeyed by my priesthood.

"And, then, I call upon my priesthood, and upon all of my people, to repent of all their sins and short-comings, of their covetousness and pride and self-will, and of all their iniquities wherein they sin against me; and to seek with all humility to fulfill my law, as my priesthood, my saints and my people; and I call upon the heads of families to put their houses in order according to the law of God, and attend to the various duties and responsibilities associated therewith, and to purify themselves before me, and to purge out iniquity from their households. And I will bless and be with you, saith the Lord, and ye shall gather together in your holy places wherein ye assemble to call upon me, and ye shall ask for such things as are right, and I will hear your prayers, and my Spirit and power shall be with you, and my blessing shall rest upon you, upon your families, your dwellings and your households, upon your flocks and herds and fields, your orchards and vineyards, and upon all that pertains to you; and you shall be my people and I will be your God."[26]

Perfecting of the Saints

To increase the Saints' understanding and conviction of the gospel, President Taylor scheduled quarterly stake conferences throughout the Church. Whenever possible, he attended these conferences. If he could not, he sent a member of the Quorum of the Twelve. Referring to this practice, Elder B. H. Roberts of the Seventy recorded: "The Saints received much teaching and instruction from the Apostles, more perhaps than at any previous time in the history of the Church. The result was a great spiritual awakening among the Saints."[27] Another significant event that occurred early in his presidency was the formal organization of the Primary in 1878 for more effective teaching of the children in the Church. President Taylor also continued to emphasize the importance of missionary work, and the number of elders sent to proclaim the gospel increased.

In his many discourses, President Taylor continually exhorted the Saints to tend to their duties in all aspects of their lives, whether as family members, Church members, neighbors, or citizens. He taught the Saints that if they would be obedient and put their trust in the Lord, they would have nothing to fear. He taught that "God will be on the side of Israel, if Israel will only be on the side of right."[28]

Defense of Liberty

No matter how strong President Taylor's convictions were, however, he always respected and spoke up for individual freedoms. In his years as an Apostle in Nauvoo, he had been called the "Champion of Liberty," and as President of the Church he continued to merit this title. At a time when Latter-day Saints formed an overwhelming majority in Utah, President Taylor repeatedly preached freedom of religion and liberty of conscience for all. He stated: "We get up sometimes a very rash feeling against people who do not think as we do. They have a right to think as they please; and so have we. Therefore, if a man does not believe as I do, that is none of my business. And if I do not believe as he does, that is none of his business. Would you protect a man that did not believe as you do? Yes, to the last bat's end. He should have equal justice with me; and then I would expect to be protected in my rights."[29]

To President Taylor, the importance of liberty applied within the Church as well. In councils, he always encouraged members to speak their minds freely. Though he understood fully the importance of unity, he felt that true unity was achieved through freedom.

Times of Trial

Circumstances for the Saints in the United States proved to be a challenge to this love of freedom. Under the direction of the Lord, the Saints had practiced plural marriage in the Church since the days of Joseph Smith in Nauvoo. During the 1860s and 1870s, the United States government passed legislation outlawing plural marriage and denying statehood and other rights to the Utah Territory and its citizens. Convinced that the legislation was a violation of the freedom of religion spoken of in the Constitution, the Church used its influence to have the issue brought before the United States Supreme Court. In 1879, just two years after President Taylor assumed the leadership of the Church, the United States Supreme Court upheld the federal government's anti-polygamy law of 1862. In 1882 and again in 1887, the United States Congress passed additional laws that allowed the federal government to disincorporate the Church as a legal entity and confiscate all Church property in excess of $50,000 (which included four temples in various stages of completion, the Tabernacle, meetinghouses, and many other properties). The legislation was designed to take away basic civil rights of Church members, including the right to vote. These developments opened legal channels for the prosecution of Latter-day Saints who were practicing plural marriage. The Church continued to make legal appeals, but to no avail.

Amid the growing strife over the issue of polygamy, President Taylor was informed that government officials planned to arrest him soon. Having exhausted all legal appeals, he had to decide whether to obey God or man. In his last public discourse, he told the Saints, "I cannot as an honorable man disobey my God . . . and trample these holy and eternal obligations under foot, that God has given me to keep, and which reach into the eternities that are to come."[30] From the day he delivered this sermon until the day of his death almost two and a half years later, he hid in various locations throughout Utah. Rather than turn away from the Lord's instructions regarding plural marriage, President Taylor chose to go into hiding as a way to obey the Lord and hopefully decrease the persecution against the Church. Elder B. H. Roberts recorded, "When President Taylor retired from public view on the evening of the 1st of February, 1885, it was not out of any consideration for his personal safety, or ease or comfort, but for the public good and in the interests of peace."[31]

Though absent from public view, President Taylor continued to provide leadership to the Church through letters and verbal instructions to trusted associates. However, the confinement, the separation from family and friends, and the stress of his responsibilities began to take their toll. Early in 1887, his health began to fail. For several months he resisted his illness and told others that he would soon recover, but by July it became apparent that his condition was serious. On the evening of 25 July 1887, President Taylor passed away peacefully at the home of Thomas Roueché in Kaysville, Utah.

Tributes to President Taylor

Some of the most apt descriptions of John Taylor's ministry were given by those who had served with and been taught by him. Speaking at President Taylor's funeral, Elder Franklin D. Richards of the Quorum of the Twelve stated: "President Taylor was a man bold and daring for the truth. He knew no fear. . . . When he and I were on our missions in Europe together, he labored in France. . . . He labored in that vicinity diligently; and at one time a number of religious divines [or clergymen] combined together to put down this heresy, as they term it. President Taylor, with that boldness which ever characterized him, consented to meet a whole pack of them. . . . He withstood them and he brought forth the truth."[32]

Elder Daniel H. Wells, who served as a counselor to Brigham Young, spoke of President Taylor as follows: "He lived a fearless, noble and God-like life—let those who still live seek to emulate his noble example. . . . He has been the champion of human rights, the champion of liberty, truth and freedom. He has lived a noble, useful life, full of honor and credit to himself and family, a satisfaction to the people and a glory to God. I take pleasure in bearing this testimony to the faithfulness and devotion of President Taylor, to his integrity to God and the love of his people."[33]

Angus M. Cannon, president of the Salt Lake Stake, was the last speaker at President Taylor's funeral and gave the following tribute to the man who had spent so many years working to establish the kingdom of God: "He has been relieved from his pains. He sleeps in God; and I can imagine seeing the portal of heaven open through which he has entered. . . . Brother Taylor took the testimony that Joseph gave him, that Jesus delivered unto Joseph, that God bade Joseph to listen to from the lips of his beloved Son—and he bore those tidings to foreign lands, and made our hearts tingle with the words which he there enunciated. I say the joy and rejoicing with which President Taylor has met with his co-laborers beyond the veil, surrounded with apostles of Jesus Christ, is great."[34]

Notes

1. B. H. Roberts, *The Life of John Taylor* (1963), 419–20.
2. In Andrew Jenson, *Latter-day Saint Biographical Encyclopedia,* 4 vols. (1901–36), 1:18–19.
3. In Hubert Howe Bancroft, *History of Utah* (1890), 682.
4. *History of Utah,* 682.
5. *Deseret News: Semi-Weekly,* 3 Jan. 1882, 1.
6. *The Life of John Taylor,* 27–28.
7. *The Life of John Taylor,* 28–29.
8. *The Life of John Taylor,* 38.
9. In Susan Arrington Madsen, *The Lord Needed a Prophet* (1996), 49.
10. *The Life of John Taylor,* 40–41.
11. *The Life of John Taylor,* 48.
12. *The Gospel Kingdom,* sel. G. Homer Durham (1941), 44.
13. *The Life of John Taylor,* 449.
14. *The Life of John Taylor,* 134–35.
15. *The Gospel Kingdom,* 360.
16. *The Gospel Kingdom,* 360.
17. See *The Gospel Kingdom,* 360.
18. *The Life of John Taylor,* 140.
19. D&C 135:3.
20. *Deseret News* (Weekly), 17 Sept. 1856, 219.
21. *The Life of John Taylor,* 208.
22. "Stories and Counsel of Prest. Taylor," *Young Woman's Journal,* May 1905, 219.
23. Julia Neville Taylor, "An Interview with Ezra Oakley Taylor, Son of President John Taylor," (The Family and Church History Department Archives of The Church of Jesus Christ of Latter-day Saints, n.d.), microfilm, 2.
24. Joseph F. Merrill, "Home Evening," *Improvement Era,* Jan. 1918, 203.
25. *The Life of John Taylor,* 347.
26. *The Life of John Taylor,* 350–51; paragraphing altered.
27. *The Life of John Taylor,* 329.
28. *Deseret News: Semi-Weekly,* 19 Sept. 1882, 1.
29. *The Gospel Kingdom,* 328–29.
30. *Deseret News: Semi-Weekly,* 17 Feb. 1885, 1.
31. *The Life of John Taylor,* 400.
32. *The Life of John Taylor,* 448.
33. *The Life of John Taylor,* 455.
34. *The Life of John Taylor,* 459–60; paragraphing altered.

"When the saint of God . . . contemplates his true position before God, angels, and men, then he soars above the things of time and sense and bursts the cords that bind him to earthly objects."

CHAPTER 1

The Origin and Destiny of Mankind

We are the offspring of God, and God in these last days has seen fit to place us in communication with himself. He has, through the revelations of himself and of his Son Jesus Christ, by the ministry of holy angels and by the restoration of the holy priesthood which emanates from God, and by which he himself is governed, placed us in a position whereby we can fulfil the object of our creation.[1]

From the Life of John Taylor

In an address he gave as President of the Quorum of the Twelve, President Taylor recalled the spiritual yearnings he felt as a child to understand life's purpose and his relationship to God. He said: "When a little boy I used to ask myself, Who am I? Where did I come from? What am I doing here? And why am I here? These things still puzzle us, at least many of them do, yet these are thoughts we cannot help reflecting upon. We see children born into the world, and we see spring and summer, autumn and winter follow each other in regular succession, and we ask ourselves, By what power were these things brought about? Why are we here and what is the object of all these things which we see around us?"[2]

President Taylor's teachings reflect the joy he found in the doctrines of the gospel that helped him understand his divine origin and destiny as a child of God. He declared that "when the saint of God considers, and the visions of eternity are open to his view and the unalterable purposes of God are developed to his mind—when he contemplates his true position before God, angels, and men, then he soars above the things of time and sense and bursts the cords that bind him to earthly objects. He contemplates God and his own destiny in the economy of heaven and rejoices in a blooming hope of an immortal glory."[3]

Teachings of John Taylor

We are children of our Heavenly Father and have the potential to become like Him.

"What is man, that thou art mindful of him? and the son of man, that thou visitest him?" (Psalm 8:4.)

In one point of view, man appears very poor, weak, and imbecile, and very insignificant: in another point of view, he appears wise, intelligent, strong, honorable, and exalted. It is just in the way that you look at a man that you are led to form your opinions concerning him. In one respect, he appears, as it were, as the grass of the field, which today is, and tomorrow is cast into the oven. He is changeable in his opinions, in his thoughts, reflections, and actions. He is idle, vain, and visionary, without being governed by any correct principle. He comes into existence, as it were, like a butterfly, flutters around for a little while, dies, and is no more.

In another point of view, we look at him as emanating from the Gods—as a God in embryo—as an eternal being who had an existence before he came here, and who will exist after his mortal remains are mingled and associated with dust, from whence he came, and from whence he will be resurrected and partake of that happiness for which he is destined, or receive the reward of his evil deeds, according to circumstances. . . .

. . . What is [man]? He had his being in the eternal worlds; he existed before he came here. He is not only the son of man, but he is the son of God also. He is a God in embryo, and possesses within him a spark of that eternal flame which was struck from the blaze of God's eternal fire in the eternal world, and is placed here upon the earth that he may possess true intelligence, true light, true knowledge,—that he may know himself—that he may know God—that he may know something about what he was

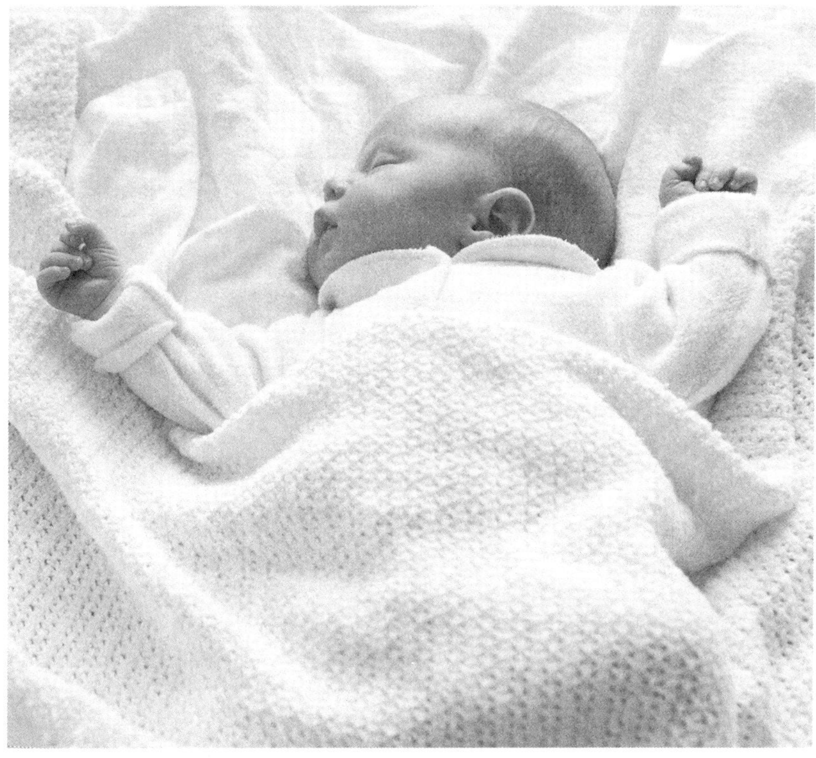

As children of God, we "did not originate from a chaotic mass of matter, moving or inert, but came forth possessing, in an embryonic state, all the faculties and powers of a God."

before he came here—that he may know something about what he is destined to enjoy in the eternal worlds.[4]

If we take man, he is said to have been made in the image of God, for the simple reason that he is a son of God, and being his son, he is, of course, his offspring, an emanation from God, in whose likeness, we are told, he is made. He did not originate from a chaotic mass of matter, moving or inert, but came forth possessing, in an embryonic state, all the faculties and powers of a God. And when he shall be perfected, and have progressed to maturity, he will be like his Father—a God, being indeed His offspring. As the horse, the ox, the sheep, and every living creature, including man, propagates its own species and perpetuates its own kind, so does God perpetuate his.[5]

[Man] stands erect on the earth in the likeness of his great Creator; beautifully constructed in all his parts, with a body possessing all the functions necessary for the wants of humanity; standing, not only by right, but by adaptability, beauty, symmetry and glory, at the head of all creation; possessing also mental powers and the capacity of reflecting upon the past, with capabilities to reason upon cause and effect, and by the inductive powers of his mind, through the inspiration of the Almighty, to comprehend the magnificent laws of nature as exhibited in the works of creation; with the capacity also of using the elements and forces of nature, and of adapting them to his own special benefit; and by his powers penetrating into the deep, ascending into the heavens, rushing with mighty velocity across the earth, making use of the separate or combined forces of nature with which he is surrounded and subjugating them to his will; as, likewise, by his intelligence, he has dominion over the fishes of the sea, over the fowls of the air, and over the cattle.[6]

We need Jesus Christ in order to reach our divine potential.

[Man] stands proudly erect as the head of all creation and the representative of God upon the earth. But while he occupies this exalted position, and is in the image of God, yet he possesses simply, as a man, only the powers which belong to man; and is subject to weakness, infirmity, disease and death. And when he dies, without some superior aid pertaining to the future, that noble structure lies silent and helpless, its organs, that heretofore were active, lively and energetic, are now dormant, inactive and powerless. And what of the mind, that before went back into eternity and reached forward into eternity? And what of its powers? Or what of that spirit, which, with its Godlike energies, its prescience [or foreknowledge] and power, could grasp infinity? What of it, and where is it? . . .

If . . . there is a spirit in man which reaches into futurity, that would grasp eternal progress, eternal enjoyments, and eternal exaltations; then those glories, those exaltations, those capabilities and those powers must be the gift of some superior being, power, or authority to that which exists in man. . . . It is of this gift that we now speak. It is of a principle that emanates from God, that originates with a superior intelligence, whose plans, and powers, and capabilities are exalted above those of mortal man, as the heavens are above the earth, or as the majestic works of the Great Creator throughout the infinitude of space are superior to the puny efforts of the children of mortality.

It is for the exaltation of man to this state of superior intelligence and Godhead that the mediation and atonement of Jesus Christ is instituted; and that noble being, man, made in the image of God, is rendered capable not only of being a son of man, but also a son of God, . . . and is rendered capable of becoming a God, possessing the power, the majesty, the exaltation and the position of a God. As it is written, "Beloved, now are we the sons of God, and it doth not yet appear what we shall be: but we know that, when he shall appear, we shall be like him; for we shall see him as he is." [1 John 3:2.]

As a man through the powers of his body he could attain to the dignity and completeness of manhood, but could go no further; as a man he is born, as a man he lives, and as a man he dies; but through the essence and power of the Godhead, which is in him, which descended to him as the gift of God from his heavenly Father, he is capable of rising from the contracted limits of manhood to the dignity of a God, and thus through the atonement of Jesus Christ . . . he is capable of eternal exaltation, eternal lives and eternal progression. But this transition from his manhood to the Godhead can alone be made through a power which is superior to man—an infinite power, an eternal power, even the power of the Godhead: for as in Adam all die, so in Christ *only* can all be made alive [see 1 Corinthians 15:22].

Through [Christ] mankind are brought into communion and communication with God; through His atonement they are enabled, as He was, to vanquish death; through that atonement and the power of the Priesthood associated therewith, they become heirs of God and joint heirs with Jesus Christ, and inheritors of thrones, powers, principalities and dominions in the eternal worlds. And instead of being subject to death, when that last enemy shall be destroyed, and death be swallowed up in victory, through that atonement they can become the fathers and mothers of lives, and be capable of perpetual and eternal progression.[7]

The Church of Jesus Christ helps us realize our divine potential.

God has ordained among you presidents, apostles, prophets, high priests, seventies, bishops and other authorities; they are of his appointment, empowered and directed by him, under his influence, teaching his law, unfolding the principles of life, and are organized and ordained expressly to lead the people in the path of exaltation and eternal glory.[8]

We were as much in the dark as other people were about the principles of salvation, and the relationship we hold to God and each other, until these things were made known to us by Joseph Smith.[9]

We are the offspring of God, and God in these last days has seen fit to place us in communication with himself. He has, through the revelations of himself and of his Son Jesus Christ, by the ministry of holy angels and by the restoration of the holy priesthood which emanates from God, and by which he himself is governed, placed us in a position whereby we can fulfill the object of our creation.[10]

We want to realize and appreciate the position we occupy before God and the great blessings and privileges that are within our reach. We have just commenced, as it were, in the great work. . . . We do not always comprehend these things, and hence we labor under difficulties pertaining to this matter, because we do not see, we do not comprehend the position and relationship that subsists between us and our God.

God is our Father; we are his children. He has brought us into his covenant, and it is our privilege to go on from wisdom to wisdom, from intelligence to intelligence, from understanding of one principle to that of another, to go forward and progress in the development of truth until we can comprehend God. For we are his children, we are his sons and daughters, and he is our father. He has organized this Church in order that we may be educated in the principles of life, that we may comprehend those principles that exist in the bosom of God, that we may be able to teach our children correct principles, in order that we may be placed in a position whereby we can be assimilated in the likeness of our heavenly Father.[11]

We should "contend earnestly" to fulfill our divine potential.

The Lord has revealed to us many blessings, and I sometimes think that we hardly appreciate the light of truth which has been developed, the glory that is connected with the gospel which has been restored, the light of revelation which has been communicated, the position that we occupy in relation to God, angels, our posterity and our progenitors; the hope that the gospel has implanted in the bosom of every faithful Latter-day Saint, which blooms with immortality and eternal life. . . .

We sometimes forget our prayers, responsibilities, duties and covenants, and we give way in many instances to things which have a tendency to darken the mind, becloud the understanding, weaken our faith and deprive us of the Spirit of God. We forget the pit whence we were dug, and the rock from which we were hewn, and it is necessary that we should reflect on the position that we occupy, upon the relationship we sustain to God, to each other and to our families, that our minds may be drawn back again to the God who made us—our Father in the heavens, who hears our prayers, and who is ready at all times to supply the wants of his faithful Saints. And it is sometimes necessary that we should reflect upon the position we hold in relation to the earth on which we live, to the existence that we had before we came here and to the eternities to come.

We should not be sluggish and dull and careless and indifferent; but as the ancient Saints were exhorted, so let us exhort you to-day—contend earnestly for the faith once delivered to the Saints [see Jude 1:3]. . . .

. . . We, as eternal beings, associated with an eternal God, having a religion that leads to that God, are desirous, as the ancients were, to know something about him, to be brought into communication with him, to fulfil the measure of our creation and our destiny on the earth, and to help the Lord to bring to pass those things that he designed from before the foundation of the world, in regard to the human family. . . . The Almighty has never altered his purpose, never changed his designs nor abrogated his laws. . . . His course is one eternal round. He has had one object in view, and that object will be accomplished in regard to man and the earth whereon he lives.

The only question with us is whether we will cooperate with God, or whether we will individually work out our own salvation or not; whether we will individually fulfil the various responsibilities that devolve upon us or not; whether we will attend to the ordinances that God has introduced or not; for ourselves to begin with, for our families, for the living and for the dead. Whether we will cooperate in building temples and administering in them; whether we will unite with the Almighty, under the direction of his holy priesthood, in bringing to pass things that have been spoken of by the holy prophets since the world was; whether we will contend earnestly for the faith once delivered to the Saints. These things rest with us to a certain extent. . . .

. . . He desires that his people shall contend earnestly for the faith once delivered to the Saints, that as immortal beings they may act in unison with the Almighty, that they may be inspired by the principle of revelation; that they should comprehend something of their dignity and manhood; of their relationship to eternity, to the world that we live in as it is and as it will be, and to the worlds that are to come. . . .

The spirit of man, possessing a body, will, through the medium of the everlasting gospel, be exalted; and that man, inasmuch as he is faithful, will, by and by, be associated with the Gods in the eternal worlds; and while we plant and sow and reap, and pursue the common avocations of life, as other men do, our main object is eternal lives and exaltations; our main object is to prepare ourselves, our posterity and our progenitors for thrones, principalities and powers in the eternal worlds.

This is what we are after, and what the ancient Saints were after. This is what Adam, Noah, Enoch, Abraham and the prophets were after, that they might fulfil their destiny on the earth, and, as one of the old prophets said, "stand in their lot in the end of days," [see Daniel 12:13] when the books should be opened, when the great white throne should appear and he who sits upon it, before whose face the heavens and the earth fled away; that we and they, and they and we might be prepared, having fulfilled the measure of our creation on the earth, to associate with the intelligences that exist in the eternal worlds; be admitted again to the presence of our Father, whence we came, and participate in those eternal realities which mankind, without revelation, know nothing about. We are here for that purpose; . . . we are building temples for that purpose; we are receiving endowments for that purpose; we are making covenants for that purpose; we are administering for the living and the dead for that purpose, and all our objects, and all our aims, like the object and aim of inspired men in former days, are altogether with reference to eternal realities as well as to time. . . .

This is what we are after, and we shall accomplish it, and no man can stop it, no organization, no power, no authority, for God is at the helm, and his kingdom is onward, onward, onward, and it will continue, and grow and increase until the kingdoms of this world shall become the kingdoms of our God and his Christ.[12]

Suggestions for Study and Discussion

- How does it help you to know that you are a child of God? How does this knowledge influence your feelings about your own potential? In what ways does this knowledge influence your prayers?
- How does the truth that all people are sons and daughters of God affect your view of others? How should this knowledge affect our relationships within our families?

- Why is it necessary that we live in a mortal state? (See also 2 Nephi 2:11–13, 24–27; Moses 5:9–11.) What role does Jesus Christ play in helping us fulfill our divine potential?
- How have the doctrines of the Church helped you understand your origin and destiny? In what ways does the Church help us fulfill our eternal destiny?
- What does it mean to you to "contend earnestly" to fulfill your divine potential? What examples have you seen of people who do this? How can we "cooperate with God" to achieve this goal?
- President Taylor taught that "our main object is to prepare ourselves, our posterity and our progenitors for thrones, principalities and powers in the eternal worlds." How can we remain focused on this objective as we pass through mortality?

Related Scriptures: Genesis 1:26; Psalm 82:6–7; Romans 8:16–17; D&C 76:22–24, 50–70

Notes

1. *The Gospel Kingdom,* sel. G. Homer Durham (1943), 70–71.
2. *Deseret News: Semi-Weekly,* 24 June 1879, 1.
3. *The Gospel Kingdom,* 63.
4. *The Gospel Kingdom,* 52–54; paragraphing altered.
5. *The Gospel Kingdom,* 52.
6. *The Gospel Kingdom,* 56–57.
7. *The Mediation and Atonement* (1882), 139–41; paragraphing altered.
8. *Deseret News* (Weekly), 8 May 1872, 186.
9. *The Gospel Kingdom,* 33.
10. *The Gospel Kingdom,* 70–71.
11. *Deseret News: Semi-Weekly,* 1 June 1880, 1; paragraphing altered.
12. *Deseret News* (Weekly), 8 May 1872, 186; paragraphing altered.

CHAPTER 2

The Everlasting Gospel

The everlasting gospel . . . was not known till the Lord revealed it from the heavens by the voice of his angel, and when we receive these principles and they abide in us, we shall then have the principles of eternal life.[1]

From the Life of John Taylor

During 1836 in Toronto, Canada, John Taylor and a number of other individuals met several times a week to study the Bible and seek to understand the truth. They believed strongly in the gathering of Israel, the gifts of the Spirit, the Savior's millennial reign, the need for apostles and prophets, and the importance of performing ordinances by proper authority from God. However, at that time they did not know of any church that taught these things. Concerning their search for the truth, John Taylor said, "We prayed to the Lord and fasted and prayed that God would teach us true principles, that He would restore the pure, ancient Gospel, and that if there was a true church upon the earth he would send unto us a messenger."

Their prayers were soon answered with the arrival of Elder Parley P. Pratt. Before Elder Pratt departed on his mission, Elder Heber C. Kimball had prophesied to him, "It is the will of the Lord that you should go to Canada, there is a people there who are diligently seeking after the truth, and many of them will believe your words, and receive the Gospel."

Elder Pratt began preaching in Toronto, and after a time was introduced to John Taylor and those who were studying with him. President Taylor later wrote: "We felt overjoyed at his preaching; but when he delivered his testimony concerning Joseph Smith and the Book of Mormon we knew not what to say.

President Taylor taught that the gospel preached by Noah and all the other ancient prophets is the "same . . . that is now being preached to all the world for a witness."

I wrote down eight of the first sermons that he preached and compared them with the scriptures. I also investigated the evidence concerning the Book of Mormon and read the Doctrine and Covenants. I made a regular business of it for three weeks and followed [Brother] Parley from place to place."[2]

John Taylor was soon convinced that the everlasting gospel had been restored. He was baptized 9 May 1836. As a missionary, as an Apostle, and eventually as the President of the Church, he rejoiced in teaching the eternal, unchanging truths of the gospel.

Teachings of John Taylor

The gospel helps us understand the attributes of God and prepares us to receive exaltation.

We, as Latter-day Saints, believe, first, in the gospel, and that is a great deal to say, for the gospel embraces principles that dive deeper, spread wider, and extend further than anything else that we can conceive. The gospel teaches us in regard to the being and attributes of God. It also teaches us our relationship to that God and the various responsibilities we are under to him as his offspring. It teaches us the various duties and responsibilities that we are under to our families and friends, to the community, to the living and the dead. It unfolds to us principles pertaining to futurity. In fact, according to the saying of one of the old disciples, it "brings life and immortality to light," [see 2 Timothy 1:10] brings us into relationship with God, and prepares us for an exaltation in the eternal world.[3]

This Gospel places man in communication with God, his Heavenly Father; this Gospel brings life and immortality to light; this Gospel is proclaimed in the interest of all men in all parts of the earth. . . . It is a message of salvation to the nations of the earth. . . . God feels interested in the welfare of the whole human family, and for this purpose He has established principles upon the earth which exist in the heavens—a Gospel that has prevailed among the Gods in the eternal worlds, containing principles which are calculated to elevate, ennoble and exalt the human family.[4]

The gospel is eternal and unchangeable.

The great principles of truth are so varied and comprehensive. . . . They reach back into the past, exist in the present, and stretch forward into the future. In the gospel of Jesus Christ is embodied all truth, so far as the salvation of the human family is concerned, and hence it is spoken of in the scriptures as being the everlasting gospel. . . .

. . . God, like his Son Jesus Christ, is "the same yesterday, to-day, and forever." [1 Nephi 10:18.] The same in intelligence, the same in purity, the same in his projects, plans and designs; he is in short, unchangeable. And I apprehend if the Saints who had communication with him in ancient days were to appear on this earth at the present time, they would find the same medium of communication, the same way of imparting intelligence, and the same unchangeable being that existed 1,800, 4,000, or 6,000 years ago.

It is true mankind have not at all times been susceptible of receiving and appreciating the same degree of light, truth, and intelligence that they have at other times. God has in certain instances withdrawn the light of his countenance—his Holy Spirit—the light and intelligence that proceeds from him—in a certain degree from the human family; but his laws are immutable and he is the same eternal, unchangeable being.

The truth does not change. What was true 1,800, 4,000, or 6,000 years ago is true today, and what was false in any age of the world is false today. Truth, like the great Eloheim, is eternal and unchangeable, and it is for us to learn its principles, to know how to appreciate it, and govern ourselves accordingly.

As the gospel is a principle that emanates from God, like its author it is "the same yesterday, to-day, and for ever,"—eternal and unchangeable. God ordained it before the morning stars sung together for joy, or ere this world rolled into existence, for the salvation of the human race. It has been in the mind of God, and as often as developed it has been manifested as an eternal, unchangeable, undeviating plan by which to save, bless, exalt and dignify man.[5]

This same Gospel was preached to Seth, and to all the antediluvian [or before the Flood] Patriarchs, and they ministered under its authority. By its power, as we have already shown. Enoch and his people were translated. Of Noah it is written: "And the Lord ordained Noah after his own order, and commanded him that he should go forth and declare his gospel unto the children of men, even as it was given unto Enoch." [Moses 8:19.] And further, to quote from the testimony of Noah before the flood: "And it came to pass that Noah continued his preaching unto the people, saying, Hearken, and give heed unto my words; believe and repent of your sins, and be baptized in the name of Jesus Christ, the Son of God, even as our fathers did, and ye shall receive the Holy Ghost, that ye may have all things made manifest; and if ye do not this, the floods will come in upon you." [See Moses 8:23–24.]

From this we learn that the principles of the Gospel in the first ages of the world were identical with those taught in our day.

The Gospel and the Holy Priesthood continued from Noah to Abraham. "Abraham received the priesthood from Melchizedek, who received it through the lineage of his fathers, even till Noah." [D&C 84:14.] . . . The knowledge and practice of the Gospel were perpetuated through Isaac, Jacob, Joseph and other Patriarchs, until the age of Moses. . . .

It was this same Gospel that the crucified Redeemer commanded His disciples to preach, when "he said unto them, Go ye into all the world, and preach the gospel to every creature. He that believeth and is baptized shall be saved; but he that believeth not shall be damned. And these signs shall follow them that believe; In my name shall they cast out devils; they shall speak with new tongues; they shall take up serpents; and if they drink any deadly thing, it shall not hurt them: they shall lay hands on the sick, and they shall recover." [Mark 16:15–18.] . . .

Hence we find on the day of Pentecost, Peter, the senior of the Apostles, in answer to the cry of the believing multitude, "Men and brethren, what shall we do?" replying in the words already quoted: "Repent and be baptized, every one of you, in the name of Jesus Christ, for the remission of sins; and ye shall receive the gift of the Holy Ghost. For the promise is unto you and your children, and to all that are afar off, even as many as the Lord our God shall call." [See Acts 2:37–39.]

Again, it was this same everlasting, unalterable, unchangeable Gospel whose restoration to the earth John, the Apostle, spoke of as follows:

"And I saw another angel fly in the midst of heaven, having the everlasting gospel to preach unto them that dwell on the earth, and to every nation, and kindred, and tongue, and people, saying with a loud voice, Fear God, and give glory to him; for the hour of his judgment is come: and worship him that made heaven, and earth, and the sea, and the fountains of waters." [Revelation 14:6–7.]

From the Bible, we turn to the Book of Mormon, and in its pages discover that the same Gospel which Jesus directed His disciples to go into all the world and preach, was preached on this continent, from the earliest ages. The Jaredites became acquainted with it through the revelations given to the brother of Jared; in one of which Jesus said unto him:

"Behold, I am he who was prepared from the foundation of the world to redeem my people. Behold, I am Jesus Christ. I am the Father and the Son. In me shall all mankind have life, and that eternally, even they who shall believe on my name; and they shall become my sons and my daughters." [Ether 3:14.] . . .

When Jesus Himself appeared to the Nephites, He preached the same identical principles that He had previously taught to the Jews, adding occasionally further truths, because of the greater faith of the first named people; "And he did expound all things, even from the beginning even until the time he should come in his glory." [See 3 Nephi 26:3.] Amongst other things He said: "Whosoever will hearken unto my words and repenteth and is baptized, the same shall be saved. Search the prophets, for many there be that testify of these things." [3 Nephi 23:5.]

And it is this same Gospel, attended by the same power and spirit, blessed by the same inspiration, and led by the same Priesthood, that is now being preached to all the world for a witness.[6]

The gospel leads us on a course of happiness, growth, and freedom.

The principles of the gospel, to the unbeliever, have neither worth nor efficacy. But with us, who believe them, they comprehend everything pertaining to the well-being of man in time and eternity. With us the gospel is the alpha and omega, the beginning and the end. It is interwoven with all our interests, happiness, and enjoyment, whether in this life or that which is to come.

We consider that, when we enter into this church and embrace the new and everlasting covenant, it is a lifelong service and affects us in all the relationships of time and eternity. And as we progress, these ideas which, at first, were a little dim and obscure, become more vivid, real, life-like, tangible and clear to our comprehensions, and we realize that we stand upon the earth as the sons and daughters of God, the representatives of heaven. We feel that God has revealed to us an everlasting gospel, and that associated with that are everlasting covenants and relationships.

The gospel, in the incipient stages of its operations, begins, as the prophet said it should, to "turn the hearts of the fathers to the children and the hearts of the children to the fathers." [See Malachi 4:6.] We no longer have to ask, as in former times, "Who am I?" "Where did I come from?" "What am I doing here?" or "What is the object of my existence?" for we have a certainty in relation to these things. It is made plain to us by the fruits of the gospel. . . . It is the knowledge of these things and of many more of a similar nature that leads us to pursue the course that we do. It is this which prevents us from bowing to the notions, caprices, ideas and follies of men.

Having been enlightened by the spirit of eternal truth, having partaken of the Holy Ghost, and our hope having entered within the veil, whither Christ, our forerunner, has gone, and knowing that we are the children of God and that we are acting in all things with reference to eternity, we pursue the even tenor of our way independent of the smiles and careless of the frowns of men.[7]

God has committed to us the gospel and the high priesthood, which is not intended, as some suppose, to bring men into bondage or to tyrannize over the consciences of men, but to make all men free as God is free; that they may drink of the streams "whereof shall make glad the city of God;" [Psalm 46:4] that they may be elevated and not debased; that they may be purified and not corrupted; that they may learn the laws of life and walk in them, and not walk in the ways of corruption and go down to death.[8]

By means of the gospel of Jesus Christ we are brought into a relationship with God. As one of the ancient apostles says: "Beloved, now are we the sons of God, and it doth not yet appear what we shall be; but we know that when he shall appear we will be like him; for we shall see him as he is." [See 1 John 3:2.] God is our Father, and a medium of communication has been opened between God and us; and inasmuch as we live our religion we shall be prepared at all times to receive blessings at his hands, and learn to understand correct principles in regard to our salvation as individuals, and the salvation of the human family.[9]

We have received the everlasting gospel, the same that existed in the days of Jesus; and it is this that has enlightened our minds, enlarged our capacities, and given us a knowledge of the past and of the future, and it has thus revealed to us the purposes of God, and through the order, and organization of this priesthood we are blessed, saved, protected, and upheld as we are at this day.[10]

Suggestions for Study and Discussion

- How did President Taylor describe the gospel? In what ways would your life be different if you had no knowledge of the gospel? What experiences have you had that show how gospel principles "elevate, ennoble and exalt the human family"?
- How does the gospel help us understand the attributes of God and our relationship to Him? Why is this knowledge necessary for our salvation? (See also John 17:3.)
- How can it help you to know that the gospel is eternal and unchangeable? How does this knowledge influence your beliefs and the decisions you make?

- President Taylor taught that the gospel is intended to "make all men free." From what does the gospel free us? What does it free us to do? How can we help others understand that the gospel brings freedom rather than restrictions?
- What have you done to receive a testimony of the gospel? What experiences have strengthened your testimony? What can we do to help ensure that the principles of the gospel continue to "abide in us"?
- How does the gospel bring us "into a relationship with God"?

Related Scriptures: John 8:31–32; 2 Timothy 1:8–10; 1 Nephi 10:18–19; 3 Nephi 27:13–22; Articles of Faith 1:4

Notes

1. *The Gospel Kingdom,* sel. G. Homer Durham (1943), 84.
2. "History of John Taylor: By Himself," Histories of the Twelve, The Family and Church History Department Archives of The Church of Jesus Christ of Latter-day Saints, 9–10.
3. *The Gospel Kingdom,* 93–94.
4. *Deseret News: Semi-Weekly,* 20 Dec. 1881, 1.
5. *Deseret News* (Weekly), 8 Feb. 1860, 385.
6. *The Mediation and Atonement* (1882), 183, 185–86, 188.
7. *The Gospel Kingdom,* 85–86; paragraphing altered.
8. *The Gospel Kingdom,* 123.
9. *Deseret News* (Weekly), 8 Feb. 1860, 386.
10. *Deseret News* (Weekly), 8 Feb. 1860, 386.

Through His teachings and His actions, the Savior gave us the perfect example of how to love one another.

CHAPTER 3

"Love Thy Neighbour as Thyself"

We ought always to live with reference to eternity, feeling full of kindness, benevolence, charity and long suffering to all.[1]

From the Life of John Taylor

President John Taylor frequently taught the Saints the importance of not only believing, but also practicing the Savior's plea to love our neighbor. "Love one another," he encouraged, "and work the works of righteousness, and look after the welfare of all, and seek to promote the happiness of all. That is what God is doing."[2] He believed strongly in the role of the Spirit in nurturing our love for others. "When you get the Spirit of God," he taught, "you feel full of kindness, charity, long-suffering, and you are willing all the day long to accord to every man that which you want yourself. You feel disposed all the day long to do unto all men as you would wish them to do unto you."[3]

From his baptism in 1836 to his death in 1887, John Taylor witnessed a great deal of persecution and unjust treatment toward the Saints. He saw mobs drive Church members from their homes; he was an eyewitness to the martyrdom of Joseph and Hyrum Smith (and was himself grievously wounded in the attack); and he was with the Saints in Utah when they continued to be persecuted. Nevertheless, he consistently exhorted Church members to love all people. In an address he gave in Utah while he was President of the Quorum of the Twelve, he said:

"David prayed that God would send his enemies to hell quickly [see Psalm 55:15]. Jesus, when he was being crucified, suffering the pain of a cruel death, said, 'Father, forgive them; for they know not what they do.' [Luke 23:34.] I like that prayer much better than the other one. . . . This is the feeling we ought to have. We ought to have it one towards another and treat one another with kindness and not get up hard feelings. . . . I hear a man say sometimes, 'I hate such a man.' Why, I do not know of a person that I hate in the world. The command is to love one another."[4]

Teachings of John Taylor

We should show love for one another as brothers and sisters.

God is our Father, we His children, and we all ought to be brethren; we ought to feel and act like brethren, and while we are striving to serve the Lord our God with all our hearts, minds, souls and strength, we ought, at the same time, to seek to love our neighbor as ourselves; we ought to feel interested in his welfare, happiness and prosperity, and in anything and everything that will tend to promote his temporal and eternal good.[5]

If we try to defraud our brother, how can we expect God to bless us in that, for he is a child of our Heavenly Father just as much as we are. And being his child he feels interested in his welfare, and if we try to take advantage to the injury of the Lord's child; do you think he would be pleased with us? . . . We want to be just and generous to each other. "Thou shalt love the Lord thy God with all thy heart, and with all thy soul, and with all thy mind, and with all thy strength." This we are told is the first commandment. And the second is like unto it, namely, "Thou shalt love thy neighbour as thyself." [Mark 12:30–31.] Do we do this? If we did, then how pleasantly we could come before the Lord. . . .

. . . We should so live that our love for each other can increase all the time, and not diminish, and have charity in our bosoms so that we may bear with one another's infirmities, feeling that we are the children of God seeking to carry out his word and will and law. And then treat everybody right.[6]

We ought to be full of charity, of brotherly kindness and affection and love one towards another and love towards all men. We ought to feel as our heavenly Father does.[7]

Seek one another's welfare, as the scripture says: "Be kindly affectionate one to another with brotherly love; in honour preferring one another." [See Romans 12:10.] You say that is rather hard; well, but you had better do it. We are told to love our neighbor as ourselves. If we can do this, and then prefer our neighbors to ourselves, and if there is a little advantage, put it on their side, we not only fulfil the law and the prophets, but the gospel. Let us cultivate the spirit of love and kindness, and let every little unpleasantness be buried.[8]

The gospel helps us cultivate love and unity.

The religion that we have embraced, in its spiritual signification, brings us into communication one with another and helps us to love one another, and I wish there was a little more of that disposition among us, and that we loved one another a little better and studied one another's interests a little more. I wish we could sympathize with our brethren, and be full of loving kindness and generosity one towards another. I wish that we could feel that brotherly love continued, and that it was spreading and increasing, flowing, from the fountain of life—from God, from heart to heart as oil is poured from vessel to vessel, that harmony, sympathy, kindness and love might be universal among us. This is what the gospel will do for us if we will only let it.[9]

At an assembly [of the Church] some little time ago there were twenty-five nationalities represented. Is there any difference of sentiment among these diverse people? No.

In speaking with a gentleman recently on some of the difficulties between the English and the Irish people, I told him that it was lamentable that such a feeling should exist. Well, said he, they are two different races and they cannot affiliate, one being Celtic and the other Anglo-Saxon, and their sympathies and feelings are dissimilar. Their ideas and feelings differ; their education and their instincts differ. That is very true so far as it goes. But what of us? We are gathered here under the inspiration of the Holy Ghost, and that as I before said, produces a unity of feeling and spirit, a oneness and sympathy that does not exist in the world and Jesus has said, "By this shall all men know that ye are my disciples, if ye have love one to another." (John 13:35.) . . .

And how is it, brethren? Are we Scandinavians; are we English; are we Scotch, Swiss or Dutch, as the case may be? No; the Spirit of God, which we obtained through obedience to the requirements of the gospel, having been born again, of the water and of the Spirit, has made us of one heart, one faith, one baptism; we have no national or class divisions of that kind among us.[10]

We are not all alike. Our faces are different, our habits are different, although made of the same material and possessing the same kind of an organization. So dissimilar are we that you can hardly find two people alike. I do not want everybody to think as I do, I am willing to grant every one a great amount of leeway in regard to these things; but I would like to see everybody do right and cleave to God. And as for a great many other little things I care very little about them.[11]

We show love by actively caring for others.

If good people are suffering for the common necessaries of life, the scriptures say, "If a man having this world's goods see his brother in need, and shutteth up his bowels of compassion, how dwelleth the love of God in him?" [See 1 John 3:17.] And in regard to those matters, we ought to look to the wants of everybody. . . . Do not let us make paupers of them; but let us treat them as brethren and sisters, as good, honorable men and women; let us see that they are provided for.

I have seen some people who would get down upon their knees and pray most heartily for God to feed the poor and clothe the naked. Now, I would never ask the Lord to do a thing that I would not do. If we have them among us, suppose we go at it and relieve them. . . . And if people sustain misfortune of any kind, look after them and bestow upon them those things necessary for their welfare and happiness. And God will bless us in so doing.

I would a great deal rather that you would take, say a sack of flour, some beef, . . . sugar, some butter and cheese, and clothing, and fuel, and such comforts and conveniences of life, and thus try to make people feel happy, than all the prayers you could offer up to the Lord about it; and he would rather see it too. That is the proper way to do things. In receiving blessings ourselves, try to distribute them, and God will bless and guide us in the ways of peace.[12]

A man came to Jesus on one occasion and asked him, which was the greatest commandment. The Savior answered him: "Thou shalt love the Lord thy God with all thy heart, and with all thy soul, and with all thy mind. This is the first and great commandment. And the second is like unto it, Thou shalt love thy neighbour as thyself." [Matthew 22:37–39.] Can we do that? It is sometimes hard work, is it not? We too frequently feel we would rather put two dollars in our own pocket than one in our neighbor's do we not? We would rather have two or three cows than that our neighbor should have one? . . .

Treat everybody well, and do what is right to everybody, and cultivate the spirit of kindness towards all. And when you see somebody's cattle in somebody's grain, feel sufficient interest in his welfare to go and drive them out; and try to promote the welfare of your neighbors and make them feel as comfortable as you can; and God will bless us, and we will bless one another.[13]

We show love by forgiving others and by seeking their forgiveness.

Treat one another aright. Have you sinned one against another? Then go and make restitution. Have you defrauded one another? Go and make it right. Have you spoken unkindly to your brother or sister? Then go and acknowledge your wrong and ask to be forgiven, promising to do better in the future. And then he or she might say, on the other hand, "Yes, and I said so and so the other day, won't you please forgive me?" How much better and how much more in keeping with the calling of a saint of God such a course would be than to harbor hard feelings in the heart.[14]

Let us treat one another with kindness and one another's reputation with respect, and feel after one another's welfare, treating everybody as we would like God to treat us. And then, when we come to the Lord, we can say, "Father, forgive us our trespasses, as we forgive them that trespass against us," [see Matthew 6:12, 14] for if we do not forgive our brother, how can we expect our Heavenly Father to forgive us? If we have had any difficulty with our neighbor, let us endeavor to make it right. Say, "Brother or sister so and so, my conscience rather troubles me about something I said about you or did to you, or some deal I had in which I got the advantage of you, and I have come to make it right, for I am determined to do right, no matter what other people do."[15]

If men, by taking a wrong course, act imprudently and seek to injure us, shall we seek to injure them? No, we will try to do them all the good we can. "But that is not natural." But then we ought to be changed from nature to grace. Jesus stated, "Ye have heard that it hath been said, Thou shalt love thy neighbour, and hate thine enemy. But I say unto you, Love your enemies, bless them that curse you, do good to them that hate you, and pray for them which despitefully use you, and persecute you," etc. [Matthew 5:43–44.] When you have done all that and met all the requirements of the law, what more can be asked of you? Nothing. . . .

. . . If there be trouble existing between me and anybody else, I would meet them half way, yes, I would meet them three quarters or even all of the way. I would feel like yielding; I would say, I do not want to quarrel, I want to be a Saint. I have set out for purity, virtue, brotherhood, and for obedience to the laws of God on earth, and for thrones and principalities and dominions in the eternal worlds, and I will not allow such paltry affairs to interfere with my prospects. I am for life, eternal lives and eternal exaltations in the kingdom of God.[16]

"Forgive us our trespasses, as we forgive those who trespass against us." Do you constantly think of that? We get down upon our knees and many of us think we are pretty decent fellows; but there is Brother So-and-so, he does not do exactly right, and I do not like him very well, and I have been talking about him a little, for he has done me an injury, and I would like to have full retribution, but, O God, won't you forgive my sins? I will, says the Lord, on condition that you forgive your brother, and only on that condition. "If thou bring thy gift to the altar, and there rememberest that thy brother hath ought against thee; leave there thy gift before the altar, and go thy way; first be reconciled to thy brother, and then come and offer thy gift." [Matthew 5:23–24.] When this law is complied with, then we can say, forgive our trespasses as we forgive those that trespass against us.

In our present condition, if the Lord were to answer our prayers, many of us would not be forgiven. If we want the entire people to be good saints, let us be good saints ourselves. Let him that says to another, "You must not steal," steal not himself. You that teach your brother not to speak evil of his neighbor, do you refrain from doing it yourself? . . .

We should operate for one another's interest, having sympathetic feelings for each other. We are supposed to be brethren in the church and kingdom of God, knit together by the indissoluble ties of the everlasting Gospel, not for time only, but for eternity. Hence all our operations should be for that end, founded on the principles of righteousness and friendship.[17]

We should follow the Savior's perfect example of love.

Our feelings towards the world of mankind, generally, ought to be the same as Jesus manifested to them. He sought to promote their welfare, and our motto ought ever to be the same as His was—"Peace on earth and good will to men." [See Luke 2:14.] No matter who they are or what they are we should seek to promote the happiness and welfare of all Adam's race.[18]

If we make any little stumbles the Savior acts not as a foolish, vindictive man, to knock another man down. He is full of kindness, long suffering, and forbearance, and treats everybody with kindness and courtesy. These are the feelings we wish to indulge in and be governed by; these are the principles, and this is the spirit that ought to actuate every elder in Israel; and by which he ought to govern his life and actions.[19]

If Jesus, when upon the earth, could patiently endure the scoffs, sneers and reproaches of men which were so indiscriminately heaped upon Him; if we are in possession of the principles which were enunciated by Him, we can afford also to cherish the same noble and magnanimous feelings that dwelt in His bosom. . . .

Jesus came here according to the foreordained plan and purpose of God pertaining to the human family as the Only Begotten of the Father full of grace and truth. He came to offer Himself a sacrifice, the just for the unjust; to meet the requirements of a broken law, that the human family were incapable of meeting, to rescue them from the ruins of the fall, to deliver them from the power of death to which all peoples had been subjected by the transgression of a law, and He Himself . . . offered himself, the Son of God, as competent propitiation for the sins of the world. And when He was opposed, rejected, cast out, spat upon and maligned; and again, when He was crucified, . . . He [said], "Father, forgive them; for they know not what they do." [Luke 23:34.]

He taught that it was written in the law in olden times, that there should be "an eye for an eye, and a tooth for a tooth:" but, says He, "I say unto you . . . Love your enemies, bless them that curse you, do good to them that hate you, and pray for them which despitefully use you, and persecute you; that ye may be the children of your Father which is in heaven: for he maketh his sun to rise on the evil and on the good, and sendeth rain on the just and on the unjust." [See Matthew 5:38–39, 44–45.] These were principles worthy of a God; these were feelings that if cherished by the human family, would elevate them from that low, groveling position in which they are laboring, would place them on a more elevated platform, would bring them into communion with their Heavenly Father and prepare them for an association with the Gods in the eternal worlds.[20]

Suggestions for Study and Discussion

- Why is it important in our associations with others to remember that all people are children of our Heavenly Father? What can we do to help us "feel as our Heavenly Father does" toward others? What are some ways you have seen people "seek one another's welfare"?
- How must we live so that "our love for each other can increase all the time and not diminish"? What can we do to accomplish this with our families?

- In what ways has the gospel helped you cultivate love for others?
- What opportunities do you have to help those who are "suffering for the common necessaries of life"? How can we know the best way to respond to these situations?
- How should we resolve conflicts with others? How can we increase our love for those who disagree with us?
- Why is it important to forgive others? How does our forgiveness of others influence our ability to feel the Spirit? How does refusing to forgive others affect us?
- How can we avoid giving offense to others or being offended ourselves? How can we overcome our pride to ask someone for forgiveness?
- What examples has the Savior provided concerning love and forgiveness? How has His example helped you love or forgive others?

Related Scriptures: Matthew 22:35–40; John 13:34–35; Mosiah 23:15; Moroni 7:45–48; D&C 12:8; 64:8–10

Notes

1. *Deseret News: Semi-Weekly,* 14 Jan. 1879, 1.
2. *The Gospel Kingdom,* sel. G. Homer Durham (1943), 341.
3. *Deseret News* (Weekly), 24 Dec. 1862, 201.
4. *Deseret News: Semi-Weekly,* 1 June 1880, 1.
5. *Deseret News: Semi-Weekly,* 29 Mar. 1870, 2.
6. *Deseret News: Semi-Weekly,* 25 June 1878, 1.
7. *Deseret News: Semi-Weekly,* 24 June 1879, 1.
8. *Deseret News: Semi-Weekly,* 8 Apr. 1879, 1.
9. *Deseret News: Semi-Weekly,* 26 Jan. 1875, 1.
10. *The Gospel Kingdom,* 247; paragraphing altered.
11. *Deseret News: Semi-Weekly,* 18 Mar. 1879, 1.
12. *Deseret News: Semi-Weekly,* 10 Aug. 1880, 1.
13. *Deseret News: Semi-Weekly,* 4 Oct. 1881, 1; paragraphing altered.
14. *The Gospel Kingdom,* 339.
15. *Deseret News: Semi-Weekly,* 8 June 1880, 1.
16. *Deseret News: Semi-Weekly,* 18 Oct. 1881, 1.
17. *Deseret News: Semi-Weekly,* 19 Dec. 1876, 1; paragraphing altered.
18. *Deseret News: Semi-Weekly,* 29 Mar. 1870, 2.
19. *Deseret News: Semi-Weekly,* 7 Sept. 1867, 2.
20. *Deseret News: Semi-Weekly,* 9 July 1881, 1; paragraphing altered.

C H A P T E R 4

Obedience, a Sacred Duty

So long as we keep the commandments of God, we need not fear any evil; for the Lord will be with us in time and in eternity.[1]

From the Life of John Taylor

John Taylor exhibited willing obedience to God throughout his life. This was especially evident when he received the call to leave his loved ones to serve the Lord as a missionary in England.

The call to serve came in July 1838 in a revelation recorded in Doctrine and Covenants section 118. In that revelation, the Apostles were commanded to depart for their missionary service from the temple site at Far West, Missouri, on 26 April 1839. Compliance with this commandment became extremely difficult with the persecution and expulsion of the Saints from Missouri in the winter of 1838–39. However, in spite of the danger they faced in returning to Missouri, Elder Taylor and his fellow Apostles trusted in the Lord and remained obedient. Shortly after midnight on 26 April 1839, they returned to Far West and met at the temple site, where they laid the cornerstone for the temple and departed for Nauvoo to make final preparations for their mission to England.[2]

Elder Taylor left for his mission from Montrose, Iowa, where he had settled with his family in old log barracks across the river from Nauvoo. Although he and his family were sick with malaria, he was obedient to the call to serve a mission to England. Commenting on the pain of departing from his family, he remarked: "The thought of the hardships they had just endured, the uncertainty of their continuing in the house they then occupied—and that only a solitary room—the prevalence of disease, the poverty of the brethren, their insecurity from mobs, together

"We have learned that it is the height of human happiness to fear God and observe his laws and keep his commandments."

with the uncertainty of what might take place during my absence, produced feelings of no ordinary character. These solicitations, paternal and conjugal, were enhanced also by the time and distance that was to separate us. But the thought of going forth at the command of the God of Israel to revisit my native land, to unfold the principles of eternal truth and make known the things that God had revealed for the salvation of the world, overcame every other feeling."[3]

President Taylor drew his strength from his deep testimony of the gospel: "When I first heard the gospel, I was compelled to admit there was something reasonable about it. I almost hoped it was not true. 'If it is true,' said I, 'as an honest man I shall be obliged to obey it, or else I cannot have any confidence in myself.' "[4]

Teachings of John Taylor

True disciples of the Lord choose to obey His will.

The Lord will bring to pass his strange purpose, and accomplish the thing he has designed. It is for us to live our religion, to fully appreciate the gospel we possess, and fully obey its requirements, submit to its laws, and yield to its dictations, following the direction of the holy priesthood, which holds the keys of the mysteries of the revelations of God, magnifying our callings, and honoring our God, that we may be prepared to fulfil our destiny upon the earth, and be enabled to be a blessing to those around us, and to pour blessings upon our posterity, and spread forth the great principles of eternity, which are calculated to bless, enlighten, ennoble, and exalt all who will yield obedience to their dictates.[5]

Jesus says, "Take my yoke upon you and learn of me, for I am meek and lowly of heart, and you shall find rest to your souls." [See Matthew 11:29.] What was the yoke placed upon the followers of Jesus? Precisely the same as that placed upon you. . . . The word was: Go forth in my name and with my authority, and my Spirit shall accompany you. And it did, and the people became one in faith, doctrine and principle, just as the Scriptures say. "Take my yoke upon you." What was it? Said he, "Blessed are the meek: for they shall inherit the earth. . . . Blessed are the pure in heart: for they shall see God. . . . Blessed are they which do hunger and thirst after righteousness: for they shall be filled." [See Matthew 5:5–6, 8.] This was the kind of yoke Jesus put upon them, and this is the kind that is put upon you—to love righteousness, keep the commands of God, live your religion and obey the principles of truth, is this a hard yoke? This is what is required of Latter-day Saints. "Take my yoke upon you and learn of me!" And how did he do it? He obeyed the will of his Father, and then he expected his disciples to obey his will.[6]

Disobedience to the laws of God brings harmful consequences.

According to the eternal laws of God and the eternal fitness of things as they exist with him in the eternal worlds and as they exist here upon the earth, all of us are or should be as much under the guidance and direction of God, and are as much obligated to listen to his law and be governed by his counsels and advice—and I should think a little more so—than we would be in making that grain of wheat to grow or ten thousand million of them to grow, for we could not do it without being governed by those laws requisite to produce the increase.

Furthermore, we all are the offspring of God, are we not? I think the scriptures read that "We are all his offspring; that he is the God and Father of the spirits of all flesh;" [see Acts 17:28; Hebrews 12:9] and being the God and Father of the spirits of all flesh, and having made a world for all flesh to inhabit, and having made provision for the sustenance of that flesh, for their food, clothing, comfort, convenience and happiness, and given them intelligence and told them to go forth and manipulate the abundance of nature to their use, has he not a right to lead and direct us, to ask obedience to his law? Would not that be a legitimate right, when we reflect upon it?

The world says, No, he has no right; I am my own master; I am an independent being; I will take my own course, etc. Some of the Latter-day Saints almost say the same thing; not quite, but they would like to get near it. "I am a free man; I will be damned if I don't do as I please, etc." Well, I will tell you another part of that story. You will be damned if you do act as you please, unless you please to do and to keep the laws of God. We cannot violate his laws with impunity nor trample under foot these eternal principles which exist in all nature. If all nature is compelled to be governed by law or suffer loss, why not man?[7]

We cannot run our own way and have the blessing of God. Every one who attempts it will find he is mistaken. God will withdraw his Spirit from such, and they will be left to themselves to wander in the dark, and go down to perdition. It is expected of us that we shall move on a higher plane, that we shall feel that we are the children of God, that God is our Father, and he will not be dishonored by disobedient children, or by those who fight against his laws and his priesthood. He expects us to live our religion, to obey His laws and keep His commandments.[8]

If we are the Saints of God, it is necessary we should begin to learn to do the will of God on the earth as it is done in the heavens: for it is not every one that sayeth, Lord, Lord, that shall enter into Christ's kingdom, but he that doeth the will of the Father who is in heaven [see Matthew 7:21]. We think sometimes we can do as we please. We may do as we please, and then God will do as He pleases; and for every word and for every secret thought we shall be brought to judgment, we are told. . . .

We are not here to do our own will, but the will of our heavenly Father. Some men who think they are doing pretty well, and doing, according to their own expression, "as they darned please," will wake up to find they have not been doing the will of God. They may have thought that they had wives and children, but they will wake up to find that they have not got them, and that they are deprived of many of those great blessings they anticipated enjoying. With all of our mercy, kindness and tender feelings towards our brethren and sisters, and towards all people, we cannot violate the law of God, nor transgress those principles that He has laid down with impunity. He expects us to do those things that are acceptable before Him, and if we don't we must pay the penalty of our departure from correct principle.[9]

If the Lord can have a people to listen to his law, there may be a chance to establish his kingdom upon the earth. If not, the only way he can establish his kingdom is to remove them from the earth, or give up his kingdom until another time; for it is impossible to establish his kingdom without having a people obedient to him. . . .

. . . Where there is not a feeling of obedience, the Spirit of God will be withdrawn. People cannot retain it and be in rebellion against the authorities and counsels of the church and kingdom of God.[10]

Obedience brings blessings in this life and in eternity.

What is a man's duty here? It is obedience to the oracles of God that are in our midst; and so long as we keep the commandments of God, we need not fear any evil; for the Lord will be with us in time and in eternity.[11]

Jesus Christ says, "my peace I give unto you: not as the world giveth, give I unto you." (John 14:27.) Wherever this peace exists, it leaves an influence that is comforting and refreshing to the souls of those who partake of it. It is like the morning dew to the thirsty plant. This peace is the gift of God alone, and it can be received only from him through obedience to his laws. If any man wishes to introduce peace into his family or among his friends, let him cultivate it in his own bosom; for sterling peace can only be had according to the legitimate rule and authority of heaven, and obedience to its laws.[12]

We have learned this, that God lives; we have learned that when we call upon him he hears our prayers; we have learned that it is the height of human happiness to fear God and observe his laws and keep his commandments; we have learned that it is a duty devolving upon us to try and make all men happy and intelligent, which happiness and intelligence can only be obtained through obedience to the laws of God.[13]

As Latter-day Saints we believe this Gospel has been restored, and further, we know that we are in possession of it. I do for one, and so do you; and through obedience to its principles and the reception of the Holy Ghost you Latter-day Saints do know that this is the work of God, and if you don't know it, it is because you are not living your religion and keeping the commandments of God; "if any man will do his will," says Christ, "he shall know of the doctrine, whether it be of God, or whether I speak of myself." [John 7:17.][14]

It is for us to magnify the callings unto which we are called, and unless we all of us are placed under the guidance and direction of the Almighty, we cannot do so—that is, those who do not yield themselves subject to the law of God, cannot do that thing. But those who yield themselves subject to the law of God, can do it and do it quite easily, for Jesus says: "Take my yoke upon you, and learn of me; for I am meek and lowly in heart: and ye shall find rest unto your souls. For my yoke is easy, and my burden is light." [Matthew 11:29–30.] Now, if we yield obedience to God and to the spirits that dwell within us, then will our light become like that of the just that shineth brighter and brighter unto the perfect day; but if we do not yield an obedience to the law and word and order of the Church and Kingdom of God upon the earth, the light that is within us will become darkness, and then, as it is said, how great is that darkness! [See Matthew 6:23.][15]

When men are humble, pure and virtuous, and seek unto the Lord for His guidance, for the light of His Holy Spirit to lead them unto the paths of life, that they may comprehend His law, His word and His will—and then obey it as it is made manifest to them—such persons, those brethren and sisters who follow this plan, are a thousand times more likely to comprehend the things of God than those that are careless, indifferent, foolish and wayward, and who neglect the blessings and the opportunities which are offered to them. The light that is in those people becomes darkness, while the path of the others is like that of the just which shineth brighter and brighter unto the perfect day. [See D&C 50:24.][16]

Our safety and happiness and our wealth depend upon our obedience to God and His laws, and our exaltation in time and eternity depends upon the same thing. If we have means placed in our hands we will ask our Father to enable us to do what is right with it, and, as I have said, we will ask Him for our daily bread, and thank Him for it; just the same as the children of Israel did. They had manna brought to them from time to time by the angels. I do not know what kind of mills they had or who were their bakers; but they brought the manna. "He that gathered much had nothing over, and he that gathered little had no lack." [Exodus 16:18.] I think that is the case sometimes with us. The angels do not feed us exactly with manna, but God does take care of us, and I feel all the day long like blessing the name of the God of Israel; and if we fear God and work righteousness, . . . we, the people of Zion, will be the richest of all people.[17]

I remember when I had the Gospel first preached to me—before I was baptized; I heard a lecture something like this: "Now, we have nothing particular to promise you, only the favor of God if you will live righteously and keep His commandments. You may be persecuted, afflicted, imprisoned or put to death for the testimony you may have to bear, for the religion you are called upon to obey; but we can promise to you that inasmuch as this is the case you will have eternal life."[18]

Suggestions for Study and Discussion

- Why do you think the Lord desires us to be obedient? What are some of the blessings He has promised us if we are obedient?
- What experiences have you had that have shown you the blessings of obedience? Why do you think you feel better when you are obedient?
- Why is agency an important part of obedience? In what ways does obedience make us free?
- In what ways does obedience help us strengthen our testimonies? What effects can disobedience have on a person's testimony? What do you think President Taylor meant when he said, "We cannot run our own way and have the blessing of God"?
- Knowing that our own salvation depends on our obedience, what can we do to teach our children this principle?
- Why do the obedient still experience trials? (See also D&C 58:2–5.) Why is it important to remain obedient even in the midst of severe trials?

Related Scriptures: Matthew 11:29–30; John 7:17; 14:15; 1 Nephi 3:7; Alma 3:26–27; D&C 58:26–29; 130:20–21

Notes

1. *The Gospel Kingdom,* sel. G. Homer Durham (1943), 212.
2. See B. H. Roberts, *The Life of John Taylor* (1963), 65–67.
3. *The Life of John Taylor,* 67–68.
4. *The Gospel Kingdom,* 369.
5. *The Gospel Kingdom,* 90–91.
6. *Deseret News* (Weekly), 1 Jan. 1873, 729.
7. *Deseret News: Semi-Weekly,* 8 June 1880, 1; paragraphing altered.
8. *The Gospel Kingdom,* 230.
9. *Deseret News* (Weekly), 2 July 1884, 370.
10. *Deseret News* (Weekly), 9 Jan. 1861, 353.
11. *The Gospel Kingdom,* 212.
12. *The Gospel Kingdom,* 319.
13. *The Gospel Kingdom,* 30.
14. *Deseret News: Semi-Weekly,* 26 Feb. 1884, 1.
15. *Deseret News: Semi-Weekly,* 24 Mar. 1885, 1.
16. *Deseret News: Semi-Weekly,* 1 Jan. 1884, 1.
17. *Deseret News: Semi-Weekly,* 14 Aug. 1883, 1.
18. *Deseret News: Semi-Weekly,* 28 Oct. 1884, 1.

Our Savior Jesus Christ "bore the weight, the responsibility, and the burden of the sins of all men, which, to us, is incomprehensible."

CHAPTER 5

The Infinite Atonement of Jesus Christ

Man, by reason of any thing that he himself could do or accomplish, could only exalt himself to the dignity and capability of man and therefore it needed the atonement of a God, before man . . . could be exalted.[1]

From the Life of John Taylor

In a Sunday meeting with members of the Church, Elder John Taylor spoke of the joy he found in pondering the Atonement of Jesus Christ: "I take pleasure in meeting with the Saints. I like to break bread with them in commemoration of the broken body of our Lord and Savior Jesus Christ, and also to partake of the cup in remembrance of his shed blood. And then to reflect upon the associations connected therewith. Our relationship to God through our Lord Jesus Christ; our relationship to each other as members of the body of Christ, and our hopes concerning the future; the second appearing of our Lord Jesus Christ, when, we are given to understand, he will gird himself and wait upon us, and we shall eat bread and drink wine with him in his Father's kingdom. I like to reflect upon all these and a thousand other things connected with the salvation, happiness and exaltation of the Saints of God in this world, and in the world to come."[2]

Teachings of John Taylor

Jesus covenanted to fulfill the Father's plan by atoning for the sins of the world.

At [the] Council in the heavens the plan that should be adopted in relation to the sons of God who were then spirits, and had not yet obtained tabernacles, was duly considered. For, in view of the creation of the world and the placing of men upon it, whereby it would be possible for them to obtain tabernacles, and in those tabernacles obey laws of life, and with them again be exalted among the Gods, we are told, that at that time, "the morning stars sang together, and all the sons of God shouted for joy." [Job 38:7.] The question then arose, how, and upon what principle, should the salvation, exaltation and eternal glory of God's sons be brought about?

It is evident that at that Council certain plans had been proposed and discussed, and that after a full discussion of those principles, and the declaration of the Father's will pertaining to His design, Lucifer came before the Father, with a plan of his own, saying, "Behold, [here am] I, send me, I will be thy Son, and I will redeem all mankind, that one soul shall not be lost, and surely I will do it; wherefore, give me thine honor." [See Moses 4:1.] But Jesus, on hearing this statement made by Lucifer, said, "Father, thy will be done, and the glory be thine forever." [Moses 4:2.]

From these remarks made by the well beloved Son, we should naturally infer that in the discussion of this subject the Father had made known His will and developed His plan and design pertaining to these matters, and all that His well beloved Son wanted to do was to carry out the will of His Father, as it would appear had been before expressed. He also wished the glory to be given to His Father, who, as God the Father, and the originator and designer of the plan, had a right to all the honor and glory.

But Lucifer wanted . . . to go contrary to the will of his Father, and presumptuously sought to deprive man of his free agency, thus making him a serf, and placing him in a position in which it was impossible for him to obtain that exaltation which God designed should be man's, through obedience to the law which He had suggested. . . . If man had not had his agency, or if he had been deprived of his agency, he could not have been tempted of the devil, or of any other power; for if the will of God prevailed, and was carried out without man's action or agency, it would have been impossible for him to have done anything wrong, for he would have been deprived of the power of doing that wrong.

This was the position that Satan desired to place, not only the spirits in the heavens, but also mankind upon the earth. And Satan said, "Surely I will save every one of them, wherefore, give me thine honor."[3]

[Satan's] plan . . . was rejected as contrary to the counsel of God, his Father. The well beloved Son then addressed the Father, and instead of proposing to carry out any plan of his own, knowing what His Father's will was, said, "Thy will be done; I will carry out thy plans and thy designs, and, as man will fall, I will offer myself as an atonement according to thy will, O God. Neither do I wish the honor, but thine be the glory;" [see Moses 4:2] and a covenant was entered into between Him and His Father, in which He agreed to atone for the sins of the world, and He thus, as stated, became the Lamb slain from before the foundation of the world [see Moses 7:47].[4]

We need the Atonement in order to overcome the effects of the Fall.

In the event of man having his free will and being subject to the power of temptation, the weakness of the flesh, the allurements of the world, and the powers of darkness, it was known that he must necessarily fall, and being fallen, it would be impossible for him to redeem himself, and that, according to an eternal law of justice, it would require an infinite, expiatory atonement to redeem man, to save him from the effects and ruin of the Fall, and to place him in a condition where he could again be reinstated in the favor of God, according to the eternal laws of justice and mercy; and find his way back to the presence of the Father. . . .

And hence, as Jesus Himself said, "Thus it is written, and thus it behoved Christ to suffer, and to rise from the dead the third day: and that repentance and remission of sins should be preached in his name among all nations, beginning at Jerusalem." [Luke 24:46–47.][5]

In the economy of God and the plan proposed by the Almighty, it was provided that man was to be placed under a law apparently simple in itself, yet the test of that law was fraught with the gravest consequences. The observance of that law would secure eternal life, and the penalty for the violation of that law was death. . . . If the law had not been broken [through the Fall], man would have lived; but would man thus living have been capable of perpetuating his species, and of thus fulfilling the designs of God in preparing tabernacles for the spirits which had been created in the spirit world? And further, could they have had the need of a mediator, who was to act as a propitiation [or atoning sacrifice] for the violation of this law, which it would appear from the circumstances was destined to be broken; or could the eternal increase and perpetuity of man have been continued, and his high exaltation to the Godhead been accomplished, without the propitiatory atonement and sacrifice of the Son of God?[6]

If it were not for the atonement of Jesus Christ, the sacrifice he made, all the human family would have to lie in the grave throughout eternity without any hope. But God having provided, through the atonement of the Lord Jesus Christ, the medium whereby we can be restored to the bosom and presence of the Father, to participate with him among the Gods in the eternal worlds—he having provided for that, has also provided for the resurrection. He proclaimed himself the resurrection and the life. Said he, "I am the resurrection, and the life: he that believeth in me, though he were dead, yet shall he live." (John 11:25.) By and by the tombs will be opened and the dead will hear the voice of the Son of God, and they shall come forth, they who have done good to the resurrection of the just, and they who have done evil to the resurrection of the unjust.[7]

To carry out the Atonement, Jesus Christ took upon Himself our sins and suffered death in the flesh.

We are told that "without shedding of blood is no remission" of sins [Hebrews 9:22]. This is beyond our comprehension. Jesus had to take away sin by the sacrifice of Himself, the just for the unjust. . . . As He in His own person bore the sins of all, and atoned for them by the sacrifice of Himself, so there came upon

Him the weight and agony of ages and generations, the indescribable agony consequent upon this great sacrificial atonement wherein He bore the sins of the world, and suffered in His own person the consequences of an eternal law of God broken by man. Hence His profound grief, His indescribable anguish, His overpowering torture, all experienced in the submission to . . . the requirements of an inexorable law.

The suffering of the Son of God was not simply the suffering of personal death; for in assuming the position that He did in making an atonement for the sins of the world He bore the weight, the responsibility, and the burden of the sins of all men, which, to us, is incomprehensible. As stated, "the Lord, your Redeemer, suffered death in the flesh; wherefore he suffereth the pains of all men;" [see D&C 18:11] and Isaiah says: "Surely he hath borne our griefs and carried our sorrows," also, "The Lord hath laid on him the iniquity of us all," and again, "He hath poured out his soul unto death, and he was numbered with the transgressors; and he bare the sins of many;" [see Isaiah 53:4, 6, 12] or, as it is written in the Second Book of Nephi: "For behold, he suffereth the pains of all men, yea, the pains of every living creature, both men, women, and children, who belong to the family of Adam;" [2 Nephi 9:21] whilst in Mosiah it is declared: "He shall suffer temptations, and pain of body, hunger, thirst and fatigue, even more than man can suffer, except it be unto death; for behold, blood cometh from every pore, so great shall be the anguish for the wickedness and abominations of his people." [See Mosiah 3:7.] . . .

. . . As a God, He descended below all things, and made Himself subject to man in man's fallen condition; as a man, He grappled with all the circumstances incident to His sufferings in the world. Anointed, indeed, with the oil of gladness above His fellows, He struggled with and overcame the powers of men and devils, of earth and hell combined; and aided by this superior power of the Godhead, He vanquished death, hell and the grave, and arose triumphant as the Son of God, the very eternal Father, the Messiah, the Prince of peace, the Redeemer, the Savior of the world; having finished and completed the work pertaining to the atonement, which His Father had given Him to do as the Son of God and the Son of man. As the Son of Man, He endured all that it was possible for flesh and blood to endure; as the Son of God He triumphed over all, and forever ascended to the right hand of God.[8]

The Savior thus becomes master of the situation—the debt is paid, the redemption made, the covenant fulfilled, justice satisfied, the will of God done, and all power is now given into the hands of the Son of God—the power of the resurrection, the power of the redemption, the power of salvation, the power to enact laws for the carrying out and accomplishment of this design. Hence life and immortality are brought to light, the Gospel is introduced, and He becomes the author of eternal life and exaltation. He is the Redeemer, the Resurrector, the Savior of man and the world. . . .

The plan, the arrangement, the agreement, the covenant was made, entered into and accepted before the foundation of the world; it was prefigured by sacrifices, and was carried out and consummated on the cross.

Hence being the mediator between God and man, He becomes by right the dictator and director on earth and in heaven for the living and for the dead, for the past, the present and the future, pertaining to man as associated with this earth or the heavens, in time or eternity, the Captain of our salvation, the Apostle and High-Priest of our profession, the Lord and Giver of life.

Is justice dishonored? No; it is satisfied, the debt is paid. Is righteousness departed from? No; this is a righteous act. All requirements are met. Is judgment violated? No; its demands are fulfilled. Is mercy triumphant? No; she simply claims her own. Justice, judgment, mercy and truth all harmonize as the attributes of Deity. "Justice and truth have met together, righteousness and peace have kissed each other." [See Psalm 85:10.] Justice and judgment triumph as well as mercy and peace; all the attributes of Deity harmonize in this great, grand, momentous, just, equitable, merciful and meritorious act.[9]

Jesus Christ was the only one who could carry out the Atonement.

It may here be asked, What difference is there between the Son of God, as the Son of God, the Redeemer, and those who believe in Him and partake of the blessings of the Gospel?

One thing, as we read, is that the Father gave Him power to have life in Himself: "For as the Father hath life in himself; so hath he given to the Son to have life in himself;" [John 5:26] and further, He had power, when all mankind had lost their life, to restore life to them again; and hence He is the Resurrection and the Life, which power no other man possesses.

Another distinction is, that having this life in Himself, He had power, as He said, to lay down His life and to take it up again, which power was also given Him by the Father. This is also a power which no other being associated with this earth possesses.

Again, He is the brightness of His Father's glory and the express image of His person. Also, He doeth what He seeth the Father do, while we only do that which we are permitted and empowered to do by Him.

He is the Elect, the Chosen, and one of the Presidency in the heavens, and in Him dwells all the fulness of the Godhead bodily, which could not be said of us in any of these particulars.

Another thing is, that all power is given to Him in heaven and upon earth, which no earthly being could say.

It is also stated that Lucifer was before Adam; so was Jesus. And Adam, as well as all other believers, was commanded to do all that he did in the name of the Son, and to call upon God in His name for ever more; which honor was not applicable to any earthly being.

He, in the nearness of His relationship to the Father, seems to occupy a position that no other person occupies. He is spoken of as His well beloved Son, as the Only Begotten of the Father—does not this mean the only begotten after the flesh? If He was the first born and obedient to the laws of His Father, did He not inherit the position by right to be the representative of God, the

Savior and Redeemer of the world? And was it not His peculiar right and privilege as the firstborn, the legitimate heir of God, the Eternal Father, to step forth, accomplish and carry out the designs of His Heavenly Father pertaining to the redemption, salvation and exaltation of man? And being Himself without sin (which no other mortal was), He took the position of Savior and Redeemer, which by right belonged to Him as the first born. And does it not seem that in having a body specially prepared, and being the offspring of God, both in body and spirit, He stood preeminently in the position of the Son of God, or in the place of God, and was God, and was thus the fit and only personage capable of making an infinite atonement? . . .

. . . Though others might be the sons of God through Him, yet it needed His body, His fulfilment of the law, the sacrifice or offering up of that body in the atonement, before any of these others, who were also sons of God by birth in the spirit world, could attain to the position of sons of God as He was; and that only through His mediation and atonement. So that in Him, and of Him, and through Him, through the principle of adoption, could we alone obtain that position which is spoken of by John: "Beloved, now are we the sons of God, and it doth not yet appear what we shall be: but we know that, when he shall appear, we shall be like him; for we shall see him as he is." Thus His atonement made it possible for us to obtain an exaltation, which we could not have possessed without it.[10]

Suggestions for Study and Discussion

- When we learned of Heavenly Father's plan—with Jesus as our Savior—"the morning stars sang together, and all the sons of God shouted for joy" (Job 38:7). Why do you think we felt so joyful?
- Satan proposed to take away mankind's agency, but Heavenly Father rejected that proposal. Why must we have agency in order to receive exaltation? (See also D&C 29:39–44.)
- What can we learn from the Savior's response to Heavenly Father's will in the Grand Council in Heaven?

- Because of the Fall of Adam and Eve, all people are subject to physical death and to spiritual death, or separation from God. What did the Savior do to overcome the effects of the Fall?
- What would have been the fate of all mankind without the Atonement? (See also 2 Nephi 9:6–10.)
- Why was Jesus Christ the only one who could carry out the Atonement?
- How do you feel when you ponder the Savior's atoning sacrifice? How can knowledge of the Atonement offer hope and reassurance as we live each day?

Related Scriptures: John 5:26; Hebrews 1:1–3; 2 Nephi 2:6–8, 25–29; 3 Nephi 11:10–11; D&C 19:15–19; Abraham 3:24–28

Notes

1. *The Mediation and Atonement* (1882), 133.
2. *Deseret News* (Weekly), 15 Jan. 1873, 760.
3. *The Mediation and Atonement,* 93–94; paragraphing altered.
4. *The Mediation and Atonement,* 97.
5. *The Mediation and Atonement,* 96–97.
6. *The Mediation and Atonement,* 128–29; paragraphing altered.
7. *The Gospel Kingdom,* sel. G. Homer Durham (1943), 118.
8. *The Mediation and Atonement,* 149–51.
9. *The Mediation and Atonement,* 171–72.
10. *The Mediation and Atonement,* 135–38.

"As Christ overcame, He has made it possible, and has placed it within the power of believers in Him, also to overcome."

CHAPTER 6

The Power of the Atonement for Us Personally

Through the great atonement, the expiatory [or atoning] sacrifice of the Son of God, it is made possible that man can be redeemed, restored, resurrected and exalted to the elevated position designed for him in the creation.[1]

From the Life of John Taylor

President John Taylor often taught of the effects of the Atonement of Jesus Christ on all mankind. He also spoke of the joy he received personally as he contemplated the mercies of the Atonement. "I rejoice that we have a Savior who had the goodness to come forth and redeem us," he said, "and I rejoice that we have a Savior that yet looks forward to the redemption of the world."[2]

Shortly before his death, President Taylor wrote the following to his family members, expressing the hope he had through the Atonement:

"I pray God the Eternal Father that when we have all finished our probation here, we may be presented to the Lord without spot or blemish, as pure and honorable representatives of the Church and kingdom of God on the earth, and then inherit a celestial glory in the kingdom of our God, and enjoy everlasting felicity with the pure and just in the realms of eternal day, through the merits and atonement of the Lord Jesus Christ, our Savior and Redeemer, in worlds without end."[3]

Teachings of John Taylor

Through the Atonement of Jesus Christ, all mankind will be resurrected.

It now becomes our duty to enquire . . . what was accomplished by the atonement.

First, the Resurrection. The penalty of the broken law in Adam's day was death; and death is passed upon all. The word of the Lord was, "In the day that thou eatest thereof thou shalt surely die." [Genesis 2:17; see also Moses 3:17.] The atonement made by Jesus Christ brought about the resurrection from the dead, and restored life. And hence Jesus said: "I am the resurrection, and the life: he that believeth in me, though he were dead, yet shall he live;" [John 11:25] and Jesus Himself became the first fruits of those who slept.

The next question that arises is, how far does this principle extend and to whom is it applicable? It extends to all the human family; to all men of every nation.[4]

All must come forth from the grave, some time or other, in the selfsame tabernacles that they possessed while living on the earth. It will be just as Ezekiel has described it—bone will come to its bone, and flesh and sinew will cover the skeleton, and at the Lord's bidding breath will enter the body, and we shall appear, many of us, a marvel to ourselves [see Ezekiel 37:1–14].

I heard Joseph Smith say, at the time he was making a tomb at Nauvoo, that he expected, when the time came when the grave would be rent asunder, that he would arise and embrace his father and mother, and shake hands with his friends. It was his written request that when he died, some kind friends would see that he was buried near his bosom friends, so that when he and they arose in the morning of the first resurrection, he could embrace them, saying, "My father! My mother!"

How consoling it is to those who are called upon to mourn the loss of dear friends in death, to know that we will again be associated with them! How encouraging to all who live according to the revealed principles of truth, perhaps more especially to those whose lives are pretty well spent, who have borne the heat and burden of the day, to know that ere long we shall burst the barriers of the tomb, and come forth living and immortal souls, to enjoy the society of our tried and trusted friends, no more to be afflicted with the seeds of death, and to finish the work the Father has given us to do![5]

The Atonement enables the faithful to overcome spiritual death and obtain exaltation.

God's plan in relation to man was that he should fall, and having fallen and obtained a knowledge of good and evil, (which knowledge he could not have obtained without placing himself in that position), then it became necessary that he should know concerning the atonement and redemption which should be brought about through the mediation of Jesus Christ.[6]

How, and in what manner are men benefitted by the atonement and by the resurrection? In this, that the atonement having restored man to his former position before the Lord, it has placed him in a position and made it possible for him to obtain that exaltation and glory which it would have been impossible for him to have received without it; even to become a son of God by adoption; and being a son then an heir of God, and a joint heir with Jesus Christ [see Romans 8:16–17]; and that, as Christ overcame, He has made it possible, and has placed it within the power of believers in Him, also to overcome; and as He is authorized to inherit His Father's glory which He had with Him before the world was, with His resurrected body, so through the adoption, may we overcome and sit down with Him upon His throne, as He has overcome and has sat down upon His Father's throne. . . .

. . . Through His atonement, believers in Christ, and those who obey His law, partake of His glory and exaltation, and are inheritors of the Godhead; whilst those who do not obey His law although resurrected cannot inherit this exaltation; they are raised from the dead, but cannot inherit a celestial glory without being obedient to a celestial law. . . . Jesus said, "Thus it is written, and thus it behoved Christ to suffer, and to rise from the dead the third day: and that repentance and remission of sins should be preached in his name among all nations, beginning at Jerusalem." [Luke 24:46–47.][7]

The Atonement redeems little children and those people who die without a knowledge of the gospel.

The Redeemer Himself, when tabernacling in the flesh, said to His disciples . . . , "Suffer little children to come unto me, and forbid them not: for of such is the kingdom of God. Verily I say unto you, Whosoever shall not receive the kingdom of God as a little child shall in no wise enter therein." [Luke 18:16–17.] And after His crucifixion and resurrection He repeated this same admonition to His Nephite disciples: "And again I say unto you, ye must repent, and be baptized in my name, and become as a little child, or ye can in nowise inherit the kingdom of God." [3 Nephi 11:38.]

Without Adam's transgression those children could not have existed; through the atonement they are placed in a state of salvation without any act of their own. These would embrace, according to the opinion of statisticians, more than one-half of the human family, who can attribute their salvation only to the mediation and atonement of the Savior. Thus, as stated elsewhere, in some mysterious, incomprehensible way, Jesus assumed the responsibility which naturally would have devolved upon Adam; but which could only be accomplished through the mediation of Himself, and by taking upon Himself their sorrows, assuming their responsibilities, and bearing their transgressions or sins.

In a manner to us incomprehensible and inexplicable, he bore the weight of the sins of the whole world; not only of Adam, but of his posterity; and in doing that, opened the kingdom of heaven, not only to all believers and all who obeyed the law of God, but to more than one-half of the human family who die before they come to years of maturity, as well as to the heathen, who, having died without law, will, through His mediation, be resurrected without law, and be judged without law, and thus participate, according to their capacity, works and worth, in the blessings of His atonement.[8]

Because the Savior has been "touched with the feeling of our infirmities," he can fully comprehend our trials.

It was necessary, when the Savior was upon the earth, that he should be tempted in all points, like unto us, and "be touched with the feeling of our infirmities," [Hebrews 4:15] to comprehend the weaknesses and strength, the perfections and imperfections of poor fallen human nature. And having accomplished the thing he came into the world to do; having had to grapple with the hypocrisy, corruption, weakness, and imbecility of man; having met with temptation and trial in all its various forms, and overcome; he has become a "faithful high priest" [Hebrews 2:17] to intercede for us in the everlasting kingdom of his Father.

He knows how to estimate and put a proper value upon human nature, for he, having been placed in the same position as we are, knows how to bear with our weaknesses and infirmities, and can fully comprehend the depth, power, and strength of the afflictions and trials that men have to cope with in this world. And thus understandingly and by experience, he can bear with them.[9]

The first principles and ordinances of the gospel are necessary for us to receive the full blessings of the Atonement.

Having noticed the great blessings, privileges, powers and exaltations that are placed within the reach of man, through the atonement of Jesus Christ, it next becomes our duty to enquire what is required of man to place him in possession of them. . . .

The conditions required of the human family to enable them to obtain the high exaltation which the atonement makes it possible for them to receive, are: First, Faith in God as our Father and the great Supreme Ruler of the universe; in whose hands are the destinies of the human family; in whom we live and move and have our being. And in His Son Jesus Christ, as the Lamb slain from before the foundation of the world, as the great Mediator and great propitiatory sacrifice provided by the Father before the creation, and consummated by the offering of Himself upon the cross. For "God so loved the world, that he gave his only begotten Son, that whosoever believeth in him should not perish, but have everlasting life." [John 3:16.] Or, to use the words of the Nephite King Benjamin:

"Believe in God; believe that he is, and that he created all things, both in heaven and in earth; believe that he has all wisdom, and all power, both in heaven and in earth; believe that man doth not comprehend all the things which the Lord can comprehend." [Mosiah 4:9.]

Or as Paul writes; "He that cometh to God must believe that he is, and that he is a rewarder of them that diligently seek him." [Hebrews 11:6.]

The second principle of the Gospel of salvation, is repentance. It is a sincere and godly sorrow for and a forsaking of sin, combined with full purpose of heart to keep God's commandments. As is written by the Prophet Isaiah: "Let the wicked forsake his way, and the unrighteous man his thoughts: and let him return unto the Lord, and he will have mercy upon him; and to our God, for he will abundantly pardon." [Isaiah 55:7.] And to quote from the Book of Mormon:

"And again, believe that ye must repent of your sins and forsake them, and humble yourselves before God; and ask in sincerity of heart that he would forgive you; and now, if you believe all these things see that ye do them." [Mosiah 4:10.]

Thirdly, Baptism for the remission of sins, of our personal transgressions, which, through this means, provided by divine mercy, are, by reason of the atonement, blotted out. To use the words of Paul: "Therefore we are buried with him by baptism into death: that like as Christ was raised up from the dead by the glory of the Father, even so we also should walk in newness of life. For if we have been planted together in the likeness of his death, we shall be also in the likeness of his resurrection." [Romans 6:4–5.]

Next, the reception of the Holy Ghost through the laying on of hands of those who have received the Holy Priesthood, and are duly authorized, ordained, and empowered to impart this blessing: Thus Peter preached on the day of Pentecost:

"Repent, and be baptized every one of you in the name of Jesus Christ for the remission of sins, and ye shall receive the gift of the Holy Ghost. For the promise is unto you, and to your children, and to all that are afar off, even as many as the Lord our God shall call." [Acts 2:38–39.]

These are the introductory or first principles of the everlasting, unchangeable Gospel of our Lord and Savior Jesus Christ, that is and has been the same to all men, amongst all nations, in all ages, whenever, or wherever it has been taught by the authority of heaven. Hence we read: It was "preached from the beginning, being declared by holy angels, sent from the presence of God, and by his own voice, and by the gift of the Holy Ghost. And thus all things were confirmed unto Adam, by an holy ordinance, and the Gospel preached, and a decree sent forth, that it should be in the world, until the end thereof." [See Moses 5:58–59.][10]

We partake of the sacrament in remembrance of the Savior's Atonement.

Sacrifices, which were offered up from the days of Adam . . . , were [representative] of the great expiatory sacrifice which He was to make by the sacrifice of Himself. They were so many types, shadows and forms of which He was the great prototype—the substance, the reality prefigured and foreshadowed by the other sacrifices which had been offered up from the beginning. . . .

But previous to the offering up of Himself, as the great expiatory sacrifice, having fulfilled the law and made it honorable, and having introduced the Gospel, He met with His disciples . . . to eat the Passover. He then told them, "With desire I have desired to eat this passover with you before I suffer." [Luke 22:15.] To eat what with you? The Passover. To eat what with you? The Sacrament of the Lord's Supper. . . . The two ceremonies centered in Him, He was the embodiment of both, He was the Being provided before the foundation of the earth, and prophesied of by men of God throughout all the preceding ages; and also on account of whom the sacrifices were offered up by all the servants of the Lord, from the fall of Adam to that time; and all the various [sacrifices] heretofore offered pointed to Him, for whom they were all made and in whom they all centered. On the other hand, He it was who introduced the more perfect law, and offering Himself once for all, an infinite atonement, He, through this sacrifice, accomplished that which was designed by the Almighty before the world was, and of which the blood of bullocks, of goats and of lambs was merely the shadow.

In view of what was almost immediately to take place, He instituted the sacrament of the Lord's Supper in commemoration of this great crowning act of redemption. When at the table, "He took bread, and gave thanks, and brake it, and gave unto them, saying, This is my body which is given for you: this do in remembrance of me;" [Luke 22:19] afterwards, "He took the cup, and gave thanks, and gave it to them, saying, Drink ye all of it; for this is my blood of the new testament, which is shed for many for the remission of sins." [Matthew 26:27–28.] . . .

As from the commencement of the world to the time when the Passover was instituted, sacrifices had been offered as a memorial or type of the sacrifice of the Son of God; so from the time of the Passover until that time when He came to offer up Himself, these sacrifices and types and shadows had been carefully observed by Prophets and Patriarchs; according to the command given to Moses and other followers of the Lord. So also did He Himself fulfil this requirement, and kept the Passover as did others; and now we, after the great sacrifice has been offered, partake of the Sacrament of the Lord's Supper in remembrance thereof. Thus this act was the great connecting link between the past and the future; thus He fulfilled the law, met the demands of justice, and obeyed the requirements of His Heavenly Father.[11]

Suggestions for Study and Discussion

- What was accomplished by the Atonement of Jesus Christ?
- In what ways does the doctrine of resurrection offer you consolation?
- How has the Atonement affected you personally? How does it help you to know that the Savior "can fully comprehend the depth, power, and strength of [your] afflictions and trials"? What experiences have you had that have strengthened your testimony of the Atonement?
- What does it mean to become a son or daughter of Christ by "adoption"? (See also Mosiah 5:1–9, 15; D&C 25:1.)
- What is required of us so we can receive the "great blessings, privileges, powers and exaltations" available to us through the Atonement? (See also Articles of Faith 1:3–4.)
- What is the relationship between the sacrament and the Atonement?

Related Scriptures: Matthew 26:26–28; Mosiah 15:22–25; Alma 34:13–15; 3 Nephi 18:1–12; Moroni 10:32–33; Moses 5:4–8

Notes

1. *The Mediation and Atonement* (1882), 170.
2. *Deseret News* (Weekly), 4 Mar. 1863, 282.
3. B. H. Roberts, *The Life of John Taylor* (1963), 398.
4. *The Mediation and Atonement,* 177–78.
5. *The Gospel Kingdom,* sel. G. Homer Durham (1943), 23–24.
6. *The Mediation and Atonement,* 187.
7. *The Mediation and Atonement,* 179–80.
8. *The Mediation and Atonement,* 148–49; paragraphing altered.
9. *The Gospel Kingdom,* 120.
10. *The Mediation and Atonement,* 180–83.
11. *The Mediation and Atonement,* 124–27.

CHAPTER 7

Integrity

Let us be pure, let us be virtuous, let us be honorable, let us maintain our integrity, let us do good to all men, and tell the truth always, and treat everybody right.[1]

From the Life of John Taylor

John Taylor lived a life of integrity that was an example to all who knew him and served with him in the Church. The day after his death in July 1887, his counselors, George Q. Cannon and Joseph F. Smith, wrote a letter to the *Deseret News* to inform the public of his passing. Part of that announcement included a tribute to President Taylor. The following is a portion of that tribute describing the stalwart character and integrity of this beloved prophet:

"Few men have ever lived who have manifested such integrity and such unflinching moral and physical courage as our beloved President who has just gone from us. He never knew the feeling of fear connected with the work of God. But in the face of angry mobs, and at other times when in imminent danger of personal violence from those who threatened his life, and upon occasions when the people were menaced with public peril, he never [flinched]—his knees never trembled, his hand never shook. Every Latter-day Saint always knew beforehand, on occasions when firmness and courage were needed, where President John Taylor would be found and what his tone would be. He met every issue squarely, boldly and in a way to call forth the admiration of all who saw and heard him. Undaunted courage, unyielding firmness were among his most prominent characteristics. . . . He was a man whom all could trust."[2]

President John Taylor, approximately 1883. In the words of his counselors, "few men have ever lived who have manifested such integrity and such unflinching moral and physical courage."

Teachings of John Taylor

Integrity means faithfully living by principles of truth and righteousness.

Let us be men of truth, honor and integrity—men that will swear to our own hurt and change not—men whose word will be our everlasting bond. . . . We are trying to raise up a people that shall be men of God, men of truth, men of integrity, men of virtue, men who will be fit to associate with the Gods in the eternal worlds.[3]

God expects to have a people who will be men of clean hands and pure hearts, who withhold their hands from the receiving of bribes, . . . who will be men of truth and integrity, of honor and virtue, and who will pursue a course that will be approved by the Gods in the eternal worlds, and by all honorable and upright men that ever did live or that now live, and having taken upon us the profession of sainthood, he expects us to be Saints, not in name, not in theory, but in reality.[4]

The great difficulty with us is that we are too fond of catering to the world, and too much of the world has crept into our hearts; the spirit of covetousness and greed, and—what shall I say?—dishonesty has spread itself like a plague throughout the length and breadth of the whole world in every direction, and we have drunk more or less into that spirit. Like a plague it has pervaded all grades of society; and instead of being governed by those high, noble, and honorable principles that dwell in the bosom of God, we are after the filthy lucre which is spoken of as being the root of all evil [see 1 Timothy 6:10]; and instead of setting our affections upon God, we set our affections upon the world, its follies and vanities. . . . Show and prove to the world, to angels and to God that you are on the side of truth and right, of honesty, purity and integrity, and that you are for God and His Kingdom.[5]

Never mind the world nor what they can say or do, for they can only do what the Lord permits them. . . . We will send out the gospel to them, and continue to advocate the principles of truth, and to organize ourselves according to the order of God, and seek to be one—for if we are not one we are not the Lord's and never can be, worlds without end. Hear it, you Latter-day Saints! And do not be figuring for yourselves and for your own aggrandizement; but feel to say in your hearts, "What can I do to help to build Zion. I am here, and everything that I have got is upon the altar, and I am prepared to do the will of God no matter what it may be, or where it sends me, to the ends of the earth or not." But we are not doing that yet; we are too much after our own affairs and drinking into the spirit of the world, and yielding and catering to that feeling and influence. Now, while we wish the world well and would desire to promote their happiness, we cannot be governed by their practices nor be under their influences. God is the Lord our God; he is to be our king and law-giver, and he must rule over us.[6]

Integrity means being honest with God, ourselves, and each other.

There is one great principle by which, I think, we all of us ought to be actuated in our worship, above everything else that we are associated with in life, and that is honesty of purpose.

The Scriptures say—"If the truth shall make you free then shall you be free indeed, the sons of God without rebuke, in the midst of a crooked and perverse generation." [See John 8:32, 36; Philippians 2:15.] We are told again that God requires truth in the inward parts [see Psalm 51:6]. It is proper that men should be honest with themselves, that they should be honest with each other in all their words, dealings, [discussions], intercommunication, business arrangements and everything else; they ought to be governed by truthfulness, honesty and integrity, and that man is very foolish indeed who would not be true to himself, true to his convictions and feelings in regard to religious matters.

We may deceive one another . . . as counterfeit coin passes for that which is considered true and valuable among men. But God searches the hearts and tries the reins of the children of men [see Jeremiah 17:10]. He knows our thoughts and comprehends our desires and feelings; he knows our acts and the motives which prompt us to perform them. He is acquainted with all the doings and operations of the human family, and all the secret thoughts and acts of the children of men, are open and naked before him, and for them he will bring them to judgment.[7]

We should be strictly honest, one with another, and with all men; let our word always be as good as our bond; avoid all ostentation of pride and vanity; and be meek, lowly, and humble; be full of integrity and honor; and deal justly and righteously with all men.[8]

If a man borrows five dollars he must give a mortgage on something, because the lender fears he will be cheated out of it. Men have no confidence in each other's word. I would not give a straw for a man if I could not trust his word. There is nothing of him, no foundation, nothing to tie to. Yet these are the very people that the prophet said should exist in the last days. They enter into covenant and never think of fulfilling it. Their word amounts to nothing, their integrity has no foundation.

I speak of these things for your information, for this is the condition of the world. And are we free from it? Not by a long way—I wish we were. I wish there were more honesty, virtue, integrity and truthfulness, and more of every principle among us that is calculated to exalt and ennoble humanity. I speak of these things as a shame to the human family; and if they exist among the Saints it is a crying, burning shame, and we all ought to be disgusted; for if anybody in the world ought to be men of integrity, truth and honesty, we should be, everywhere and under all circumstances. And if we say a thing it ought to be as worthy of belief as if we had sworn to it, and as if we were bound by ten thousand ties to accomplish it.[9]

What do we believe in? We believe in purity, in virtue, in honesty, in integrity, in truthfulness and in not giving way to falsehood; we believe in treating all men justly, uprightly and honorably; we believe in fearing God, observing His laws and keeping His commandments. Do we all do it? No, not quite. I wish we did. But a great majority of the Latter-day Saints are doing this; and if there are those that are not, let them look well to their path. . . . And as we are here for the purpose of building up Zion, He expects that we will be upright and honorable in all our dealings with one another and with all men.[10]

We must have integrity to overcome evil and build the kingdom of God.

We are living in a critical and an important age. Men sometimes are astonished when they see the corruption, wickedness and evil, the departure from honesty and integrity, and the villainy that everywhere exist; but why should they be? . . . Has it not been preached to us that the nations of the earth had the elements of destruction within themselves and that they were bound to crumble? And when we see honor trampled under foot, and integrity and truth standing afar off, while the wicked, corrupt and froward [or disobedient] manage and direct affairs, we may expect that the axe is laid at the root of the tree and that [the tree] is decaying and will soon fall [see D&C 97:7]. And that is what is being accomplished among the nations today. We need not whine or think there is anything strange or remarkable about it. We have expected these things to transpire, and they will be a great deal worse than they are to-day. But we are engaged in introducing correct principles.[11]

We are living in the dispensation of the fullness of times, when God is gathering all things together in one, and he has brought us from different nations, countries, climes and peoples. What to do? To make fools of ourselves? Is our object to live as the wicked do—to be "covetous, boasters, proud, blasphemers, disobedient to parents, heady, highminded, despisers of those who are good, to have a form of godliness without the power?" [See 2 Timothy 3:2–5.] No, we came here that we might learn the laws of the Almighty, and prepare ourselves and our posterity for thrones, principalities, powers and dominions in the celestial kingdom of our God.

We talk sometimes about Zion, that has got to be built up in Jackson County; also about a New Jerusalem that has to be built and prepared to meet a Jerusalem that shall descend from the heavens. How do our lives and actions compare with these things? Are our hearts, feelings and affections drawn out after them, or are we forgetful and our minds swallowed up with the affairs of time and sense?

Are we preparing our children for this time, and spreading an influence around us wherever we go to lead people in the paths of life and lift them up to God? Or are we taking a downward course—come day, go day, just as it happens? I think we ought to wake up and be alive, and endeavor to pursue a course that will secure the smile and approbation of the Almighty. . . .

We ought to be preparing our youth to tread in our footsteps, if they are right, that they may be honorable members in society, that when we get through in this world and to go into the other, we may leave behind [posterity] who are full of integrity, and who will keep the commandments of God. We ought to teach our children meekness and humility, integrity, virtue and the fear of God, that they may teach those principles to their children. . . . Seek to implant in the hearts of your youth principles that will be calculated to make them honorable, highminded, intelligent, virtuous, modest, pure men and women, full of integrity and truth . . . that they with you may have an inheritance in the kingdom of God.[12]

We forget, sometimes, that we are engaged, with many others, in establishing righteousness and planting the kingdom of God upon the earth; and we condescend to little meannesses, and become forgetful of the great and glorious calling to which we are called. Many of us give way to temptation; we falter and get into darkness, and lose the Spirit of the Lord. We forget that God and angels are looking upon us; we forget that the spirits of just men made perfect and our ancient fathers, who are looking forward for the establishment of the kingdom of God upon the earth, are gazing upon us, and that our acts are open to the inspection of all the authorized agencies of the invisible world.

And, forgetting these things sometimes, we act the part of fools, and the Spirit of God is grieved; it withdraws from us, and we are then left to grope our way in the dark. But if we could live our religion, fear God, be strictly honest, observe his laws and his statutes, and keep his commandments to do them, we should feel very different. We should feel comfortable and happy. Our spirits would be peaceful and buoyant. And from day to day, from week to week, and from year to year, our joys would increase.[13]

God will bless those whose lives reflect integrity and purity.

In relation to events that will yet take place and the kind of trials, troubles, and sufferings which we shall have to cope with, it is to me a matter of very little moment; these things are in the hands of God. . . . If we are found to be willing and obedient, and on the Lord's side for right, for truth, and integrity, for virtue and purity and holiness, adhering to the principles of truth and the laws of life, then God will be with us, and he will sustain all those who adhere to these principles. . . . The pure and virtuous, the honorable and upright, will go forth from conquering to conquer until they shall accomplish all that God designs them to do on this earth.[14]

Be honest with yourselves, honest before God. Be virtuous, be truthful and full of integrity, and fear the Lord your God in your hearts, and his blessing will be with you, and his Spirit will attend you, and your generations after you, worlds without end. Amen.[15]

Suggestions for Study and Discussion

- Based on what you have learned from President Taylor, how would you define integrity? In what areas of life can it be especially challenging to maintain integrity?
- What do you think it means to be honest with ourselves? with others? with God? Why is it important to be honest in all aspects of our lives? How are we blessed as we are honest?
- How would life be different if everyone were committed to the principles of honesty and integrity? How would such a commitment affect your actions?
- What challenges to integrity do children face today? What can we do to teach children the value of honesty and integrity?
- How do our lives and actions compare with our goal to build the kingdom of God? Why is it important to make this comparison often?

Related Scriptures: Psalm 15:1–5; Proverbs 20:7; Alma 41:14; D&C 10:28; 136:25–26; Articles of Faith 1:13

Notes

1. *Deseret News: Semi-Weekly,* 24 Oct. 1882, 1.
2. B. H. Roberts, *The Life of John Taylor* (1963), 410–11.
3. *Deseret News: Semi-Weekly,* 21 Oct. 1884, 1.
4. *The Gospel Kingdom,* sel. G. Homer Durham (1943), 123.
5. *Deseret News: Semi-Weekly,* 15 Mar. 1881, 1.
6. *Deseret News: Semi-Weekly,* 31 Aug. 1880, 1.
7. *Deseret News: Semi-Weekly,* 16 Dec. 1873, 1; paragraphing altered.
8. *The Gospel Kingdom,* 343.
9. *Deseret News: Semi-Weekly,* 11 Feb. 1873, 2.
10. *Deseret News* (Weekly), 26 Apr. 1882, 210.
11. *Deseret News: Semi-Weekly,* 26 Jan. 1875, 1.
12. *Deseret News* (Weekly), 15 Jan. 1873, 761; paragraphing altered.
13. *The Gospel Kingdom,* 179.
14. *Deseret News: Semi-Weekly,* 19 Dec. 1876, 1.
15. *Deseret News: Semi-Weekly,* 11 Dec. 1877, 1.

Of missionaries, President Taylor said, "When these brethren go forth, it may be a new work to them . . . , yet these elders go forth as the sent messengers of the Lord Jesus Christ."

CHAPTER 8

Our Missionary Duty

I never see the elders go forth on missions to preach the gospel [without considering] that they are going forth to take part in one of the greatest works ever committed to the human family.[1]

From the Life of John Taylor

Elder John Taylor served as a missionary within the United States and abroad, fulfilling several full-time missions between 1839 and 1857. He demonstrated his great faith and testimony while often preaching under trying circumstances, sometimes without money or food. He trusted that the Lord would protect him and his family and provide the means for him to preach the gospel.

One such instance of the Lord's sustaining power occurred shortly after Elder Taylor left his family in Montrose, Iowa, to fulfill a mission in England. As he was traveling through Indiana, he became very ill and was forced to spend several weeks recovering at a hotel. During this time, Elder Taylor taught the gospel in meetings he held next to the hotel, even though he had to sit part of the time while he spoke. His listeners noticed that despite his difficult circumstances, he never asked for money. Finally, one of them approached him and said: "Mr. Taylor, you do not act as most preachers do; you have said nothing about your circumstances or money, yet you have been here some time sick; your doctor's, hotel and other bills must be heavy. Some friends and myself have talked these matters over and would like to assist you."

Elder Taylor gratefully accepted this help and was soon able to resume his journey, having paid all his bills. Regarding this experience, Elder Taylor said, "I would rather put my trust in the Lord than in any of the kings of the earth."[2] With his trust in the Lord and his dedication to teaching the gospel to others, John Taylor is a powerful example of how we should do missionary work.

Teachings of John Taylor

Missionary work brings knowledge of life and immortality to all mankind.

We are here for a certain purpose; the world was organized for a certain purpose; . . . the gospel has been introduced for a certain purpose in the different ages of time, and among the different peoples to whom it has been revealed and communicated, and we, today, are in subjection to the general rule. The Lord has led us along as he once led Israel, and as he led the Nephites from the land of Jerusalem, and the ten tribes, and other peoples, who went to different places. He has led us along, and the first thing he did with us . . . was to send his gospel, having revealed it first to Joseph Smith, and he, being authorized by the Almighty, and having received his appointment through the holy priesthood that exists in the heavens, and with that appointment authority to confer it upon others, did confer it upon others, and they in turn upon others, and hence the gospel was sent to us in the various nations where we resided.

And when these men went forth to proclaim this gospel, they went, as Jesus said, not to do their "will, but the will of the Father who sent them," [see John 5:30] and to cooperate with the holy priesthood here upon the earth in introducing correct principles. Hence they went among the nations, and thousands and tens of thousands and millions listened to their testimonies; but as it was in former days, so it has been in latter days. Says Jesus—"Strait is the gate and narrow the way that leads to life, and few there be that find it; while wide is the gate and broad is the way that leads to destruction, and many there be that go in thereat." [See Matthew 7:13–14.] This has been the case in all ages and among all peoples, wherever and whenever the gospel has been preached to them.[3]

God has restored the gospel for the purpose of bringing life and immortality to light; and without the knowledge of the gospel there is no knowledge of life and immortality; for men cannot comprehend these principles only as they are made known unto them. . . . When the heavens were opened and the Father and Son appeared and revealed unto Joseph the principles of the gospel, and when the holy Priesthood was restored and the Church and kingdom of God established upon the earth, there were the greatest blessings bestowed upon this generation that it was possible for man to receive. If they could comprehend it, it was the greatest blessing which God could confer upon humanity.[4]

It is our duty to assist the Lord through missionary work.

Now then, the Lord has been desirous, in this age, as he has in other ages, to gather to himself a people who would do his will, keep his commandments, listen to his counsel and carry out his behests. . . . The Lord, in this age as on former occasions, sends by whom he will send; he selects his own messengers and sends them among the people. And when the elders of Israel went forth, he said to them in a certain revelation—"Go forth, and mine angels shall go before you, and my spirit shall accompany you." [See D&C 84:88.] And they went forth, and God was true to his word, and many of you, at that time in distant nations, listened to the words of life, and when you heard them you knew and understood then, just as Jesus said—"My sheep hear my voice and know me, and they follow me, but a stranger will they not follow, because they know not the voice of a stranger." [See John 10:5, 27.] You heard the voice of truth accompanied by the spirit of God, and that caused a chord to vibrate within your own bosoms and you yielded obedience. . . .

Now, then, we are gathered together to help, what to do? To look after our own individual interest? No. To accumulate wealth? No. To possess and wallow in the good things of this life? No, but to do the will of God and devote ourselves, our talents and abilities, our intelligence and influence in every possible way to carry out the designs of Jehovah and help to establish peace and righteousness upon the earth. This, as I understand it, is what we are here for, and not to attend to our own individual affairs and let God and his kingdom do as they please. We are all interested in the great latter-day work of God, and we all ought to be co-workers therein.[5]

I was ordained an Elder by the proper authorities, and I went forth to preach this Gospel. Other Elders went forth as I did to the civilized nations, preaching the same doctrine and holding out the same promises. Some of them were not very learned; some were not very profoundly educated. We send a singular class of people in our Elders. Sometimes a missionary is a merchant, sometimes a legislator, a blacksmith, an adobe maker, a plasterer, a farmer, or common laborer, as the case may be. But all under the same influence and spirit, all going forth as missionaries to preach the Gospel of light, of life and of salvation. They have received the treasures of eternal life, and they are enabled to communicate them to others; and they hold out the same promises.

You who hear me this afternoon as well as thousands upon thousands of others, have listened to those principles, you have had held out unto you those promises; and when you obeyed the Gospel, you received this same spirit; and you are my witnesses of the truth of the things that I now proclaim in your hearing and of the Spirit and power of God attending the obedience to the Gospel, and you will not deny it. This congregation will not deny it. When you yielded obedience to the laws of God, obeyed His commandments, and were baptized for the remission of your sins and had hands laid upon you for the reception of the Holy Ghost, you did receive it; and you are living witnesses before God. This is a secret that the world does not comprehend. . . . We are in possession of the principles of eternal life, and are operating for eternity; and then we are operating to build up the Zion of God, where righteousness can be taught, and where men can be protected, and where liberty can be proclaimed to all men of every color, of every creed and of every nation.[6]

Our duty is to preach the Gospel to all men. . . . And we are doing this in spite of the opposition of men, and in the name of

God we will do it. . . . And if they love the devil better than God, they can do so and sup trouble and sorrow and calamity and war and bloodshed. For nation will rise against nation, country against country; and thrones will be cast down; and empires will be scattered to the four winds, and the powers of the earth everywhere will be shaken; and the Lord will come forth by and by to judge the nations; and it behooves us to know what we are doing, and while we profess to be the saints of God not to be hypocrites, but be full of truth and full of integrity and magnify our calling and honor our God.

This is what God expects of us. And then to build temples, and what then? Administer in them. Send the gospel to the nations of the earth. And then gather the people in. What then? Build more temples. What then? Have men administer in them.[7]

Missionaries teach eternal truth with the power and authority of God.

There is a very great difference between our mode of promulgating the gospel, and that pursued by the world. Many of these men . . . would be very unlikely instruments for preaching the gospel according to popular notions; but the grand difference between us and them is that we go forth in the name of Israel's God, sustained by His power, wisdom and intelligence, to proclaim the principles of eternal truth communicated to us by Him; while they go forth to proclaim what they have learned in colleges.

Our Elders go forth in weakness. . . . When [they] go forth, they have no preparation beyond the common rudiments of education that all are supposed to learn; but it is not words they go to teach, it is principles. And although before an audience learned in the laws of God, they may feel a good deal of tremor and bashfulness in trying to express themselves, yet, when they go forth and stand before congregations in the world, the Spirit of the Lord God will go with them, the Lord will sustain them and will give unto them wisdom, "that all their adversaries will not be able to gainsay, nor resist." [See Luke 21:15.] That is the promise made to the servants of the Lord who go forth trusting in Him.[8]

These young men are just like the rest of us: they have received the spirit of life, light and intelligence, the gift of the Holy Ghost, and they are the messengers of the Great Jehovah, whom He has selected, set apart, and ordained to go and proclaim His will to the nations of the earth. They go not in their own name or strength, but in the name, strength and power of Israel's God. That is their position, and if they cleave to God and magnify their callings, adhere to the principles of truth, and shun temptation and corruption of every kind, the power of God will be with them, and God shall open their mouths, and enable them to confound the wisdom of the wise, and they will say things that will astonish themselves and those who listen to them.

I would say to these brethren, let it be your study to fulfill your mission. Never mind the world; never mind the dollars and cents, the pounds, shillings, and pence. You cleave to God, live your religion, magnify your callings, humble yourselves before God, call upon Him in secret and He will open your path before you.[9]

We need to prepare ourselves spiritually in order to be effective missionaries.

I would say, however, to those going on missions that they should study the Bible, Book of Mormon, Book of Doctrine and Covenants, and all our works, that they may become acquainted with the principles of our faith. I would also say to other young men who are not now going on missions, but who will probably have to go at some time in the future, that these things are of more importance to them than they realize at the present time. We ought to be built up and fortified by the truth. We ought to become acquainted with the principles, doctrines, and ordinances pertaining to the Church and Kingdom of God.

We are told in the Book of Doctrine and Covenants to search after wisdom as we would for hidden treasures, both by study and by faith; to become acquainted with the history and laws of the nation we live in, and of the nations of the earth [see D&C 88:78–80, 118]. I know that when young men are working around here, going to the canyon, working on the farm, going to the theatre, and so on, their minds are not much occupied with these things; but when they are called upon to take a part in the drama themselves, many of them will wish they had paid more attention to the instructions they have received, and had made themselves more familiar with the Bible, Book of Mormon, and the Book of Doctrine and Covenants.[10]

The kind of men we want as bearers of this gospel message are men who have faith in God; men who have faith in their religion; men who honor their priesthood; men in whom the people who know them have faith and in whom God has confidence. . . . We want men full of the Holy Ghost and the power of God. . . . Men who bear the words of life among the nations, ought to be men of honor, integrity, virtue and purity; and this being the command of God to us, we shall try and carry it out.[11]

We must have faith and courage to fulfill our missionary duty.

There is a terrible time approaching the nations of the earth, . . . worse than has ever entered into the heart of man to conceive of—war, bloodshed, and desolation, mourning and misery, pestilence, famine, and earthquakes, and all those calamities spoken of by the prophets will most assuredly be fulfilled. . . . And it is for us, Latter-day Saints, to understand the position we occupy. . . .

. . . There are some things that make it extremely difficult for men sometimes to perform the kind of missions that they did formerly, owing to age, infirmities, and circumstances. Yet I have frequently felt ashamed when I have seen the acts of many of these quorums to which I refer, when they have been called upon to go on missions. One has one excuse, and another, another. It was easier some twenty years ago to raise two or three hundred men than it is now among all those thousands in Israel. How do you account for this? Partly in consequence of an apathy that exists.[12]

There are lots of able-bodied men who, if they could only have a little more faith in God, and could realize the calamities that are coming upon the earth, and the responsibilities of that priesthood that God has conferred upon them, they would be ready to break all barriers and say, Here I am, send me; I wish to benefit the human family. If Jesus came to seek and save those who are lost, let me be possessed of the same spirit.[13]

I, myself, have traveled hundreds of thousands of miles preaching the gospel; and without purse or scrip, trusting in the Lord. Did he ever forsake me? Never, no never. I always was provided for, for which I feel to praise God my Heavenly Father. I was engaged in his work, and he told me that he would sustain me in it. He has been true to his trust; and if I have not been true to mine, I hope he will forgive me and help me to do better. But the Lord has been true and faithful, and I have never needed anything to eat or drink or wear, and was never prevented for want of means of traveling where I pleased.[14]

I have a great deal more confidence in men who rise here feeling their weakness and inability, than I have in those who feel that they are well informed and capable of teaching anything and everything. Why? Because when men trust to themselves they trust in a broken reed; and when they trust in the Lord they will never fail. . . . The Lord is over all, He watches over His people, and if these brethren will continue to trust in God . . . , His Spirit will rest upon them, enlighten their minds, enlarge their capacities and give to them wisdom and intelligence in time of need. They need not be under any apprehension with regard to the wisdom of the world; for there is no wisdom in the world equal to that which the Lord gives to His Saints; and as long as these brethren keep from evil, live their religion, and cleave to the Lord by keeping His commandments, there is no fear as to the results; and this will apply to all the Saints as well as to these brethren.[15]

Whatever their feelings may be, [missionaries] go forth as the angels of mercy bearing the precious seeds of the gospel, and they shall be the means of bringing many from darkness to light, from error and superstition to life, light, truth, and intelligence, and finally, to exaltation in the celestial kingdom of our God.

When these brethren go forth, it may be a new work to them. They will have to combat the errors of ages, contend with the

Office of the Millennial Star *in Liverpool, approximately 1885. Early in his ministry, John Taylor served as a missionary in the British Isles, where he used his talents in writing and speaking to further the work of the Lord.*

prejudices which they themselves state to you held such a powerful influence over them; they will also have to preach to and reason with men who have no regard for truth, much less for the religion which we have embraced, yet these elders go forth as the sent messengers of the Lord Jesus Christ. They go to proclaim that God has established his work upon the earth, that he has spoken from the heavens, and that the visions of the Almighty have been opened to our view; the light of ages is being revealed to the servants of the Most High, the darkness which has enshrouded the world for ages is being dispersed; and these chosen elders of Israel are sent forth to proclaim these glad tidings of salvation to the dark and benighted nations of the earth. . . . They go forth and they shall come back rejoicing, bearing precious sheaves with them, and they will bless the name of the God of Israel, that they have had the privilege of taking a part in warning this generation.[16]

Suggestions for Study and Discussion

- How does missionary work help fulfill the Lord's purposes? As one who has received the gospel, what missionary duties do you have in the Lord's plan?
- Why does the Church send young and inexperienced people as full-time missionaries?
- Why is faith in the Lord fundamental to missionary work?
- How does our personal preparation and worthiness affect our ability to be effective instruments for the Lord?
- In addition to serving a full-time mission, what other opportunities do we have to share the gospel?
- What are some of the reasons members give for not participating in missionary work? What can you do to overcome your own obstacles in this area?
- How have you seen the Lord bless those who give their time, talents, energy, and means to share the gospel?

Related Scriptures: Alma 26:5–7; 3 Nephi 20:29–31; D&C 1:18–23; 4:1–7; 75:2–5; 133:7–9

Notes

1. *The Gospel Kingdom,* sel. G. Homer Durham (1943), 238.
2. See B. H. Roberts, *The Life of John Taylor* (1963), 69–71.
3. *Deseret News: Semi-Weekly,* 9 May 1876, 1; paragraphing altered.
4. *Deseret News: Semi-Weekly,* 4 Oct. 1881, 1.
5. *Deseret News: Semi-Weekly,* 9 May 1876, 1.
6. *Deseret News: Semi-Weekly,* 18 Apr. 1882, 1; paragraphing altered.
7. *The Gospel Kingdom,* 234–35; paragraphing altered.
8. *Deseret News: Semi-Weekly,* 15 June 1867, 2.
9. *Deseret News* (Weekly), 19 June 1867, 194.
10. *Deseret News: Semi-Weekly,* 15 June 1867, 2. Note: At the time of this statement, the Pearl of Great Price had not yet been canonized; it became a standard work of the Church in 1880.
11. *Deseret News: Semi-Weekly,* 15 Mar. 1881, 1.
12. *The Gospel Kingdom,* 237.
13. *Deseret News: Semi-Weekly,* 24 Sept. 1878, 1.
14. *The Gospel Kingdom,* 234.
15. *Deseret News: Semi-Weekly,* 15 June 1867, 2; paragraphing altered.
16. *The Gospel Kingdom,* 238–39.

CHAPTER 9

Joseph Smith, the Prophet of the Restoration

Joseph Smith, the Prophet and Seer of the Lord, has done more, save Jesus only, for the salvation of men in this world, than any other man that ever lived in it.[1]

From the Life of John Taylor

In March 1837, John Taylor went to Kirtland, Ohio, and had the opportunity to meet the Prophet Joseph Smith for the first time and learn more about the principles of the newly restored gospel. At the time of John Taylor's visit to Kirtland, many Church members had become critical of the Prophet Joseph. Even some members of the Quorum of the Twelve were caught up in this dissenting spirit, including Parley P. Pratt, who had initially taught John Taylor the gospel. When Elder Pratt approached him and shared some of his doubts about the Prophet, Brother Taylor replied:

"I am surprised to hear you speak so, Brother Parley. Before you left Canada you bore a strong testimony to Joseph Smith being a Prophet of God, and to the truth of the work he has inaugurated; and you said you knew these things by revelation, and the gift of the Holy Ghost. You gave to me a strict charge to the effect that though you or an angel from heaven was to declare anything else I was not to believe it. Now Brother Parley, it is not man that I am following, but the Lord. The principles you taught me led me to Him, and I now have the same testimony that you then rejoiced in. If the work was true six months ago, it is true today; if Joseph Smith was then a prophet, he is now a prophet."[2] To Elder Pratt's credit, he soon repented of his feelings and continued to be a valiant servant of the Lord.

The Prophet Joseph Smith "lived great, and he died great in the eyes of God and his people; and like most of the Lord's anointed in ancient times, has sealed his mission and his works with his own blood" (D&C 135:3).

John Taylor remained loyal to the Prophet Joseph Smith from the day he met him, and they were together when the Prophet was martyred. In a discourse given almost 20 years after the Prophet Joseph's death, Elder Taylor said, "If there is no other man under the heavens that knows that Joseph Smith is a prophet of God I do, and I bear testimony of it to God, angels and men."[3] Throughout Elder Taylor's ministry, he delighted in teaching that "God restored his ancient Gospel to Joseph Smith, giving him revelation, opening the heavens to him, and making him acquainted with the plan of salvation and exaltation of the children of men."[4]

Teachings of John Taylor

Joseph Smith was foreordained to be the prophet of the Restoration.

There was nothing particular about [Joseph Smith], he was a man like the balance of us. But the Lord, for certain reasons of his own, I suppose, selected him to be his mouthpiece to the nations in this age of the world. Perhaps Joseph, as well as many others, was set apart to a certain office before the world was. Christ was the Lamb slain from before the foundation of the world. Abraham was set apart to his office, and a great many others in the same way; and Joseph Smith came to do his work.[5]

We all look upon Joseph Smith as being a prophet of God. God called him to occupy the position that he did. How long ago? Thousands of years ago before this world was formed. The prophets prophesied about his coming, that a man should arise whose name should be Joseph, and that his father's name should be Joseph, and also that he should be a descendant of that Joseph who was sold into Egypt. This prophecy you will find recorded in the Book of Mormon [see 2 Nephi 3:15]. He had very great and precious promises made to him by the Lord.[6]

The Lord restored the fulness of His gospel through the Prophet Joseph Smith.

What condition was the world in before the gospel we now preach was introduced? . . . Where could we find anything resembling that which was taught by Jesus? Nowhere on the face of the wide earth. Apostles, prophets, pastors, teachers etc., were nowhere to be found. Do I know this? I do know it, for I lived in the world at that time! I knew what was going on. I was mixed up with their teachers and was well acquainted with the different societies and organizations. Did they have the gospel as laid down in the scriptures? No.[7]

I did not know that it was necessary to be baptised for the remission of sins until the gospel taught it to me, yet I knew the Bible from A to Z. I could read a great many things in the prophecies, and make calculations about the millennium and the gathering of Israel, but did not know the first principle of the gospel of Christ; and there is not a man here that knew them. I have traveled extensively in the world and have never met with a priest, or scientific man that knew the first principles of the gospel of Christ in any country.

What could the Lord do with such a pack of ignorant fools as we were? There was one man that had a little good sense, and a spark of faith in the promises of God, and that was Joseph Smith—a backwoods man. He believed a certain portion of Scripture which said—"If any man lack wisdom let him ask of God who giveth to all men liberally and upbraideth not." [See James 1:5.] He was fool enough in the eyes of the world, and wise enough in the eyes of God and angels, and all true intelligence, to go into a secret place to ask God for wisdom, believing that God would hear him. The Lord did hear him, and told him what to do.[8]

A message was announced to us by Joseph Smith the Prophet, as a revelation from God wherein he stated that holy angels had appeared to him and revealed the everlasting Gospel as it existed in former ages; and that God the Father and God the Son had also appeared to him: the Father pointing to the Son said, "This is my beloved Son, hear ye him." [See Joseph Smith—History 1:17.] Moroni, a prophet that had lived on this continent, revealed unto him the plates containing the Book of Mormon, and by the gift and power of God Joseph was enabled to translate them into what is known as the Book of Mormon. . . .

. . . The Father having presented His Son to Joseph Smith, and commanded him to hear Him, Joseph was obedient to the heavenly call, and listened to the various communications made by men holding the Holy Priesthood in the various ages under the direction of the Only Begotten. He and Oliver Cowdery were commanded to baptize each other, which they did. John the Baptist came and conferred upon them the Aaronic Priesthood. Then Peter, James and John, upon whom was conferred in the Savior's day, the keys of the Melchizedek Priesthood came and conferred the Melchizedek Priesthood upon them. Then Adam, Noah, Abraham, Moses, Elijah, Elias and many of the leading characters mentioned in the Scriptures, who had operated in the various dispensations, came and conferred upon Joseph the various keys, powers, rights, privileges and immunities which they enjoyed in their times.

Again, Joseph was commanded to preach this Gospel and to bear this testimony to the world. He was taught the same principles that were taught to Adam, the same principles that were taught to Noah, to Enoch, to Abraham, to Moses, to the Prophets, and to Elijah: the same principles that were taught by Jesus Christ and the Apostles in former times . . . , accompanied with the same Priesthood and the same organization, only more fully, because the present dispensation is a combination of the various dispensations that have existed in the different ages of the world, and which is designated in the Scriptures as the dispensation of the fulness of times, in which God would gather together all things in one, whether they be things in heaven or things on earth. Therefore, whatever of knowledge, of intelligence, of Priesthood, of powers, of revelations were conferred upon those men in the different ages, were again restored to the earth by the ministration and through the medium of those who held the holy Priesthood of God in the different dispensations in which they lived.[9]

Joseph Smith was taught by the Lord.

Who was Joseph Smith? An unlettered youth. Could he do anything to accomplish [the establishment of God's kingdom]?

Not unless God had revealed it to him. He asked wisdom of God and received it. Till that time he knew no more about these things than you or I. It was God and God alone that did these things. "He can take the weak things of this earth, the base things and the things that are not, to bring to naught the things that are, that no flesh may glory in his presence." [See 1 Corinthians 1:28–29.] He took Joseph. Why? Because the time had come to begin a work, in which all the holy Priesthood of God that had lived in former ages were concerned. Joseph was the honored instrument chosen to take the initiative.[10]

Joseph Smith was quite an uneducated man. He was uneducated when he was a boy. He was brought up in the Green Mountains of Vermont, and he did not have any of the advantages of what we call an education. The Lord took him into His school, and He taught him things that I have seen puzzle many of the wisest scientists, profoundest thinkers, and the most learned men that I have met with in this world. Why? Because he was taught of God. What did those principles refer to? To the earth on which we live; to the elements of which it is composed; to the heavens above us; to the Gods that exist in the eternal worlds; to the principles by which the earth was organized, sustained, upheld and governed, and its relationship to other planets and systems; and speaking of governments, laws and principles, he possessed more intelligence than ninety-nine hundredths of the people of to-day. And he sought to teach others.[11]

Joseph Smith was an honorable and virtuous man who was persecuted for the principles he taught.

I was acquainted with Joseph Smith for years. I have traveled with him; I have been with him in private and in public; I have associated with him in councils of all kinds; I have listened hundreds of times to his public teachings, and his advice to his friends and associates of a more private nature. I have been at his house and seen his deportment in his family. I have seen him arraigned before the tribunals of his country, and have seen him honorably acquitted, and delivered from the pernicious breath of slander, and the machinations and falsehoods of wicked and corrupt men. I was with him living, and with him when he died, when he was murdered in Carthage jail by a ruthless mob. . . .

I have seen him, then, under these various circumstances, and I testify before God, angels, and men, that he was a good, honorable, virtuous man—that his doctrines were good, scriptural, and wholesome—that his precepts were such as became a man of God—that his private and public character was unimpeachable—and that he lived and died as a man of God and a gentleman. This is my testimony. If it is disputed, bring me a person authorized to receive an affidavit, and I will make one to this effect. I therefore testify of things which I know and of things which I have seen.[12]

When I reflected that our noble chieftain, the Prophet of the living God, had fallen, and that I had seen his brother in the cold embrace of death, it seemed as though there was a void or vacuum in the great field of human existence to me, and a dark gloomy chasm in the kingdom, and that we were left alone. Oh, how lonely was that feeling! How cold, barren, and desolate! In the midst of difficulties he was always the first in motion; in critical positions his counsel was always sought. As our prophet he approached our God, and obtained for us his will; but now our prophet, our counselor, our general, our leader, was gone, and amid the fiery ordeal that we then had to pass through, we were left alone without his aid, and as our future guide for things spiritual or temporal, and for all things pertaining to this world, or the next, he had spoken for the last time on earth.

These reflections and a thousand others flashed upon my mind. I thought, why must God's nobility, the salt of the earth, the most exalted of the human family, and the most perfect types of all excellence, fall victims to the cruel, fiendish hate of incarnate devils?[13]

Joseph Smith was a virtuous, high-minded, honorable man, a gentleman and a Christian. But he introduced principles which strike at the root of the corrupt systems of men. This necessarily comes in contact with their prepossessions, prejudices, and interests; and as they cannot overturn his principles, they attack his character. And that is one reason why we have so many books written against his character, without touching his principles, and also why we meet with so much opposition. But truth, eternal truth, is invulnerable. It cannot be destroyed, but like the throne of Jehovah, it will outride all the storms of men, and live for ever.[14]

The martyrdom of the Prophet Joseph could not stop the advancement of the kingdom of God.

I remember the time very well when Joseph Smith was taken from us. . . . But these things are matters, although of great importance to us, yet relatively they have not a very great deal to do with the building up of the Church and kingdom of God upon the earth, and with His work in which we are all engaged.

When the Lord revealed the everlasting Gospel to Joseph Smith, he unfolded unto him his purposes and designs in relation to the earth whereon we live, and gave unto him a knowledge of his law and the ordinances of the Gospel and the doctrine thereof. It was not for the object simply of elevating him as a man, but it was done for the interest of society, in the interest of the world, and in the interest of the living and the dead, according to the decrees and designs of Jehovah which he formed before the world rolled into existence, or the morning stars sang together for joy.

The Lord had his designs in relation to the earth and the inhabitants thereof, and in these last days he saw proper to reveal and restore, through his servant Joseph Smith, what we term the new and everlasting Gospel; new to the world at present, because of their traditions, their follies and weaknesses, and their creeds, opinions and notions, but everlasting because it existed with God, and because it existed with him before the world was, and will continue when change shall have succeeded change upon this earth, and when the earth shall have been redeemed and all things made new, and while life and thought and being last, and immortality endures.

Therefore, although the Gospel is new to the world, it is everlasting. And it was introduced, as I have stated, in the interests of humanity—our fathers, the ancient Prophets and Apostles, and men of God who have lived in the various ages of the world, who have administered in the holy Priesthood while they lived upon the earth, and who are now administering in the heavens, and who had a hand in the introduction of this work, together with God our heavenly Father, and Jesus the Mediator of the New Covenant; and to-day they feel interested in the rolling forth of this work, and in the accomplishment of these purposes which God designed before the foundation of the world. And it is to God and his Son, and to these men, that we are indebted for the light and the intelligence that has been communicated to us, and to them we shall be indebted through all time for the same kind of knowledge and intelligence to sustain and direct us.[15]

The idea of the Church being disorganized and broken up because of the Prophet and the patriarch being slain is preposterous. This Church has the seeds of immortality in its midst. It is not of man, nor by man—it is the offspring of Deity. It is organized after the pattern of heavenly things, through the principles of revelation; by the opening of the heavens; by the ministering of angels, and the revelations of Jehovah. It is not affected by the death of one or two, or fifty individuals. It possesses a priesthood after the order of Melchizedek, having the power of an endless life, "without beginning of days or end of years." [D&C 84:17.] It is organized for the purpose of saving this generation, and generations that are past. It exists in time and will exist in eternity. This church fail? No! Times and seasons may change, revolution may succeed revolution; thrones may be cast down; and empires be dissolved; earthquakes may rend the earth from center to circumference; the mountains may be hurled out of their places, and the mighty ocean be moved from its bed, but amidst the crash of worlds and the crack of matter, truth, eternal truth, must remain unchanged, and those principles which God has revealed to his saints be unscathed amidst the warring elements, and remain as firm as the throne of Jehovah.[16]

Suggestions for Study and Discussion

- What impresses you about John Taylor's feelings about the Prophet Joseph Smith? In what ways can we follow his example of defending the Prophet Joseph?
- Why is it important to you to know that Joseph Smith was foreordained to serve as a prophet? (See also D&C 138:53–56.)

- Why is it important to have a testimony that Joseph Smith was a prophet of God? How did you gain your testimony of this truth?
- How can you help those who are struggling to gain or strengthen their testimony of the Prophet Joseph? What blessings have you experienced from bearing testimony of the Prophet Joseph Smith?
- Why is our time period described as the "dispensation of the fulness of times"?
- How have you and your family been blessed by the truths and powers restored through Joseph Smith?
- Why wasn't it necessary for Joseph Smith to be formally educated? (See also D&C 1:24–28; 136:32–33.) What qualities did Joseph have that helped prepare him to fulfill his calling? How might his example help us fulfill our callings?
- What does it mean to you to know that the Church has continued to grow despite the death of the Prophet Joseph Smith?

Related Scriptures: D&C 1:29–30, 38; 21:1–8; 65:2; 128:19–23; 135; Joseph Smith—History 1:1–75

Notes

1. D&C 135:3.
2. See B. H. Roberts, *The Life of John Taylor* (1963), 39–40.
3. *Deseret News* (Weekly), 25 Mar. 1863, 306.
4. *The Gospel Kingdom,* sel. G. Homer Durham (1943), 33.
5. *Deseret News: Semi-Weekly,* 1 June 1875, 1.
6. *The Gospel Kingdom,* 121.
7. *The Gospel Kingdom,* 125.
8. *Deseret News* (Weekly), 28 Dec. 1859, 337; paragraphing altered.
9. *Deseret News: Semi-Weekly,* 18 Apr. 1882, 1.
10. *Deseret News: Semi-Weekly,* 22 Aug. 1876, 1.
11. *Deseret News: Semi-Weekly,* 22 July 1884, 1.
12. *The Gospel Kingdom,* 355; paragraphing altered.
13. *The Gospel Kingdom,* 362.
14. *The Gospel Kingdom,* 355–56.
15. *Deseret News: Semi-Weekly,* 16 Apr. 1878, 1; paragraphing altered.
16. *The Gospel Kingdom,* 364–65.

CHAPTER 10

The Value of Education

We are here, as a people, . . . that we may put ourselves in possession of every truth, of every virtue, of every principle of intelligence known among men, together with those that God has revealed for our special guidance, and apply them to our everyday life, and thus educate ourselves and our children in everything that tends to exalt man.[1]

From the Life of John Taylor

In 1877, President John Taylor was elected to the office of territorial superintendent of district schools in Utah. In that position, he sought to appoint the most qualified teachers to teach the children and youth. He also continually monitored educational statistics—not only from Utah, but from all the states and territories in the United States—to help him better understand the level of education among the Latter-day Saints. For his administration of the school system, he received a letter of commendation from the acting commissioner of education of the United States.[2] The letter was a fitting recognition for President Taylor, whose life reflected his love of learning and teaching.

From his childhood schooling in England to his service as President of the Church, John Taylor consistently studied and worked to magnify the intelligence the Lord had given him. His diligence in learning enabled him to help the growth of the Church in many ways. One such instance occurred while he was serving a mission in France. Although he had been in the country only a short time, he participated in the translation of the Book of Mormon into French and German and initiated the publication of two monthly Church periodicals in those languages.[3]

President Taylor believed strongly in education and lifelong learning. He was a skilled craftsman, businessman, writer, and speaker.

John Taylor's many writings on gospel subjects included letters, tracts, hymns, pamphlets, newspaper articles, and books. One of his books, entitled *The Government of God,* was praised by a noted American historian, who wrote: "As a dissertation on a general and abstract subject, it probably has not its equal in point of ability within the whole range of Mormon literature. The style is lofty and clear, and every page betokens the great learning of the author. As a student of ancient and modern history, theologian, and moral philosopher, President Taylor is justly entitled to the front rank."[4]

In addition to his many writings, President Taylor's command of language, coupled with his testimony of the gospel, resulted in countless inspiring and instructive sermons. Elder B. H. Roberts wrote: "The Saints who listened to him for half a century will remember as long as they live his commanding presence, his personal magnetism, the vigor and power of his discourses and the grand principles of which they treated. . . . His eloquence was a majestic river full to the point of overflowing its banks, sweeping grandly through rich regions of thought."[5]

Teachings of John Taylor

We must be "alive in the cause of education" for ourselves and our children.

We want . . . to be alive in the cause of education. We are commanded of the Lord to obtain knowledge, both by study and by faith, seeking it out of the best books [see D&C 88:118]. And it becomes us to teach our children, and afford them instruction in every branch of education calculated to promote their welfare.[6]

We are here, as a people, . . . not to imitate the world, unless it be in that which is good . . . but that we may put ourselves in possession of every truth, of every virtue, of every principle of intelligence known among men, together with those that God has revealed for our special guidance, and apply them to our everyday life, and thus educate ourselves and our children in everything that tends to exalt man. . . . We should seek to know more about ourselves and our bodies, about what is most conducive to health and how to preserve health and how to avoid disease; and to know what to eat and what to drink, and what to abstain from taking into our systems. We should become acquainted with the physiology of the human system, and live in accordance with the laws that govern our bodies, that our days may be long in the land which the Lord our God has given us. And in order to fully comprehend ourselves we must study from the best books, and also by faith. And then let education be fostered and encouraged in our midst.

Train your children to be intelligent and industrious. First teach them the value of healthful bodies, and how to preserve them in soundness and vigor; teach them to entertain the highest regard for virtue and chastity and likewise encourage them to develop the intellectual faculties with which they are endowed. They should also be taught regarding the earth on which they live, its properties, and the laws that govern it; and they ought to be instructed concerning God who made the earth, and His designs and purposes in its creation and the placing of man upon it. . . . And whatever labor they pursue they should be taught to do so intelligently; and every incentive, at the command of parents to induce children to labor intelligently and understandingly, should be held out to them. . . .

It is highly necessary that we should learn to read and write and speak our own language correctly; and where people are deficient themselves in education they should strive all the more to see that the deficiency be not perpetuated in their offspring. We ought to take more pains than we do in the training and education of our youth. All that we can possibly do by way of placing them in a position to become the equals, at least, of [mankind], we ought to take pleasure in doing; for in elevating them we bring honor to our own name, and glory to God the Father. To do this requires labor and means, and it also requires perseverance and determination on the part of all concerned.[7]

Whatever you do, be choice in your selection of teachers. We do not want infidels to mold the minds of our children. They are a precious charge bestowed upon us by the Lord, and we cannot be too careful in rearing and training them. I would rather have my children taught the simple rudiments of a common education by men of God, and have them under their influence, than have them taught in the most abstruse [or complex] sciences by men who have not the fear of God in their hearts. . . .

We need to pay more attention to educational matters, and do all we can to procure the services of competent teachers. Some people say, we cannot afford to pay them. You cannot afford not to employ them. We want our children to grow up intelligently, and to walk abreast with the peoples of any nation. God expects us to do it; and therefore I call attention to this matter. I have heard intelligent practical men say, it is quite as cheap to keep a good horse as a poor one, or to raise good stock as inferior animals. Is it not quite as cheap to raise good intelligent children as to rear children in ignorance?[8]

All true intelligence comes from God and expands our minds and souls.

Man, by philosophy and the exercise of his natural intelligence, may gain an understanding, to some extent, of the laws of Nature. But to comprehend God, heavenly wisdom and intelligence are necessary.[9]

It is good for men to be taught in the history and laws of nations, to become acquainted with the principles of justice and equity, with the nature of disease and the medicinal properties of plants, etc. But there is no need of their being without the knowledge of God, for in fact every branch of true knowledge known to man has originated in God, and men have come in possession of it from his word or from his works. . . . All the intelligence which men possess on the earth, whether religious, scientific, or political—proceeds from God. Every good and perfect gift proceeds from him, the fountain of light and truth, wherein there is no variableness nor shadow of turning. The knowledge of the human system has proceeded from the human system itself, which God has organized.[10]

There is no man living, and there never was a man living, who was capable of teaching the things of God only as he was taught, instructed and directed by the spirit of revelation proceeding from the Almighty. And then there are no people competent to receive true intelligence and to form a correct judgment in relation to the sacred principles of eternal life, unless they are under the influence of the same spirit, and hence speakers and hearers are all in the hands of the Almighty.[11]

The principles of the gospel are calculated to expand the mind, enlarge the heart, unfold the capacity and make all men feel their relationship to God and to each other, that we may all be partakers of the same blessings; that we may all be intelligent, that we may all be learned in the things of the kingdom of God and all be prepared for the celestial inheritance in the eternal worlds. This is the difference between the system that we have embraced and the systems of the world—they are of men, this is of God. . . . The kingdom of God exalts the good, blesses all, enlightens all, expands the minds of all and puts within the reach of all the blessings of eternity. . . . I appreciate all true intelligence, whether moral, social, scientific, political or philosophical. . . .

Truth and intelligence [have] a tendency to enlarge the capacity, to expand the soul and to show man his real position, his relationship to himself and to his God, both in relation to the present and the future, that he may know how to live on the earth and be prepared to mingle with the Gods in the eternal worlds. . . .

It is the principles of truth which cement us together and make us act in union and strength; it is those principles that buoy up our feelings, animate our souls and make us feel joyous and jubilant under all circumstances; it is light, it is truth, it is intelligence, it comes from and leads to God, exaltation and celestial glory. We feel joyous because we have the principles of eternal life within us; it is because we have partaken at the fountain of life, and know our relationship to the Lord.[12]

The Church helps educate us about this world and the world to come.

We need teaching continually, line upon line, precept upon precept, here a little and there a little. Hence we have our various organizations of the priesthood, . . . to teach, to instruct, and to enter into all the ramifications of life whether they pertain to this world or the world to come.[13]

Students and teachers at the Plain City School in Utah in 1884. President Taylor exhorted the Saints to "foster education and intelligence of every kind . . . and magnify the gifts which God [had] given them."

We have here our Relief Societies. . . . I was in Nauvoo at the time the Relief Society was organized by the Prophet Joseph Smith, and I was present at the occasion. . . .

With regard to those Societies, I will say, they have done a good work and are a great assistance to our bishops, as well as being peculiarly adapted to console, bless, and encourage those of their sisters who need their care, and also to visit the sick, as well as to counsel and instruct the younger women in the things pertaining to their calling as children and saints of the Most High. I am happy to say that we have a great many honorable and noble women engaged in these labors of love, and the Lord blesses them in their labors, and I bless them in the name of the Lord. And I say to our sisters, continue to be diligent and faithful in seeking the well-being and happiness of your sex, instruct and train your own daughters in the fear of God, and teach your sisters to do likewise, that we may be the blessed of the Lord and our offspring with us.[14]

Then, we have our Sunday Schools, and many of our brethren and sisters in this direction are doing a good work. I would advise the [presidents] of Sunday Schools to endeavor to collect the best talent they can to teach and instruct our children. What greater or more honorable work can we be engaged in than in teaching the children the principles of salvation? You that are diligent and that give your hearts to these things, God will bless, and the day will come when the youth of Israel will rise up and call you blessed.[15]

Education, used righteously, can help us build Zion.

It is good for the elders to become acquainted with the languages, for they may have to go abroad, and should be able to talk to the people, and not look like fools. . . . You may say, I thought the Lord would give us the gift of tongues. He won't if we are too indolent to study them. I never ask the Lord to do a thing I could do for myself.

We should be acquainted with all things, should obtain intelligence both by faith and by study. We are instructed to gather it out of the best books, and become acquainted with governments, nations, and laws. The elders of this church have need to study these things, that when they go to the nations, they may not wish to return home before they have accomplished a good work.[16]

God expects Zion to become the praise and glory of the whole earth so that kings, hearing of her fame, will come and gaze upon her glory. . . . He wants us to observe his laws and fear him, and standing as messengers to go forth to the nations; clothed upon with the power of the priesthood which has been conferred upon us; seeking "first the kingdom of God, and his righteousness;" [Matthew 6:33] seeking first the welfare and happiness of our fellow-men. . . .

This being the case, we ought to foster education and intelligence of every kind; cultivate literary tastes, and men of literary and scientific talent should improve that talent, and all should magnify the gifts which God has given unto them. Educate your children, and seek for those to teach them who have faith in God and in his promises, as well as intelligence. . . . If there is anything good and praiseworthy in morals, religions, science, or anything calculated to exalt and ennoble man, we are after it. But with all our getting, we want to get understanding [see Proverbs 4:7]; and that understanding which flows from God.[17]

The great principle that we have to come to is the knowledge of God, of the relationship that we sustain to each other, of the various duties we have to attend to in the various spheres of life in which we are called to act as mortal and immortal, intelligent, eternal beings, in order that we may magnify our calling and approve ourselves before God and the holy angels, and if we obtain knowledge of this kind, we shall do well, for this is the greatest good of the whole, it embraces everything that we want.[18]

Suggestions for Study and Discussion

- What does it mean to you to be "alive in the cause of education"? What experiences have shown you the importance of education?
- What opportunities exist for you to expand your education? How can you better take advantage of these opportunities? Why is it important that we continue learning throughout our lives? How can our education and learning help build the kingdom of God?
- Why is it important to educate ourselves and our children about good health? In what ways can we do this?
- Why is it important that we have good teachers for our children? What can we do to help ensure that our children have qualified and moral teachers? What else can we do to participate in our children's education?
- What knowledge have you gained by participating in different organizations within the Church? Why do some people seem to gain so little from their Church instruction and others gain so much? How can we and our children receive the most out of our Church classes and programs?
- What can you do to show your appreciation to those who labor to teach you and your children?

- President Taylor taught that "the great principle that we have to come to is the knowledge of God." Why should the Lord and His teachings be central to all of our study and learning? What does it mean to you to learn "by study and by faith"?

Related Scriptures: Proverbs 4:7; John 8:31–32; D&C 88:77–80; 93:36; 130:18–21

Notes

1. *Deseret News: Semi-Weekly,* 12 June 1883, 1.
2. See B. H. Roberts, *The Life of John Taylor* (1963), 323.
3. See *The Life of John Taylor,* 228–32.
4. Hubert Howe Bancroft, *History of Utah* (1890), 433.
5. See *The Life of John Taylor,* 430–33.
6. *Deseret News: Semi-Weekly,* 4 June 1878, 1.
7. *Deseret News: Semi-Weekly,* 12 June 1883, 1.
8. *The Gospel Kingdom,* sel. G. Homer Durham (1943), 273.
9. *The Gospel Kingdom,* 73.
10. *The Gospel Kingdom,* 271.
11. *The Gospel Kingdom,* 275.
12. *Deseret News* (Weekly), 30 Sept. 1857, 238.
13. *The Gospel Kingdom,* 134.
14. *The Gospel Kingdom,* 178–79.
15. *The Gospel Kingdom,* 276.
16. *The Gospel Kingdom,* 78–79; paragraphing altered.
17. *Deseret News: Semi-Weekly,* 24 Sept. 1878, 1.
18. *Deseret News* (Weekly), 30 Sept. 1857, 238.

CHAPTER 11

Finding Joy in Life

It is for [the Saints] to grasp at everything that is good, and calculated to promote the happiness of the human family.[1]

From the Life of John Taylor

In late June of 1847, a large group of Saints led by Elder John Taylor and Elder Parley P. Pratt left Winter Quarters to travel west. By September 1847 they had reached the east side of the Rocky Mountains, between 300 and 400 miles away from the Salt Lake Valley. During the first week of September, several inches of snow had fallen, and many of the Saints began to feel disheartened. At this same time, President Brigham Young and several members of the Twelve were returning from the Salt Lake Valley to Winter Quarters and met Elder Taylor's group. Amid the snow and the growing concern of those who were traveling to the Salt Lake Valley, Elder Taylor encouraged everyone to be of good cheer and met in council with President Young, the accompanying members of the Twelve, and the other leading brethren in the group.

While the brethren were meeting, the clouds dispersed and the sun soon melted the snow. Without telling the rest of the group, several of the sisters went to a secluded grassy area fringed with bushes. There they began setting up makeshift tables decorated with white linen and fine tableware. A historical account records that " 'the fatted calf' was killed; game and fish were prepared in abundance; fruits, jellies and relishes reserved for special occasions were brought out until truly it was a royal feast."

When the council meeting had ended, the brethren who had been in the meeting and more than 100 other members of the group were led to the surprise gathering, where they enjoyed a

"God designs that we should enjoy ourselves. I do not believe in a religion that makes people gloomy, melancholy, [or] miserable."

fine meal. The account records the following: "Supper over and cleared away, preparations were made for dancing; and soon was added to the sweet confusion of laughter and cheerful conversation the merry strains of the violin. . . . Dancing was interspersed with songs and recitations. 'We felt mutually edified and blessed,' writes Elder Taylor, 'we praised the Lord and blessed one another.' "[2]

Latter-day Saints have always believed in finding happiness in life, whether it be through enjoying the beauty and abundance of nature, gathering for wholesome social activities, or pondering the truths of the gospel. John Taylor taught, "It is 'life and the pursuit of happiness' that ought to occupy the attention of all intellectual beings." While he believed that we can experience great joy in this life, he also taught that "the greatest happiness that we can attain to is in securing the approbation of our Heavenly Father, in fearing God, in being made acquainted with his laws—with the principles of eternal truth, and with those things that we consider will best promote not only our temporal, but our eternal happiness."[3]

Teachings of John Taylor

God wants us to enjoy life.

We like enjoyment here. That is right. God designs that we should enjoy ourselves. I do not believe in a religion that makes people gloomy, melancholy, miserable and ascetic. . . . I should not think there was anything great or good associated with that, while everything around, the trees, birds, flowers and green fields, were so pleasing, the insects and bees buzzing and fluttering, the lambs frolicking and playing. While everything else enjoyed life, why should not we? But we want to do it correctly and not pervert any of these principles that God has planted in the human family.[4]

Is there anything gloomy in the works that God has made? Turn where we will, we see harmony, loveliness, cheerfulness, and beauty.

The blessings of providence were made for man, and his enjoyment; he is placed as head of creation. For him the earth teems with the richest profusion; the golden grain, the luscious fruit, the choicest vines; for him, the herbs, and flowers bedeck the earth, shed their odoriferous perfumes, and display their gorgeous beauty; . . . For him, the shrub and vine bloom and blossom, and nature clothes herself in her richest attire; the rippling stream, the pure fountain, the crystal river flow for him, all nature spreads her richest charms, and invites him to partake of her joyousness, beauty, and innocence, and to worship her God.

Talk about melancholy in the fear of God, and in his service! It is the corruption of the world, that has made men unhappy; and the corruption of religion that has made it gloomy: these are the miseries entailed by men, not the blessings of God. Talk about gloom! Is there gloom in the warbling of the birds, in the prancing of the horse, in the playfulness of the lamb, or kid; in the beauty of flowers, in any of Nature's gifts, or rich attire, or in God, that made them, or in his service?[5]

Social enjoyment can be compatible with true religion.

Why, there are some people who think that the fiddle, for instance, is an instrument of the devil and it is quite wrong to use it. I do not think so, I think it is a splendid thing to dance by. But some folks think that we should not dance. Yes, we should enjoy life in any way we can. Some people object to music. Why, music prevails in the heavens, and among the birds! God has filled them with it. There is nothing more pleasing and delightful than it is to go into the woods or among the bushes early in the morning and listen to the warbling and rich melody of the birds, and it is strictly in accordance with the sympathies of our nature.

We have no idea of the excellence of the music we shall have in heaven. It may be said of that, as one of the Apostles has said in relation to something else—"Eye hath not seen, nor ear heard, neither hath it entered into the heart of man to conceive of those things which are prepared for those who love and fear

God." [See 1 Corinthians 2:9.] We have no idea of the excellency, beauty, harmony and symphony of the music in the heavens.

Our object is to get and cleave to everything that is good, and to reject everything that is bad. One reason why religious people in the world are opposed to music and theatres is because of the corruption that is mixed up with them. Wicked and corrupt men associate themselves with these things, and degrade them; but is this any reason that the Saints should not enjoy the gifts of God? Is that a correct principle? Certainly not. It is for them to grasp at everything that is good, and calculated to promote the happiness of the human family. . . .

In all our amusements we should see that things are conducted right, and we should never forget to act the part of ladies and gentlemen, and we should do away with frowardness [or disobedience] and impudence, and treat everybody with kindness, courtesy and respect.[6]

Social enjoyment and amusements are not incompatible with correct conduct and true religion. Instead of forbidding the theatre and placing it under ban, it has been the aim of the Latter-day Saints to control it and keep it free from impure influences, and to preserve it as a place where all could meet for the purpose of healthful enjoyment. Our leading men have, therefore, gone to these places with the view, by their presence, of restraining all practices and influences that would be injurious to the young and rising generation. Too great care cannot be exercised that liberty shall not degenerate into license, and not to convert that which should furnish enjoyment and simple pleasure into a means of producing unhealthful excitement or corrupting morals. . . . Committee-men and officers in charge should see that dances of every kind are conducted in a modest and becoming manner and that no behavior be permitted that would lead to evil or that would offend the most delicate susceptibilities.[7]

Being united in the gospel brings us joy.

It is very pleasant for the Saints of God to reflect upon the principles of eternal truth, that have been developed unto them. If there is anything connected with happiness and humanity, if there is anything calculated to expand the views and feelings of the human family, to raise our hopes and aspirations, and to give peace, joy, and confidence, it is the thought that God has revealed unto us the precepts of eternal truth; that He has planted them within our bosoms and given unto us a certainty in regard to those things we profess to believe in, and assuredly do know.[8]

I cannot conceive of anything more beautiful and heavenly than a united brotherhood, organized after the pattern laid down in the Doctrine and Covenants; when all act for the benefit of all—when while we love God with all our hearts we love our neighbor as ourselves; where our time, our property, our talents, our mental and bodily powers are all exerted for the good of all; where no man grabs or takes advantage of another; where there is a common interest, a common purse, a common stock; where, as they did on this continent, it is said of them that "they all dealt justly to each other," and all acted for the general weal, "when every man in every place could meet a brother and a friend," when all the generous and benevolent influences and sympathies of our nature are carried out, and covetousness, arrogance, hatred, and pride, and every evil are subdued and brought into subjection to the will and Spirit of God. These principles are very beautiful and would be very happifying for a community, a territory, a state, nation, or the world.[9]

I have felt joyful in the Lord, and I bless the name of the God of Israel that I am associated with his church and kingdom on the earth. These feelings I wish at all times to cherish in my bosom and carry out in my life; and I believe there are hundreds, if not thousands, before me to-day, who have the same spirit and feeling, and the same desires. . . .

What makes us so buoyant and joyful on occasions like this? . . . It is because there is a union of good feelings, good desires and aspirations and one spirit inspires the whole, forming a phalanx [or organized body] of power, of faith, and of the Spirit of the Lord. A single taper [or candle] will give a light, and it is pleasant to look upon, but thousands of the same kind of light make a general illumination. With us, it is a time of union, of light, of life, of intelligence, of the Spirit of the living God; our feelings are one, our faith is one, and a great multitude possessing this oneness forms an array of power that no power on this side of earth or hell is able to cope with, or overcome. . . .

We believe that we as a body of people, embracing all the various quorums of this church and kingdom are engaged in this one great work; and hence there is a feeling of faith, union, and intensity, or power, if you please, of the Spirit of the living God, that quickens and vivifies the mind, gives energy to the body, and joy to the bosom. In this we all feel to participate. The Lord is here by his Spirit and power, and our hearts are joyful.[10]

Understanding the principles of truth brings happiness and joy.

When we look at ourselves aright—when we understand the principles of truth aright—what is there we would not give for salvation? When the Spirit has beamed forth powerfully upon the hearts of the saints—when the light and intelligence of heaven has manifested itself—when the Lord has [shone] upon the souls of the saints when assembled together, what have they felt like? that they are the blessed of the Lord. How oft when they have met together on special occasions to receive certain blessings from the hands of God, has the spirit of revelation rested upon them, and the future been opened to their view in all its beauty, glory, richness, and excellency; and when their hearts have been warmed up by that spirit, how have they felt to rejoice! How have they looked upon the things of this world, and the prospect that awaited them! upon their privileges as saints of the Most High God; and upon the glory they will inherit if they are faithful to the end!

You may have experienced the feeling that such thoughts and prospects would naturally create in the human heart. Why is it we feel otherwise at any time? It is because we forget to pray and call upon God, and dedicate ourselves to him, or because we fall into transgression, commit iniquity, and lose the Spirit of God, and forget our calling's glorious hope; but if we could all the time see and realize and understand our true position before God, our minds would be continually on the stretch after the things of God, and we should be seeking to know all the day long, what we could do to promote the happiness and salvation of the world, what we could do to honor our calling—to honor the priesthood of the Son of God, and what to do to honor our God, and to improve the remaining time we have upon the earth, and the energies of our bodies for the accomplishment of his purposes, and for the rolling forth of his kingdom—for the advancement of his designs, that when we stand before him, he may say to us, "well done thou good and faithful servant, enter into the joy of thy Lord; thou hast been faithful over a few things, I will make thee ruler over many things." [See Matthew 25:21.][11]

So far as I am personally concerned, I am here as a candidate for eternity, for heaven and for happiness. I want to secure by my acts a peace in another world that will impart that happiness and bliss for which I am seeking.[12]

Suggestions for Study and Discussion

- President Taylor taught that God created the earth and its beauty for our enjoyment. What experiences have you had in which you found joy in the beauty of the earth and felt closer to the Lord?
- How can wholesome music, poetry, drama, or other forms of entertainment bring us joy? What can we do to bring the power and joy of uplifting music into our lives and the lives of our family members? How can we support and promote wholesome entertainment?
- Why do you think music is such an important part of our religious worship? How have the hymns of the Church comforted or strengthened you during times of trial?
- How has your fellowship with other Saints brought you joy? What can you do to encourage greater unity among the members of your ward or branch?
- What does it mean to you to feel "joyful in the Lord"? What are some doctrines of the gospel that bring you joy? As we seek joy in this life, why is it important to think also of eternity?

- What are some events in your life that have brought you joy? What can we do to retain a spirit of joy in our lives in spite of our trials? What can we do to help our children find joy in their lives?

Related Scriptures: Psalm 118:24; Isaiah 12:2–3; Matthew 25:21; 2 Nephi 2:25; Mosiah 2:41; Articles of Faith 1:13

Notes

1. *Deseret News* (Weekly), 15 Jan. 1873, 760.
2. See B. H. Roberts, *The Life of John Taylor* (1963), 186, 188–92; see also B. H. Roberts, *A Comprehensive History of the Church,* 3:293–98.
3. *The Gospel Kingdom,* sel. G. Homer Durham (1943), 342.
4. *Deseret News* (Weekly), 15 Jan. 1873, 760.
5. *The Government of God* (1852), 30.
6. *Deseret News* (Weekly), 15 Jan. 1873, 760.
7. In James R. Clark, comp., *Messages of the First Presidency of The Church of Jesus Christ of Latter-day Saints,* 6 vols. (1965–75), 3:121–22.
8. *Deseret News* (Weekly), 8 Nov. 1871, 463.
9. *The Gospel Kingdom,* 258.
10. *Deseret News* (Weekly), 28 Dec. 1859, 337.
11. *Deseret News* (Weekly), 25 May 1854, 2; paragraphing altered.
12. *Deseret News* (Weekly), 11 Apr. 1860, 41.

"In partaking of the sacrament we not only commemorate the death and sufferings of our Lord and Savior Jesus Christ, but we also [look toward] the time when he will come again."

CHAPTER 12

The Sabbath Is a Holy Day

We are commanded to remember the Sabbath day to keep it holy.[1]

From the Life of John Taylor

As mentioned in the previous chapter, beginning in late June 1847, Elders John Taylor and Parley P. Pratt led a group of more than 1,500 Saints from Winter Quarters to the Salt Lake Valley. Describing the beginning of this journey, Elder B. H. Roberts wrote:

"It was late in the season for starting on such an expedition. It was too late for them to put in crops that season, even if they stopped far short of the eastern base of the Rocky Mountains. They barely had provisions to last them a year and a half, and if their first crop failed, starvation must follow, for they would be from ten to fifteen hundred miles from the nearest point where food could be obtained. . . .

"They had their all upon the altar, including their wives and children, who must share their hardships and their fate. They knew not their destination, they entrusted all on a single venture, from which there was no chance of retreat. If they should fail to find a suitable location and raise a crop the first season, there was no getting provisions to them, nor them to provisions. They must succeed, or perish in the wilderness to which they had started."

In spite of these perilous circumstances and the need to arrive in the Salt Lake Valley before the onset of winter, travel was halted each Sunday for observance of the Sabbath day. Elder Roberts continued, "Sunday was observed as a day of rest, religious services were held in each camp, and the stillness of the great wilderness of the west was broken by Saints singing the songs of Zion." On 5 October 1847, the Taylor and Pratt companies safely arrived in the Salt Lake Valley and began the necessary preparations for winter.[2]

For President John Taylor, the Sabbath was a day of worship, rest, and thoughtful recollection. He encouraged the Saints to "keep the Sabbath day holy, set it aside as a day of rest, a day of meeting together to perform your sacraments and listen to the words of life, and thus be found keeping the commandments, and setting a good example before your children."[3]

Teachings of John Taylor

The Sabbath is a day to worship God with all our hearts.

The best of us are not too good; we all of us might be better, and do better and enjoy life better, having more of the Spirit of the Lord in our own homes and in our own hearts, and do more to promote the welfare of all who come within our reach and influence. To serve the Lord is one of the great objects of our existence; and I appreciate as a great privilege the opportunity we enjoy of worshiping God on the Sabbath day. And when we do meet to worship God, I like to see us worship him with all our hearts. I think it altogether out of place on such occasions to hear people talk about secular things; these are times, above all others perhaps, when our feelings and affections should be drawn out towards God. If we sing praises to God, let us do it in the proper spirit; if we pray, let every soul be engaged in prayer, doing it with all our hearts, that through our union our spirits may be blended in one, that our prayers and our worship may be available with God, whose Spirit permeates all things, and is always present in the assemblies of good and faithful Saints.

I will tell you how I feel on a Sabbath morning. I realize this is a day set apart to worship Almighty God: now I ought to worship God myself, and I ought to look after my family and discover whether they are engaged in the same thing or not. For we are commanded to keep holy the Sabbath day and to rest from all our labors, as God did when He created the earth upon which we dwell. He has given us six days to attend to the various labors and duties of life, and if we [undertake] to keep the Sabbath, let us do it acceptably to God our Father, dedicating ourselves to him at least, for that day, and placing our feelings and affections upon him. And then, the Elders of Israel throughout the broad earth are engaged this day in trying to teach the principles of salvation, and I feel like praying for them, and also for our missionaries who are going abroad among the Saints in this land, as well those who speak, as those who dictate in the assemblies of the Saints in this land and in all other lands, that as this is a day set apart for the worship of God, all Israel everywhere may be under the influence and guidance of the Spirit of the living God, and that those especially who speak may be under the divine influence of the Holy Ghost, and present to the various congregations the words of eternal life.[4]

The Sabbath is a day to teach and learn by the Spirit.

It is pleasant for the Saints to meet together to commune with each other, to listen to the words of life, to reflect also upon their position and relationship to God, to His Church and Kingdom, as well as to examine into their own feelings, and, under the guidance of the Lord and of His Holy Spirit, try to find out what relationship they sustain to their Heavenly Father, and whether they are performing the various duties devolving upon them and are seeking to carry out the word, the will, and the law of God.[5]

When we are . . . assembled together we may expect to receive guidance and blessings from God, from whom, the Scriptures inform us, "every good and perfect gift proceeds;" and in Him, we are also informed, "there is no variableness nor shadow of turning." [See James 1:17.] In our assemblies they who speak and they who hear ought to be under the guidance and direction of the Lord, the Fountain of Light. Of all people under the heavens we, Latter-day Saints, do continually realize the necessity of leaning upon God; for I look upon it that, no matter what intelligence may be communicated, no matter how brilliant the speech and edifying the ideas communicated may be, they will not benefit those who hear unless they are under the guidance and inspiration of the spirit of God.[6]

There is no man living, and there never was a man living, who was capable of teaching the things of God only as he was taught, instructed and directed by the spirit of revelation proceeding from the Almighty. And then there are no people competent to receive true intelligence and to form a correct judgment in relation to the sacred principles of eternal life, unless they are under the influence of the same spirit, and hence speakers and hearers are all in the hands of the Almighty.[7]

We meet together, as intelligent beings, desirous of understanding something of our common origin, our present existence, and our future destiny. We meet to find out something in relation to our Heavenly Father, in relation to his providential dealings with the human family, in relation to his policy and designs pertaining to us, and in relation to the object of our creation; and to know something, if possible, pertaining to that world that lies beyond our present scene of action. These are some things among the many that we are desirous to know, to comprehend, to find out, if possible.[8]

I do not know of any way whereby we can be taught, instructed, and be made to comprehend our true position, only by being under the influence of the Spirit of the living God. A man may speak by the Spirit of God, but it requires a portion of that Spirit also in those who hear, to enable them to comprehend correctly the importance of the things that are delivered to them, and hence the difficulty the Lord and his saints have always had in making the people comprehend the things that are especially for their interests. We all consider that if we could be taught of God it would be very well. I suppose the world generally would consider it to be a great blessing. Then the question arises in their minds, whether the teachings they receive come from God or not. How are they to know that? I know of no other way than that which is spoken in the scriptures, "But there is a spirit in man: and the inspiration of the Almighty giveth them understanding." (Job 32:8) And, again, we are told in the New Testament, that "No man knoweth the things of God but by the Spirit of God." [See 1 Corinthians 2:11.]

Hence all the wisdom, all the intelligence, all the reasoning, all the philosophy and all the arguments that could be brought to bear on the human mind would be of no avail unless the mind of man is prepared to receive this teaching—prepared by the Spirit of the Lord, the same Spirit which conveys the intelligence.[9]

We partake of the sacrament on the Sabbath in memory of Jesus Christ.

It would seem that the coming of the Savior to the world, his suffering, death, resurrection, and ascension to the position he occupies in the eternal world before his Heavenly Father has a great deal to do with our interests and happiness; and hence this continued memorial that we partake of every Sabbath. This sacrament is the fulfillment of the request of Jesus Christ to his disciples. "For as often as ye eat this bread, and drink this cup, ye do shew the Lord's death till he come." (1 Corinthians 11:26.) Faith in this ordinance would necessarily imply that we have faith in Jesus Christ, that he is the Only Begotten of the Father, that he came from the heavens to the earth to accomplish a certain purpose which God had designed—even to secure the salvation and exaltation of the human family. All this has a great deal to do with our welfare and happiness here and hereafter. The death of Jesus Christ would not have taken place had it not been necessary. That this ceremony should be instituted to keep that circumstance before the minds of his people, bespeaks its importance.[10]

We have met to partake of the sacrament of the Lord's supper, and we should endeavor to draw away our feelings and affections from things of time and sense. For in partaking of the sacrament we not only commemorate the death and sufferings of our Lord and Savior Jesus Christ, but we also shadow forth the time when he will come again and when we shall meet and eat bread with him in the kingdom of God [see Luke 14:15; Matthew 26:29]. When we are thus assembled together, we may expect to receive guidance and blessings from God.[11]

Ancient people of God, in whose hearts was enkindled the flame of inspiration, looked forward to that memorable event when the Lamb slain from before the foundation of the world

An early photo of the Pinto Ward, St. George Utah Stake. President Taylor taught that the Sabbath is a time to rest from our labors and strengthen our relationship with God.

would offer himself as a sacrifice, whilst we look back to the same thing. We break bread and eat, and we drink water in the presence of each other every Sabbath day, and we do it in remembrance of the broken body and shed blood of our Lord and Saviour Jesus Christ; and this we will continue to do until he comes again. When he does come, the Latter-day Saints expect to be among that favored number that will eat and drink with him at his own table in our Father's kingdom. I expect this just as much as I expect to eat my supper tonight.[12]

We ought to be careful that we do not partake of these emblems [of the sacrament] to our condemnation. Do you ever quarrel with your brethren, or act in such a way as to get up feelings, and perhaps speak harsh words one about another, and in other ways do that which is wrong, and then meet together in solemn mockery before God and eat condemnation to your souls? We want to be careful about these things; and hence we should understand that when we bring our gift to the altar, and there remember that we have ought against our brother, we should first go and be reconciled to him and then come and offer our gift [see Matthew 5:23–24]. Not come in any kind of hypocrisy, but come with clean hands and pure hearts, and feel to say "O God search me and try me and prove me, and if there is any way of wickedness in me, let it depart, and let me be thy true representative upon the earth, and let me partake of the spirit that dwelleth in Christ, and live in the enjoyment of that upon the earth; that when he comes again I, with my brethren, may meet him with clean hands and pure hearts."[13]

To receive the blessings of God, we must do more than simply attend our meetings and partake of the sacrament.

Too many of us feel after the world. Can the world give you the light that you have received, and the gospel and the hopes of heaven you have received, and the priesthood you have received? And will you barter these things for a mess of pottage, and wallow in the filth, corruption, iniquity, and evils which abound in the world? What have we come here for? To worship God and to keep his commandments. And how is it with many of us? We forget, in many instances, our high calling's glorious hope, and we give way to follies, foibles, weakness, and iniquity, and we are governed more or less by covetousness, drunkenness, Sabbath-breaking, and evils of various kinds. I sometimes see Elders of Israel bringing in loads of wood and loads of hay on the Sabbath day. Why, it is a burning shame in the eyes of God, holy angels, and all other intelligent beings. . . . What do you think about a lying Elder, a swearing High Priest, a Sabbath-breaking Seventy, and a covetous Saint? The souls of such men ought to be inspired with the light of revelation, and they ought to be living witnesses, epistles known and read of all men! Do you think you can live your religion, have the Spirit of God and obtain eternal life, and follow after these things? I tell you nay.[14]

It is customary for men in the world from which we have gathered out, to talk on Sunday about spiritual things, when they are dressed in their Sunday coats and at meeting, and then on Monday to pack up their religion with their Sunday clothes in their trunks, to have nothing more to do with it until next Sunday. . . . O, the folly of man in not acknowledging God in all things, in laying aside God and his religion, and trusting in their own judgment and intelligence.[15]

There is something that goes a little further than we think about sometimes; and that is, while we profess to be followers of the Lord, while we profess to have received the Gospel and to be governed by it, a profession will amount to nothing unless we have washed our robes and made them white in the blood of the Lamb. It is not enough for us to be connected with the Zion of God, for the Zion of God must consist of men that are pure in heart and pure in life and spotless before God, at least that is what we have got to arrive at. We are not there yet, but we must get there before we shall be prepared to inherit glory and exaltation; therefore a form of godliness will amount to but little with any of us, for he that knoweth the master's will and doeth it not shall be beaten with many stripes [see Luke 12:47]. It is "not every one that saith unto me, Lord, Lord, shall enter into the kingdom of heaven: but He that doeth the will of my Father which is in heaven." [Matthew 7:21.] These are doctrines of the Gospel as I understand them. And it is not enough for us to embrace the Gospel and to be gathered here to the land of Zion and be associated with the people of God, attend our meetings and partake of the Sacrament of the Lord's supper, and endeavor to move along without much blame of any kind attached to us; for notwithstanding all this, if our hearts are not right, if we are not pure in heart before God, if we have not pure hearts and pure consciences, fearing God and keeping His commandments, we shall not, unless we repent, participate in these blessings about which I have spoken, and of which the Prophets bear testimony.[16]

It is our business to be Saints. And to be worthy of that character it is our duty to live by the principles of virtue, truth, integrity, holiness, purity, and honor that we may at all times secure the favor of Almighty God; that His blessings may be with us and dwell in our bosoms; that the peace of God may abide in our habitations; . . . and that we, as a people, may be under His divine protection.[17]

Suggestions for Study and Discussion

- What are some of the blessings we can experience from faithful observance of the Sabbath? (See also D&C 59:9–13.) How have you personally been blessed for keeping the Sabbath day holy?
- What can you do to worship God more fully on the Sabbath? How can you prepare yourself to be more in tune with the Holy Spirit before Church meetings begin?
- What can parents and grandparents do to influence their children and grandchildren to keep the Sabbath holy? How can we make the Sabbath different from other days for our families? How can observance of the Sabbath strengthen families and protect us from the world?
- Why is it necessary to learn by the Spirit in our Sabbath worship? What can you do in your role as a teacher or learner to invite the influence of the Holy Spirit on the Sabbath?
- What covenants do we make as we partake of the sacrament? (See also Moroni 4–5 or D&C 20:76–79.) How do these covenants relate to our baptismal covenants? (See also Mosiah 18:7–10.)
- Why is it important that we regularly partake of the sacrament? What can you do to feel closer to the Lord as you partake of the sacrament?
- What is the difference between merely attending meetings and truly keeping the Sabbath holy? How can you keep the spirit of the Sabbath with you during the week?

Related Scriptures: Exodus 20:8–11; Isaiah 58:13–14; Matthew 12:10–13; 3 Nephi 18:1–12; D&C 27:1–14; 59:9–20

Notes

1. *Deseret News: Semi-Weekly,* 15 Mar. 1881, 1.
2. See B. H. Roberts, *The Life of John Taylor* (1963), 188–92.
3. *The Gospel Kingdom,* sel. G. Homer Durham (1943), 339.
4. *Deseret News: Semi-Weekly,* 18 Oct. 1881, 1.
5. *Deseret News: Semi-Weekly,* 26 Feb. 1884, 1.
6. *Deseret News: Semi-Weekly,* 29 Mar. 1870, 2.
7. *The Gospel Kingdom,* 275.
8. *The Gospel Kingdom,* 226.
9. *The Gospel Kingdom,* 45–46.
10. *The Gospel Kingdom,* 109.
11. *The Gospel Kingdom,* 227.
12. *Deseret News: Semi-Weekly,* 20 Mar. 1877, 1.
13. *Deseret News: Semi-Weekly,* 31 Aug. 1880, 1.
14. *Deseret News: Semi-Weekly,* 1 Feb. 1876, 1.
15. *Deseret News* (Weekly), 25 Nov. 1863, 142; paragraphing altered.
16. *Deseret News: Semi-Weekly,* 17 Mar. 1885, 1.
17. *Deseret News: Semi-Weekly,* 9 July 1881, 1.

C H A P T E R 1 3

Priesthood, the Government and Power of God

The priesthood . . . is living power.[1]

From the Life of John Taylor

To John Taylor, the priesthood, in addition to being the authority to act in God's name, was also a powerful force by which great things could be accomplished. He taught that priesthood bearers should be active in using the priesthood to serve others and to bring to pass God's righteous purposes. He encouraged all priesthood holders to attend to their duties and magnify their callings, stating that "the teacher or deacon who fulfils his duties is a great deal more honorable than a president or any of the twelve who does not."[2]

President Taylor also recognized and appreciated the authority of those who used their priesthood to serve him and his family. His humble respect for priesthood authority was exemplified by a story that his son Moses W. Taylor once related regarding an evening in the Taylor home when the family was visited by the home teachers. "One of the two was a boy sixteen years of age," the younger Taylor recalled, "and that night it was his turn to preside. Father called the family together and informed the teachers that we were all there and said: 'We are in your hands and await your instructions.' "

The boy then asked President Taylor if they prayed as a family and privately, if they treated their neighbors well, attended church regularly, and supported the authorities of the Church. "These questions were answered one after another by my father just as humbly as the youngest member of the family would have answered them. After the teachers had concluded their labors,

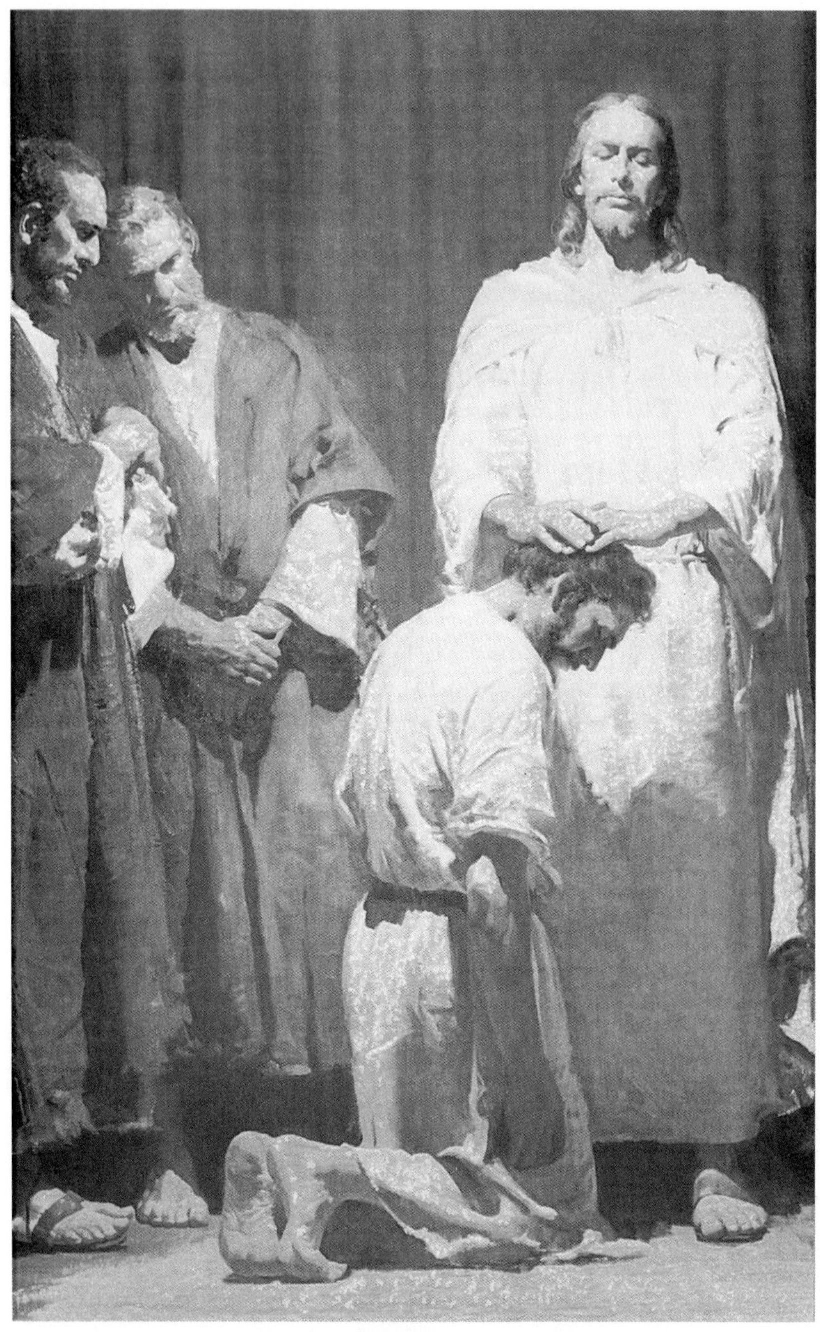

Bearers of the priesthood must remember the source of all priesthood power. As President Taylor taught, "If we have any honor proceeding from or through the priesthood, it comes from God."

they then requested my father to give them some instructions.

"He told them that he was pleased with them for their faithfulness and thanked them for calling and urged them to call on the family as often as they could for he realized the great good that a man holding the priesthood—which is the power of God—could do his family, and told them that there was no office in the church where greater good could be done than in that of a teacher. He told them to pay particular attention to his children and counsel them as a father.

" 'I am not often home,' said he, 'for my church duties call me away so much and I fear if my children do not frequently get good counsel, they may be led astray.' "[3]

Teachings of John Taylor

Priesthood is the power of God.

What is priesthood? . . . I shall briefly answer that it is the government of God, whether on the earth or in the heavens, for it is by that power, agency, or principle that all things are governed on the earth and in the heavens, and by that power that all things are upheld and sustained. It governs all things—it directs all things—it sustains all things—and has to do with all things that God and truth are associated with. It is the power of God delegated to intelligences in the heavens and to men on the earth; and when we arrive in the celestial kingdom of God, we shall find the most perfect order and harmony existing, because there is the perfect pattern, the most perfect order of government carried out, and when or wherever those principles have been developed in the earth, in proportion as they have spread and been acted upon, just in that proportion have they produced blessings and salvation to the human family. And when the government of God shall be more extensively adopted, and when Jesus' prayer, that he taught his disciples, is answered, and God's kingdom comes on the earth, and his will is done here as in heaven [see Matthew 6:10], then, and not till then, will universal love, peace, harmony, and union prevail.[4]

[Priesthood] is . . . the principle and power by which [God] regulates, controls, dictates and manages His affairs, His worlds, His kingdoms, His principalities, His powers, His intelligences, and all things that are underneath Him and above Him, and with which He has to do.[5]

The power manifested by the priesthood is simply the power of God, for he is the head of the priesthood . . . ; and it is upon this principle that all the works of God have been accomplished, whether on the earth or in the heavens; and any manifestation of power through the priesthood on the earth is simply a delegated power from the priesthood in the heavens, and the more the priesthood on the earth becomes assimilated with and subject to the priesthood in the heavens the more of this power shall we possess.[6]

The living priesthood on earth is directed from heaven.

God has organized a priesthood, and that priesthood bears rule in all things pertaining to the earth and the heavens; one part of it exists in the heavens, another part on the earth; they both co-operate together for the building up of Zion, the redemption of the dead and the living, and the bringing to pass the "times of the restitution of all things;" [see Acts 3:21] and as they are thus closely united, it is necessary that there should be a communication between the one and the other, and that those on the earth should receive instructions from those in the heavens, who are acquainted with earthly as well as heavenly things, having had the experience of both, as they once officiated in the same priesthood on the earth.[7]

It is the intercourse and communication of the priesthood in heaven, that gives power, life, and efficacy to the living priesthood on the earth, and without which they would be as dead and withered branches: and if any man has life, or power, it is the power and life of the priesthood, the gift and power of God communicated through the regular channels of the priesthood, both in heaven and on earth; and to seek it without, would be like a stream seeking to be supplied with water when its fountain was dried up, or like a branch seeking to obtain virtue when the trunk of the tree was cut off by the root: and to talk of a church without this is to talk of a thing of naught—a dried fountain, a dead and withered tree.[8]

No man [can] guide this kingdom. He cannot unless God be with him and on the side of the elders of Israel. But with him on their side, all things will move on aright, and the intelligence and the revelations of God will be poured out. His law will be made known and the principles of truth be developed; or it is not the kingdom of God. And we all of us ought to humble ourselves before God, and seek for the guidance of the Almighty. . . .

There is a principle associated with the kingdom of God that recognizes God in all things, and that recognizes the priesthood in all things, and those who do not do it had better repent or they will come to a stand very quickly; I tell you that in the name of the Lord. Do not think you are wise and that you can manage and manipulate the priesthood, for you cannot do it. God must manage, regulate, dictate, and stand at the head, and every man in his place. The ark of God does not need steadying [see 2 Samuel 6:3, 6–7], especially by incompetent men without revelation and without knowledge of the kingdom of God and its laws. It is a great work that we are engaged in, and it is for us to prepare ourselves for the labor before us, and to acknowledge God, his authority, his law and his priesthood in all things.[9]

We want to minister for God in time and throughout the eternities that are to come. We have started in, and we will try by the help of God and the light of His Holy Spirit, and the revelations that He will give to us from time to time—we will try and operate and co-operate with the Priesthood in the eternal worlds either on this earth or in the heavens. We shall operate until the work that God has designed pertaining to this earth shall be accomplished, and the living and the dead saved so far as they are capable of being saved according to eternal laws that exist in the heavens, and according to the decrees of the Almighty. . . .

I say continually, "O God, lead me in the right path: O God, preserve me from all error; O God, I am a poor, feeble, weak, erring human creature, surrounded with infirmities. I need Thy help all the day long. O God, help me." That is my feeling, and the feeling of my brethren of the First Presidency, and of the Twelve and others. We feel that we need the help of the Almighty. We will try and be humble, and be faithful and true to our covenants. And if we listen to counsel and obey the laws of God, and do the things that He requires at our hands, He will help us and bless us, and He will bless Zion and preserve Israel.[10]

Priesthood is given to enable us to build up Zion.

What is this priesthood given us for? That we may be enabled to build up the Zion of our God. What for? To put down wrong and corruption, lasciviousness, lying, thieving, dishonesty, and covetousness, with every kind of evil, and also to encourage faith, meekness, charity, purity, brotherly kindness, truthfulness, integrity, honesty, and everything that is calculated to exalt and ennoble mankind, that we may be the true and proper representatives of God our Father here upon the earth, that we may learn to know his will and do it; that his will may be done on earth as in heaven.[11]

To bring about this desirable end—to restore creation to its pristine excellency and to fulfil the object of creation—to redeem, save, exalt, and glorify man—to save and redeem the dead and the living, and all that shall live according to its laws, is the design and object of the establishment of the priesthood on the earth in the last days. It is for the purpose of fulfilling what has not heretofore been done—that God's works may be perfected—that the times of the restitution of all things may be brought about, and that, in conjunction with the eternal priesthood in the heavens (who without us, nor we without them, could not be made perfect), we may bring to pass all things which have been in the mind of God, or spoken of by the Spirit of God, through the mouth of all the holy prophets since the world was. . . .

The priesthood in the heavens are uniting with us to bring about these purposes, and as they are governed by the same principle, that our works may agree—that there may be a reciprocity of action, and that God's will (so far as we are concerned) may be done on the earth as it is in heaven. It is this which we have to learn, and this which we must do to fulfil our calling, and render our works acceptable in the sight of God and of the holy angels, and also in the sight of our brethren, who are associated with us in the priesthood in the kingdom of God on the earth.[12]

The priesthood is placed in the church for this purpose, to dig, to plant, to nourish, to teach correct principles, and to develop the order of the kingdom of God, to fight the devils, and maintain and support the authorities of the church of Christ upon the earth. It is our duty all to act together to form one great unit—one great united phalanx [or organized body], having sworn allegiance to the kingdom of God; then everything will move on quietly, peaceably, and easily, and then there will be very little trouble.[13]

Priesthood is given for the blessing of the human family.

The Priesthood always was given for the blessing of the human family. People talk about it as though it was for the special benefit of individuals. What was said of Abraham? "In thee and in thy seed"—what? I will confer blessings upon thee. O, that is all right so far as it goes. But "in thee and in thy seed shall all the families of the earth be blessed." [See Abraham 2:11.] Let us act in the capacity of benefactors, and if we are descended of Abraham, let us walk in his footsteps and make ourselves worthy of the promises, let us extend our feelings wide as eternity, and seek to bless and benefit, lift up and ennoble all around us; that we may all rejoice together and be exalted by the same principles which have been revealed for the benefit of all men. . . .

If I were a Bishop—I do not know what I would do, but I know what I should do. I should feel like saying, Father, thou hast committed a number of souls to my care; help me to look after their temporal interests and also to promote their spiritual welfare, and see that they are properly instructed in the laws of life: help me also to teach the teachers that go among the people, that they may go full of the Holy Spirit to bless and benefit the people, that with the aid of my brethren I may be a Savior among them. That is the way I ought to feel and to do if I were a Bishop; and that is the way you Bishops ought to feel and to act, and do it humbly with a desire to do good. And then, if I were a Priest, Teacher or Deacon, and was going around as an instructor among the people, I would want to watch over their welfare.[14]

[Jesus said], "Simon, son of Jonas, lovest thou me more than these? He saith unto him, yea, Lord; thou knowest that I love thee." If you love me, if you are my friend and my disciple, "Feed my Lambs." That was not very hard to do; he had been called for that purpose. "He saith to him again the second time, Simon, son of Jonas, lovest thou me? He saith unto him, yea, Lord, thou knowest that I love thee. He said unto him, Feed my Sheep." And the third time the Savior put the same question to Peter, and which on being answered as before, he said to him, "Feed my Sheep." [See John 21:15–17.] What is the duty of the Apostles; the Presidents of Stakes, the High Priests, and Seventies, especially of those that are generally presiding? If Jesus was here, he would tell you to lay aside your nonsense, your follies and weaknesses, and act more like men and Saints and go to work and "Feed my Sheep."[15]

God gives power to those who magnify the priesthood.

If we understand ourselves and our position, it ought to be with us, the kingdom of God first and ourselves afterwards. If we can learn to accomplish a little thing, the Lord will probably tell us to do a greater, because we are prepared to do it. . . . If we are the people of God, and he is trusting to us to accomplish these great purposes, we have got to do a little more than we have done, and we have got to be willing and obedient to the dictation of the Spirit of the Lord and his servants whom he had placed over us. If we do this, every labor we engage in will be joyous and pleasant to us, peace will reign in our bosoms and the peace of God will abide in our habitations; the Spirit of the

Lord will brood over us, and we shall be full of joy and rejoicing all the day long, and so it will be to the end of the chapter. I know of no other way to accomplish all this work, only to be taught of the Lord, and for that purpose he has organized his holy priesthood.[16]

There is as much devolving upon the priests, the teachers, and the deacons, and those of the lesser priesthood as there is upon any other members of the church. When they do not fulfil their duties, what is the result? People go to the twelve, or to the First Presidency; they pass the more immediate authorities; and confusion and disorder exist; and valuable time is occupied almost needlessly; . . . and all this for the want of men's knowing their duties and doing them.

But while we are contending over little things what becomes of us? We are losing sight of our callings; we forget that this kingdom was established upon the earth for the purpose of introducing righteousness and the laws of heaven upon the earth, and of blessing mankind and of saving the living and the dead. We forget what we are here for, and what the kingdom of God is established for. It is not for you or for me or anybody else alone; it is for the interests of the world and the salvation of mankind. We are expected, every one of us, to perform the various duties and responsibilities devolving upon us. If we neglect them, are we not guilty before God? Whence come the difficulties that we have in our midst? Because as I have said in many instances the priesthood do not perform their duties, are not vigilant and faithful.[17]

I have noticed some in my travels, those, who, like the disciples of Jesus of old, evince a great desire for power, and manifest a very anxious disposition to know who among them shall be greatest. This is folly, for honor proceeds not from office, but by a person magnifying his office and calling. If we have any honor proceeding from or through the priesthood, it comes from God, and we certainly should be vain to boast of a gift when we have no hand in the gift, only in receiving it. If it comes from God, he ought to have the glory and not us, and our magnifying our calling is the only way or medium through which we can obtain honor or influence.[18]

Suggestions for Study and Discussion

- What is the priesthood of God? What blessings are available to us through the priesthood? How do you feel when you consider that God has entrusted to man the power of the priesthood?
- What can each family member do to strengthen the power of the priesthood in the home?
- Why is it important that priesthood holders receive continual guidance from the Lord?
- How does the priesthood help to "redeem, save, exalt, and glorify man"?
- How have you and your loved ones been blessed through the righteous use of the priesthood? How can women share in the blessings of the priesthood?
- What are some opportunities for priesthood service in your area? What can priesthood holders do to help strengthen homes where there is no priesthood bearer?
- Read D&C 84:33–34. What does it mean to magnify a priesthood calling? What does it mean to magnify any calling in the Church? In what ways can we help those in our ward or branch who are attempting to magnify their callings?

Related Scriptures: 1 Corinthians 4:20; 1 Timothy 4:12–16; Jacob 1:18–19; D&C 58:26–28; 84:18–21, 26–27, 33–34; 107:99–100

Notes

1. *The Gospel Kingdom,* sel. G. Homer Durham (1943), 127.
2. *The Gospel Kingdom,* 166.
3. "Stories and Counsel of Prest. Taylor," *Young Woman's Journal,* May 1905, 219; paragraphing altered.
4. *The Gospel Kingdom,* 129.
5. *Deseret News* (Weekly), 28 Dec. 1859, 338.
6. *The Gospel Kingdom,* 130.
7. "On Priesthood," *Millennial Star,* 1 Nov. 1847, 323.
8. *The Gospel Kingdom,* 130.
9. *The Gospel Kingdom,* 166.
10. *Deseret News* (Weekly), 18 June 1884, 339; paragraphing altered.
11. *The Gospel Kingdom,* 130–31.
12. *The Gospel Kingdom,* 132.
13. *The Gospel Kingdom,* 129.
14. *Deseret News: Semi-Weekly,* 18 Oct. 1881, 1; paragraphing altered.
15. *Deseret News: Semi-Weekly,* 19 Aug. 1879, 1.
16. *The Gospel Kingdom,* 131–32.
17. *The Gospel Kingdom,* 154.
18. *The Gospel Kingdom,* 133.

C H A P T E R 1 4

The Responsibilities and Order of the Priesthood

The organization of the church is . . . according to the principles that God has revealed.[1]

From the Life of John Taylor

President Taylor felt strongly about order and organization within the priesthood, teaching that the priesthood "is a pattern of things in the heavens" and the means "through which the blessings of God flow to his people on the earth."[2] He began the practice of weekly priesthood meetings in the wards, together with monthly stake priesthood meetings and quarterly stake conferences, to encourage priesthood holders to learn and fulfill their duties.

With the death of Brigham Young in August 1877, the First Presidency was dissolved and the Quorum of the Twelve Apostles, with John Taylor as their President, became the presiding body of the Church. Although President Taylor knew that in such circumstances the Twelve as a quorum were then equal in authority to the First Presidency (see D&C 107:22–24), he also knew that the proper order of the priesthood provided that the Church be led by a President and his two counselors. At the same time, he humbly sought to do only the will of the Lord and did not want to take any position unto himself.

A little more than three years after the death of Brigham Young, the First Presidency was reorganized. On 10 October 1880, President John Taylor was sustained as President of the Church, with George Q. Cannon and Joseph F. Smith as counselors. Speaking on the day of this sustaining, President Taylor said: "Had it not been our duty to have the church organized fully and completely in all its departments, I should have much preferred

"If we have received any office, or calling, or authority, or any power to administer in any of the ordinances, we have received that from the hand of God."

to have continued with the brethren of the twelve, speaking of it merely as a matter of personal feeling. But there are questions arising in regard to these matters that are not for us to say how they shall be, or what course shall be pursued. When God has given us an order and has appointed an organization in his church, with the various quorums of priesthood as presented to us by revelation through the Prophet Joseph Smith, I do not think that either the First Presidency, the twelve, the high priests, the seventies, the bishops, or anybody else, have a right to change or alter that plan which the Lord has introduced and established."

He then noted that since the death of Brigham Young, the priesthood had been fully organized, with the exception of the First Presidency and that it was necessary that the quorum of the First Presidency, as well as all other quorums, should occupy the place assigned it by the Almighty.

President Taylor continued: "These were the suggestions of the Spirit of the Lord to me. I expressed my feelings to the twelve, who coincided with me, and indeed, several of them had had the same feelings as those with which I was actuated. It is not with us, or ought not to be, a matter of place, position, or honor, although it is a great honor to be a servant of God. It is a great honor to hold the priesthood of God. But while it is an honor to be God's servants, holding his priesthood, it is not honorable for any man or any set of men to seek for position in the holy priesthood. Jesus said, Ye have not called me, but I have called you [see John 15:16]. And as I said before, had I consulted my own personal feelings, I would have said, things are going on very pleasantly, smoothly, and agreeably; and I have a number of good associates whom I respect and esteem, as my brethren, and I rejoice in their counsels. Let things remain as they are. But it is not for me to say, it is not for you to say what we would individually prefer, but it is for us holding the holy priesthood to see that all the organizations of that priesthood are preserved intact and that everything in the church and kingdom of God is organized according to the plan which he has revealed. Therefore we have taken the course which you have been called upon to sanction by your votes today."[3]

Teachings of John Taylor

There are two priesthoods, namely the Melchizedek and Aaronic.

First.—We find that there are two distinctive general priesthoods, namely, the Melchizedek and Aaronic. . . . Second—That they are both conferred by the Lord; that both are everlasting, and administer in time and eternity. Third—That the Melchizedek priesthood holds the right of presidency, and has power and authority *over all the offices in the church,* in all ages of the world, *to administer in spiritual things.* Fourth—That the second priesthood is called the priesthood of Aaron, because it was conferred upon Aaron and his seed throughout all their generations. Fifth—That the lesser [or Aaronic] priesthood is a part of, or an appendage to the greater, or the Melchizedek priesthood, and has power in administering outward ordinances. . . . Sixth—That there is a presidency over each of these priesthoods, both over the Melchizedek and the Aaronic.

Seventh—That while the power of the higher, or Melchizedek, is to hold the keys *of all* the spiritual *blessings of the church;* to have the privilege of receiving the mysteries of the kingdom of heaven, to have the heavens opened to them, to commune with the general assembly and church of the firstborn and to enjoy the communion and presence of God the Father, and Jesus the Mediator of the new covenant, and to preside over all the spiritual officers of the church, yet the *presidency* of the high priesthood, after the order of Melchizedek, have a right to officiate in *all the offices in the church,* both spiritual and temporal.

"Then comes the High Priesthood, which is the greatest of all. Wherefore, it must needs be that one be appointed of the High Priesthood to preside over the priesthood, and he shall be called President of the High Priesthood of the Church; Or, in other words, the Presiding High Priest over the High Priesthood of the Church." [D&C 107:64–66.]

It is thus evident that this priesthood presides over all presidents, all bishops, including the presiding bishop; over all councils, organizations, and authorities in the whole Church, in all the world.

That the bishopric is the presidency of the Aaronic priesthood, which is an appendage to the greater or Melchizedek priesthood [see D&C 107:14], and that no man has a legal right to hold the keys of the Aaronic priesthood, which presides over all bishops and all the lesser priesthood, except he be a literal descendant of Aaron. But, that as a high priest of the Melchizedek priesthood has authority to officiate in all the lesser offices, he may officiate in the office of bishop . . . if called, set apart, and ordained unto this power by the hands of the presidency of the Melchizedek priesthood. [See D&C 107:17.][4]

This high [or Melchizedek] priesthood, we are told, has held the right of presidency in all ages of the world [see D&C 107:8]. But there is a difference between the general powers of the priesthood, and the particular office and calling to which men are set apart. . . . Because a man is a high priest, is he an apostle? No. Because a man is a high priest, is he the president of a stake, or the counselor to the president of a stake? No. Because he is a high priest, is he a bishop? No, not by any means. And so on, in all the various offices. The high priesthood holds the authority to administer in those ordinances, offices, and places, when they are appointed by the proper authorities, and at no other time; and while they are sustained also by the people. . . . It is not because a man holds a certain class of priesthood that he is to administer in all the offices of that priesthood. He administers in them only as he is called and set apart for that purpose.[5]

Priesthood offices have been given for the perfecting of the Saints.

The Lord has placed in his church apostles and prophets, high priests, seventies, elders, etc. What for? For the perfecting of the Saints. [See Ephesians 4:11–12.] Are we all perfect to begin with? No. These various officers are for perfecting of the Saints. What else? For the work of the ministry, that men might be qualified and informed and be full of intelligence, wisdom, and light, and learn to proclaim the principles of eternal truth and to bring out from the treasury of God things new and old, things calculated to promote the welfare of the people. Now, then, these offices having been placed in the church, every man ought to be respected in his office.[6]

God has communicated to the Latter-day Saints principles that the world are ignorant of, and being ignorant of them they know not how to appreciate our feelings. They call good evil, light darkness, error truth, and truth error, because they have not the means of seeing the difference between one and the other. "But you are a chosen people, a royal generation, a holy priesthood," [see 1 Peter 2:9] separate and set apart by the Almighty for the accomplishment of his purposes. God has ordained among you presidents, apostles, prophets, high priests, seventies, bishops and other authorities; they are of his appointment, empowered and directed by him, under his influence, teaching his law, unfolding the principles of life, and are organized and ordained expressly to lead the people in the path of exaltation and eternal glory.[7]

Oh, if we could comprehend the glory, the intelligence, the power, the majesty and dominion of our heavenly Father! If we could contemplate the exaltation, the glory, the happiness that awaits the righteous, the pure and the virtuous of those that fear God, even the Saints of the Most High! If we could comprehend the great blessings that God has in store for those people that fear Him and observe His laws and keep His commandments, we should feel very different from what we do. But then, we do not. The Lord has brought us from among the different nations, that we may be educated in the things of the kingdom of God. He has conferred the Holy Priesthood for that purpose. And the very organizations that we have, of Stakes and Wards, with their Presidency and Bishops, High Councils, High Priests, Seventies, Elders, Priests, Teachers and Deacons, etc., are placed in the Church by the Almighty to educate and elevate us.[8]

We are organized with apostles and prophets: with presidents and their counselors, with bishops and their counselors, with elders, priests, teachers and deacons. We are organized according to the order of God, and these very principles that look small to us emanate from God. We have seventies and high priests, and all these men hold certain positions which it is expected of them that they will fulfil and magnify, here in the flesh, in the interests of truth and righteousness; in the interests of the kingdom of God and in the establishment of correct principles among the Saints of the most High. We are here to cooperate with God in the salvation of the living, in the redemption of the dead, in the blessings of our ancestors, in the pouring out blessings upon our children; we are here for the purpose of redeeming and regenerating the earth on which we live, and God has placed his authority and his counsels here upon the earth for that purpose, that men may learn to do the will of God on the earth as it is done in heaven. This is the object of our existence. And it is for us to comprehend the position.[9]

The priesthood has been organized according to the order of God.

[The priesthood] is an order, as I understand it, that is introduced by the Almighty, and by Him alone. It is not of man, nor did it proceed from man; and as it did not proceed from man, neither can it progress nor be perfected by man without the direction of the Almighty. In fact, with all these helps, with all these organizations, with all these principles, owing to the weakness and infirmities of man, we find it difficult to preserve in purity those sacred institutions that God has given unto us, and we continually need the greatest care, humility, self-denial, perseverance, watchfulness and reliance upon God.[10]

If we have received any office, or calling, or authority, or any power to administer in any of the ordinances, we have received that from the hand of God, and we can only perform these ordinances according to the priesthood we are permitted to possess. . . . If we perform our duties, each one of us in our proper position, God gives us power to accomplish the object we have in view, no matter what it is, or what priesthood we hold, no matter whether it is the President of the Church, or the President of the stake, a Bishop, a High Councilor, a High Priest, a Seventy, or an Elder, Priest, Teacher or Deacon; no matter what, if they perform duties with an eye single to the glory of God, he will sustain them in their operations and administrations.[11]

The First Presidency of the Church from 1880 to 1887: President John Taylor (center) and his counselors, George Q. Cannon (left) and Joseph F. Smith (right).

You and I may violate our covenants; you and I may trample upon the principles of the Gospel and violate the order of the Priesthood and thc commands of God; but among the hosts of Israel there will be thousands and tens of thousands who will be true to the principles of truth, and God in the heavens, the holy angels and the ancient Priesthood that now live where God lives are all united together for the accomplishment of this purpose. The Lord will roll forth His purposes in His own way and in His own time. And having thus organized, as I before stated, it is not for us to act as we may think individually, but as God shall dictate.

We have a regular order in the Church. You brethren, who hold the holy Priesthood, understand these things. Has God not given to every man a portion of His Spirit to profit withal? Yes. Has He not done more than this to the saints who are true and faithful? Has He not given to them the gift of the Holy Ghost? He has, and they know it and realize it. They are brought into communion with each other, and into communion with God and the heavenly hosts. But having this Spirit do we need others to guide us? Yes, all the time. Why? Because of the powers of darkness, the influence of Satan and the weakness of human nature. We need watchmen upon the towers of Zion, who are on the alert to look after the interests of Israel, and to see that God's people do not go astray. . . . All the officers necessary for the work of the ministry are to be found in the Church, and everything has been organized according to the order of God.[12]

Priesthood should be exercised in kindness, with fidelity to God.

We should have a common sympathy one for another, and feel a kindly regard for the lowest of God's creations, and especially for the Saints of God, no matter what position they occupy. If any are in error, try to reclaim them by kindness; if they have a bad spirit, show them a better one; if any do not do right, do right yourselves and say, "Come, follow me, as I follow Christ." Would not that be the right course to pursue? I think it would; that is the way I understand the Gospel. We do not, any of us, have the priesthood for self aggrandizement, or to be used to oppress or take advantage of anybody, or to use improper language; but with all kindness and long suffering and forbearance and with love unfeigned. I will read from the Doctrine and Covenants. . . .

"Behold, there are many called, but few are chosen. And why are they not chosen? Because their hearts are set so much upon the things of this world, and aspire to the honors of men, and they do not learn this one lesson—" just the very thing I have been talking about—"That the rights of the priesthood are inseparably connected with the powers of heaven, and that the powers of heaven cannot be controlled nor handled only upon the principles of righteousness." Do you think that God will give power to any man only to carry out his own contracted or selfish purposes? I tell you he never will, never, no never. "That they may be conferred on us it is true; but when we undertake to cover our sins, or to gratify our pride, our vain ambition, or to exercise control, or dominion or compulsion, upon the souls of the children of men, in any degree of unrighteousness, behold the heavens withdraw themselves, the Spirit of the Lord is grieved; and when it is withdrawn, Amen to the priesthood of that man." [See D&C 121:34–37.]

We think sometimes, we are standing in heavenly places in Christ Jesus; and so we are. But there is no priesthood of the Son of God that authorizes one man to oppress another or to intrude upon his rights in any way. There is no such thing in the category; it does not exist; as it is said—"Behold, ere he is aware, he is left unto himself, to kick against the pricks, to persecute the saints, and to fight against God." [D&C 121:38.][13]

There is no authority associated with the Holy Priesthood except on the principle of persuasion, and no man has a right to plume himself upon any position he occupies in this Church, for he is simply a servant of God, and a servant of the people, and if any man attempts to use any kind of arbitrary authority and act with any degree of unrighteousness God will hold that man to an account for it, and we all of us have to be judged according to the deeds done in the body. We are here as saviors of men, and not as tyrants and oppressors. . . .

. . . It is for us who hold the Holy Priesthood to be pure. "Be ye pure that bear the vessels of the Lord." [See Isaiah 52:11.] It is for each of us to be pure, and then say to others, "follow me, as I follow Jesus." It is for us to live our religion and obey the laws of God, and perform the duties that devolve upon us.[14]

I do not believe in any kind of tyranny. I believe in long-suffering, in mercy, in kindness, in gentleness, and in the love and fear of God. I do not believe that the Priesthood was given to man to exercise dominion and authority over the souls of other men. Everything ought to be done with kindness and long-suffering, yet with fidelity to God.[15]

Suggestions for Study and Discussion

- Why is it important that order exist within the priesthood? How can this order assist each of us in meeting the needs of those for whom we have responsibility?

- Why are there various offices in the priesthood? (See also Ephesians 4:11–12.) How have you seen that the different priesthood offices assist in "perfecting the Saints"?
- What experiences have you had in which you were blessed for following the counsel of priesthood leaders, even when you didn't understand or agree with the counsel at first?
- In discussing Christlike leadership, President Taylor encouraged priesthood bearers to live by the words "Come, follow me, as I follow Christ." How can this counsel bless our relationships with our families and with others? How does honoring women help men honor the priesthood?
- Why does pride diminish or destroy one's priesthood power? How can we develop the character traits of kindness, long-suffering, forbearance, and love unfeigned? In what ways can we encourage these traits among those with whom we serve in the Church?
- In what ways can you help the Aaronic Priesthood holders in your family and ward prepare for the privilege of holding the Melchizedek Priesthood?

Related Scriptures: Ephesians 4:11–15; D&C 20:38–67; 84:18–32, 109–110; 107; 121:33–46

Notes

1. *The Gospel Kingdom,* sel. G. Homer Durham (1943), 159.
2. *Deseret News* (Weekly), 28 Dec. 1859, 337.
3. *The Gospel Kingdom,* 141–42.
4. *The Gospel Kingdom,* 155–56; paragraphing and punctuation altered.
5. *The Gospel Kingdom,* 197–98.
6. *The Gospel Kingdom,* 165.
7. *Deseret News* (Weekly), 8 May 1872, 181.
8. *Deseret News: Semi-Weekly,* 3 Jan. 1882, 1.
9. *Deseret News: Semi-Weekly,* 1 June 1880, 1.
10. *Deseret News: Semi-Weekly,* 8 Mar. 1881, 1.
11. *Deseret News: Semi-Weekly,* 10 Aug. 1880, 1.
12. *Deseret News: Semi-Weekly,* 21 Oct. 1884, 1; paragraphing altered.
13. *Deseret News: Semi-Weekly,* 19 Aug. 1879, 1.
14. *Deseret News: Semi-Weekly,* 14 Aug. 1883, 1.
15. *Deseret News: Semi-Weekly,* 24 Mar. 1885, 1.

CHAPTER 15

Agency and Accountability

It is our privilege to determine our own exaltation or degradation; it is our privilege to determine our own happiness or misery in the world to come.[1]

From the Life of John Taylor

"We talk sometimes about free will," observed President John Taylor. "Is that a correct principle? Yes. And it is a principle that has always existed, and proceeded from God, our Heavenly Father."[2] President Taylor cherished the principle of moral agency—the power Heavenly Father has given His children to choose good or evil and to act for themselves. However, he also taught that individuals are accountable to God for their acts. He affirmed, "God never gave man unlimited control of the affairs of this world; but always speaks of man as being under his guidance, inhabiting his territory, and responsible to him for his acts."[3]

To emphasize the relationship between agency and accountability, President Taylor shared the following analogy: "A man lets or rents a vineyard or farm, the man occupying it has a certain agency and discretionary power vested in his hands, but always subject to certain conditions imposed by the owner of the property. Hence God made a covenant with Noah, Abraham, the Children of Israel, and the primitive saints. The making of a covenant naturally implies two parties: in such cases, God is one, the people the other. If the people fulfil their covenant, the Lord is bound to fulfil his; but if man transgresses then the Lord is not bound to fulfil his engagement. . . . Man, then, acts as a moral agent, to improve upon the blessings which God puts within his power, or not, as he pleases."[4]

In President Taylor's day, some people claimed that the gospel and the priesthood were intended to "bring men into bondage or to tyrannize over the consciences of men." He boldly refuted this idea, declaring that the purpose of the gospel is "to make all men free as God is free; that they may drink of the streams 'whereof shall make glad the city of God'; [Psalm 46:4] that they may be elevated and not debased; that they may be purified and not corrupted; that they may learn the laws of life and walk in them, and not walk in the ways of corruption and go down to death."[5]

Teachings of John Taylor

From the beginning, God has given us the gift of agency.

The Father . . . made a decree . . . that both the inhabitants of heaven and the inhabitants of earth should have their free agency. It was against this that Lucifer rebelled; and he could not have rebelled against a plan or commandment that had not been given; for rebellion signifies a violation of law, command, or authority; and he was cast out of heaven because of this rebellion. This rebellion could not have existed without a free agency; for without a free agency they would all have been compelled to do the will of the Father. But having the free agency, they used it; and Lucifer and a third part of the angels were cast out because they rebelled and used this agency in opposition to their heavenly Father. And not only because they rebelled, but because, as stated, "they sought to destroy the agency of man;" [see Moses 4:3] and their agency would have been used in opposition to the interests, happiness and eternal exaltation of mankind, which were proposed to be accomplished through the atonement and redemption provided by Jesus Christ.[6]

[God] has given us the ability to choose the good and refuse the evil. We can work iniquity or righteousness, just as we please; and the Devil has taken advantage of this, and tried to surround men's minds with such influences as would bring about their ruin, that he might lead them captive at his will. The Lord has not bound them, nor controlled them; but the result of their actions he has controlled, whenever they have taken a course that was of itself calculated to injure his people.

The Lord . . . will let mankind pursue happiness in their own way, and according to their desire he will let them drink the cup of their own iniquity in their own way. On the other hand, he has manifested his goodness and will continue to do it to all his children. What does he design to accomplish? The building up of this kingdom upon the earth, the establishment of righteousness, the driving back of the adversary and the banishing of [Satan] from the earth. By this means, the principles of truth will be extended throughout the length and breadth of the earth, and all will bow to God and his Christ, and the chosen ones will administer the ordinances of his house forever and ever. The Almighty had this object in view long ago.[7]

God gives us guidance, but He will not force the human mind.

We received the gospel. Was any one forced to obey it? Was there any coercion in any possible way manifested toward us? Not that I know of. Was Oliver Cowdery, who was the second elder in the church, obliged to receive this gospel? No, he was not. Was Hyrum Smith obliged to receive it? No, he was not. Were any of the witnesses to the Book of Mormon—the Whitmers and others? No. And after they did identify themselves with this church, were they compelled to stay in it? No. Have any of the members of the quorum of the twelve, the seventies, the high priests, or the members of the high councils, or the presidents of the seventies, or any class of men in this church, been compelled to occupy the position to which they have been called? I do not know of any, do you? I know there was no coercion used with me further than the force of truth recommending itself to my mind; neither was there with you, further than the power of truth operating upon your minds.[8]

I would not wish to control the human mind. I would not control the actions of men. God does not do it, he leaves them to their own agency to combat with the trials, temptations, adversities, and evils of every kind that are in the world, to which humanity is, or can be incident. He puts within their reach, however, certain principles and would like to lead them to himself if they would be led. If not, he then does the very best with them that he can.[9]

Man has a moral agency; acting under the Lord, and is, consequently, responsible to him for his acts, as a moral agent. But does he leave him alone and unassisted to carry out his designs? No. Looking upon man as his son, he has from time to time offered his services and instructions, as a father. He has given revelations, instructing and warning his people. He has given promises to the obedient, and threatened the disobedient. He has instructed kings, rulers, and prophets. He has also protected the righteous, and punished, by judgments, the wicked. He has promised to Abraham and others lands and possessions. He has held out promises of eternal life to the faithful; but has never coerced or forced the human mind.[10]

God holds us accountable for our use of agency and recompenses us according to our decisions.

Are we not the framers of our own destiny? Are we not the arbitrators of our fate? . . . It is our privilege to determine our own exaltation or degradation; it is our privilege to determine our own happiness or misery in the world to come.[11]

By a careful examination of the Scriptures, we shall find that man has had certain powers vested in his hands, which he holds subject to the control and guidance of the Lord; and that if he has acted without the counsel, guidance, or instruction of God, he has gone beyond the limits assigned him by the Lord, and is as much culpable as [a government official] would be who should exceed the limits of his instructions; or a man holding a farm, or vineyard, by a certain lease, if he should disregard the conditions of that lease, and destroy the farm, or vineyard; for the earth is the Lord's, and man was put on it by the Lord. It is not man's possession, only as he holds it from God. . . . If man is placed as an agent to act for the Lord, and also for himself, and then should neglect the Lord, he would certainly be held responsible to his Creator.[12]

Let your memories run back, and you can remember the time when you did a good action, you can remember the time when you did a bad action; the thing is printed there and you can bring it out and gaze upon it whenever you please. . . . If you have studied language you can call that out at pleasure, you can show the distinction between the different parts of speech very readily. If you have studied mechanism your mind will go to the place where you saw a certain machine, and you will go to work and make one like it. If you have travelled in cities you can tell what kind of houses, and streets, composed the different cities you passed through, and the character of the people you associated with; and you can ruminate upon them, and reflect upon them by day or by night whenever you think proper, and call the things up which you did and saw. Where do you read all this? In your own book, you do not go to somebody else's book or library, it is written in your own record, and you there read it. Your eyes and ears have taken it in, and your hands have touched it, and then your judgment, as it is called, has acted upon it—your reflective powers.

Now, if you are in possession of a spirit or intellectuality of that kind, whereby you are enabled to read your own acts, do you not think that that being who has placed that spirit and that intelligence within you holds the keys of that intelligence, and can read it whenever he pleases? Is not that philosophical, reasonable and scriptural? I think it is. . . .

Man sleeps the sleep of death but the spirit lives where the record of his deeds is kept—that does not die—man cannot kill it, there is no decay associated with it, and it still retains in all its vividness, the remembrance of that which transpired before the separation by death, of the body and the ever-living spirit.[13]

We are God's people, and he is bound by everything that is calculated to bind either man or God. He is bound to take care of his people, if they take care of themselves; if they honour their calling and priesthood; if they magnify and do credit to the power and authority that is conferred upon them; if they do not deviate from correct principles, God is bound to fulfill all things according to the obligations that he is under; one of which is to provide for his Saints. . . . Who has ever known God to depart from correct principles? . . . I never have, and I am well satisfied that you never did.[14]

Suggestions for Study and Discussion

- Why is agency essential to our exaltation? How are agency and the Atonement of Jesus Christ related?
- In what ways does Satan continue to try to influence our agency? How can we resist those attempts?
- What forms of guidance does the Lord give us to help us use our agency righteously? How does He reward our righteous use of agency?
- Why is it important for individuals to have the opportunity to make their own decisions? How can we honor the agency of family members and at the same time encourage them to make correct decisions? How can you help family members understand the consequences of their decisions?
- Although we are free to make decisions, why might unrighteous decisions restrict our freedom? How have you felt your freedom increase through righteous decisions?

Related Scriptures: Joshua 24:15; Galatians 6:7; 2 Nephi 2:14–16, 26–27; Helaman 14:30–31; D&C 58:26–28; 101:78; Moses 4:1–4; 6:33

Notes

1. *Deseret News* (Weekly), 9 Jan. 1861, 353.
2. *The Gospel Kingdom,* sel. G. Homer Durham (1943), 59.
3. *The Government of God* (1852), 49.
4. *The Government of God,* 49–50.
5. *The Gospel Kingdom,* 123.
6. *The Mediation and Atonement* (1882), 95.
7. *Deseret News* (Weekly), 9 Jan. 1861, 353; paragraphing altered.
8. *The Gospel Kingdom,* 59–60.
9. *The Gospel Kingdom,* 337.
10. *The Government of God,* 54–55.
11. *Deseret News* (Weekly), 9 Jan. 1861, 353.
12. *The Government of God,* 47.
13. *Deseret News* (Weekly), 8 Mar. 1865, 178–79; paragraphing altered.
14. *Deseret News* (Weekly), 9 Jan. 1861, 353.

Through regular personal prayer, we can strengthen our relationship with our Heavenly Father.

CHAPTER 16

Strengthening Our Relationship with God

I would rather have God for my friend than all other influences and powers outside.[1]

From the Life of John Taylor

John Taylor had a deep and personal love for our Heavenly Father. He referred to Him as "our father, friend and benefactor." He said, "We lean upon his arm, and we know that he will guide and direct, influence and control the affairs of his people, therefore we rely upon him."[2]

Bearing testimony of God's love and concern for His children, President Taylor stated: "There is not a man upon the earth that has put his trust in God, I do not care what part of the world he has been in, but what can say that he delivered him. I know that has been the case with me, emphatically so. I have been satisfied, when in foreign lands and in strange countries, where I had no access but to the Almighty, that he was on my side, and I know that he has answered my prayers."[3]

This trust in God was evident in 1839, when Elder Taylor left with Elder Wilford Woodruff for a mission in the British Isles. Elder Taylor became seriously ill on the journey from Nauvoo to New York, where they were to take passage on a ship to England. Elder Woodruff went ahead to New York and waited for Elder Taylor, who was delayed in his journey due to his illness.

When Elder Taylor reached New York, Elder Woodruff was anxious to depart and immediately obtained his own passage to England. Although Elder Taylor had no money, he told Elder

Woodruff, "Well, Brother Woodruff, if you think it best for me to go, I will accompany you." Elder Woodruff inquired as to how Elder Taylor would obtain the money for the journey, to which Elder Taylor answered: "Oh, there will be no difficulty about that. Go and take a passage for me on your vessel, and I will furnish you the means."

Hearing the conversation between Elder Taylor and Elder Woodruff, a Brother Theodore Turley expressed a desire to accompany the Apostles on their journey and offered to cook for them, although he had no money either. In response to Brother Turley's desire to be involved in the work, Elder Taylor told Elder Woodruff to obtain a passage for Brother Turley also.

In a short time, the Lord provided the means for the journey. Elder B. H. Roberts of the Seventy recorded: "At the time of making these arrangements Elder Taylor had no money, but the Spirit had whispered [to] him that means would be forthcoming, and when had that still, small voice failed him! In that he trusted, and he did not trust in vain. Although he did not ask for a penny of anyone, from various persons in voluntary donations he received money enough to meet his engagements for the passage of himself and Brother Turley, but no more."[4]

Teachings of John Taylor

God is our Father and He cherishes a paternal regard for us.

Our religion . . . does not set up God as some austere being that we cannot approach, but it tells us he is our Father, and that we are his children, and that he cherishes in his bosom a paternal regard for us; and we have experienced something of the feelings that exist between father and son, mother and daughter, parents and children.[5]

How does God feel towards the human family? He feels that they are his children. What, all? Yes, the white, the black, the red, the Jew, the gentile, the heathen, the Christian, and all classes and grades of men. He feels interested in all. He has done so from the beginning and will continue to do so to the end. He will do all that lies in his power for the benefit, blessing, and exaltation of the human family, both in time and eternity.[6]

We are all the children of God. He is our Father and has a right to direct us, not only us, but has a perfect right to direct and control the affairs of all the human family that exist upon the face of the earth for they are all his offspring.[7]

The object that God has in view is to benefit mankind as much as lies in His power. We talk sometimes about moving heaven and earth but God has moved heaven and earth for the accomplishment of that object. . . . God desires our welfare, and He has instituted laws for that purpose. He has introduced the everlasting Gospel for that purpose; and He has restored the Holy Priesthood that existed anciently, together with all the principles, blessings, powers, rites, ordinances, and privileges that have graced the earth from the commencement of time.[8]

If we understand ourselves correctly, we must look upon ourselves as eternal beings, and upon God as our Father, for we have been taught when we pray to say, "Our Father, who art in heaven, hallowed be thy name." [See Matthew 6:9.] "We have fathers in the flesh, and we do them reverence, how much more shall we be in subjection to the Father of Spirits and live." [See Hebrews 12:9.] I need not enter into any proof in relation to this, for it is well understood by the saints that God is the father of our spirits, and that when we go back into his presence, we shall know him, as we have known our earthly parents. We are taught to approach him as we would an earthly parent to ask of him such blessings as we need; and he has said "if a son ask bread of his father shall he give him a stone, or if he ask for fish, a scorpion. If ye then, being evil, know how to give good gifts unto your children, how much more will your Heavenly Father give his Holy Spirit to them that ask him." [See Matthew 7:9–11.][9]

Our Heavenly Father will bless us when we seek Him in humble prayer.

We should feel that God is our Father and that we are his children, and that he has promised to listen to our prayers, and that we are called upon to be obedient to his will and to carry out his designs. And then we ought, in order that our prayers may be effectual, perform the various duties devolving upon us, such as have been referred to, and we should be honest and honorable in our dealings one with another. If we try to defraud our brother, how can we expect God to bless us in that, for [our brother] is a child of our Heavenly Father just as much as we are. . . . [God] feels interested in his welfare, and if we try to take advantage to the injury of the Lord's child; do you think [the Lord] would be pleased with us?[10]

I am reminded of my boyhood. At that early period of my life I learned to approach God. Many a time I have gone into the fields, and, concealing myself behind some bush, would bow before the Lord and call upon him to guide and direct me. And he heard my prayer. At times I would get other boys to accompany me. It would not hurt you, boys and girls, to call upon the Lord in your secret places, as I did. That was the spirit which I had when a little boy. And God has led me from one thing to another. . . . My spirit was drawn out after God then; and I feel the same yet.[11]

I will tell you the first thing I used to do when I went preaching, particularly when I went to a [new] place—and that was to go aside to some place, anywhere I could get, into a field, a barn, into the woods, or my closet, and ask God to bless me and give me wisdom to meet all the circumstances with which I might have to contend; and the Lord gave me the wisdom I needed and sustained me. If you pursue a course of this kind, he will bless you also. Do not trust in yourselves, but study the best books—the Bible and Book of Mormon—and get all the information you can, and then cleave to God and keep yourselves free from corruption and pollution of every kind, and the blessings of the Most High will be with you.[12]

Do not forget to call upon the Lord in your family circles, dedicating yourselves and all you have to God every day of your lives; and seek to do right, and cultivate the spirit of union and love, and the peace and blessing of the Living God will be with us, and He will lead us in the paths of life; and we shall be sustained and upheld by all the holy angels and the ancient patriarchs and men of God, and the veil will become thinner between us and our God, and we will approach nearer to him, and our souls will magnify the Lord of hosts.[13]

We must trust and have faith in God.

I do not believe in a religion that has not got all my affections, but I believe in a religion that I can live for, or die for. I am not talking about things that I do not understand; I have wrestled with death, and had the devil aiming at me, and I cared nothing for it. Let me be deprived of this hope and my religion is vain. . . . It is for us to act upon the principle that we started upon; to trust and have faith in God; to let this influence us in our acts one towards another.[14]

If we will perform our part, the Lord will not fail to do His. Because others act foolishly we cannot afford to imitate them. We profess to be the Zion of God, the pure in heart. We profess to be men and women of integrity, of truth and virtue, and to have faith in God. This must not only be our profession, but our practice; we must carry out and fulfil the word and will and law of God.[15]

Faith without works being dead [see James 2:17, 26], it is evident that living faith and that which is acceptable to God, is that which not only believes in God, but acts upon that belief. It is not only the cause of action, but includes both cause and action. Or in other words it is belief or faith made perfect by works.[16]

We have got to put our trust in God, let the consequences be as they may. And as long as we do this, and as long as we keep the holy covenants we have entered into with him and with one another, Zion will triumph. . . .

But I will tell you what we have to do, my brethren and sisters, we must fear God in our hearts; we must lay aside our covetousness and our waywardness, our self-will and foolishness of every kind. . . . We must humble ourselves before the Lord, repenting of our sins, and henceforth preserve our bodies and spirits pure, that we may be fit receptacles for the Spirit of the living God, and be guided by him in all our labors both for the living and the dead. Our desires must be for God and his righteousness, until we shall exclaim with one of old: O God, search me, and try me, and if there be any way of wickedness in me, bid it depart [see Psalm 139:23–24]. It is for us, as fathers and mothers, to go before the Lord in all humility and call upon him that his peace may be in our hearts; and wherein we may have done wrong, confess that wrong and repair it as far as we possibly can; and in this way let every man and woman in Israel begin to set their houses in order, and forever cultivate the spirit of peace, the spirit of union and love.

And if the families of Israel do this throughout all the land of Zion, all fearing God and working righteousness, cherishing the spirit of humility and meekness, and putting our trust in him, there is no power in existence that can injure us.[17]

Peace is the gift of God to those who walk according to His light.

Peace is the gift of God. Do you want peace? Go to God. Do you want peace in your families? Go to God. Do you want peace to brood over your families? If you do, live your religion, and the very peace of God will dwell and abide with you, for that is where peace comes from, and it [does not] dwell anywhere else. . . . Peace is good, and I say seek for it, cherish it in your bosoms, in your neighborhoods, and wherever you go among your friends and associates. If we only get that peace that dwells in the bosom of God all will be right. . . .

Some, in speaking of war and troubles, will say, are you not afraid? No, I am a servant of God, and this is enough, for Father is at the helm. It is for me to be as clay in the hands of the potter, to be pliable and walk in the light of the countenance of the Spirit of the Lord, and then no matter what comes. Let the lightnings flash and the earthquakes bellow, God is at the helm, and I feel like saying but little, for the Lord God Omnipotent reigneth and will continue his work until he has put all enemies under his feet, and his kingdom extends from the rivers to the ends of the earth.[18]

All we have to do is to live our religion, to obey the counsel of our President, be humble and faithful and not exalted in our own strength, but ask wisdom of God and see that we have peace with God, with our families, with one another, that peace may reign in our bosoms and in our community.[19]

When we live our religion, when we walk according to the light of the Spirit of God, when we purge ourselves [of] impurity and corruption, and the sweet whispering of the Spirit of the Lord pours intelligence into our bosoms, broods over us, causing peace and joy to be with us, we have then, more or less, a faint glimpse of those things that are laid up for the faithful, and it is then we feel as though we and all that we have are in the hands of the Lord and that we are ready to offer ourselves [as] a sacrifice for the accomplishment of his purposes upon the earth.[20]

Peace is a desirable thing; it is the gift of God, and the greatest gift that God can bestow upon mortals. What is more desirable than peace? Peace in nations, peace in cities, peace in families. Like the soft murmuring zephyr [or west wind], its soothing influence calms the brow of care, dries the eye of sorrow, and chases trouble from the bosom; and let it be universally experienced, and it would drive sorrow from the world, and make this earth a paradise. But peace is the gift of God.[21]

Suggestions for Study and Discussion

- What are some ways that God manifests His paternal love for us? How can knowing that He has a caring Father's regard for us help us in times of spiritual and physical need?
- Why do we sometimes fail to have meaningful, regular prayer? What can we do to make our prayers more meaningful?
- What can we learn from John Taylor's experiences with prayer? How can we teach children to approach God in prayer as young John Taylor did?
- How can we build our trust in God? How have you been blessed as you have put your trust in God?
- What does it mean to be willing to "walk according to the light of the Spirit of God"? How does faith affect this level of willingness? What are some specific ways that you can put your faith into action?

- In what ways have you experienced peace as a gift from God? How has this peace influenced your love for Him?
- How can you improve the level of peace in your family?

Related Scriptures: Proverbs 3:5–6; Philippians 4:6–7; 2 Nephi 32:8–9; Mosiah 4:9–10; D&C 19:23; 20:17–18; 59:23–24

Notes

1. *The Gospel Kingdom,* sel. G. Homer Durham (1943), 343.
2. *Deseret News* (Weekly), 27 Dec. 1871, 550.
3. *The Gospel Kingdom,* 45.
4. See B. H. Roberts, *The Life of John Taylor* (1963), 65–74.
5. *The Gospel Kingdom,* 30.
6. *The Gospel Kingdom,* 63.
7. *The Gospel Kingdom,* 79.
8. *The Gospel Kingdom,* 30.
9. *Deseret News* (Weekly), 22 Dec. 1853, 101.
10. *Deseret News: Semi-Weekly,* 25 June 1878, 1.
11. *The Gospel Kingdom,* 46.
12. *The Gospel Kingdom,* 240.
13. *Deseret News: Semi-Weekly,* 23 Dec 1879, 1.
14. *Deseret News* (Weekly), 11 Apr. 1860, 42.
15. *Deseret News: Semi-Weekly,* 15 May 1883, 1.
16. *The Gospel Kingdom,* 332.
17. *The Gospel Kingdom,* 347–48.
18. *Deseret News* (Weekly), 24 Dec. 1862, 202.
19. *Deseret News* (Weekly), 23 Sept. 1857, 231.
20. *Deseret News* (Weekly), 3 Feb. 1858, 382.
21. *The Government of God* (1852), 20.

C H A P T E R 1 7

Revelation through the Holy Ghost

Revelation . . . is the very foundation of our religion.[1]

From the Life of John Taylor

President John Taylor said: "I well remember a remark that Joseph Smith made to me. . . . Said he, 'Elder Taylor, you have been baptized, you have had hands laid upon your head for the reception of the Holy Ghost, and you have been ordained to the holy priesthood. Now, if you will continue to follow the leadings of that spirit, it will always lead you right. Sometimes it might be contrary to your judgment; never mind that, follow its dictates; and if you be true to its whisperings it will in time become in you a principle of revelation so that you will know all things.' "[2]

John Taylor followed the counsel of Joseph Smith and relied on revelation through the Holy Ghost for guidance in his personal life and in his calling as a prophet, seer, and revelator. President Heber J. Grant, the seventh President of the Church, commented on President Taylor's sensitivity to the promptings of the Spirit: "I was called into the Council of the Twelve Apostles by a revelation of the Lord to President John Taylor. From the time that I entered the Council of the Twelve, two years after John Taylor was made President of the Church, until the day of his death, I met with him, week after week, . . . and I know that he was a servant of the living God. I know that the inspiration of the Lord came to him; and I know that upon all occasions, whenever he said: 'This is what the Lord desires,' and his associates in the council of the apostles sustained his position, that upon every occasion he was vindicated and the inspiration of the Lord to him

President Taylor compared revelation to light, describing it as "the candle of the Lord" that helps us to "walk according to the light of eternal truth."

showed that his wisdom by the power of God had been superior to the wisdom of other men. . . .

"I could relate circumstances when the apostles have been sent out to accomplish certain labors under the inspiration of the Lord to John Taylor, when they thought they could not accomplish the labors. They have returned and been able to bear testimony that by and with the help of the Lord they had been able to accomplish the labor placed upon them by President Taylor, the prophet of the Lord."[3]

The Teachings of John Taylor

There is a difference between the Spirit that leads men to do right and the gift of the Holy Ghost.

In regard to the operation of the Spirit upon man, let me draw your attention to a fact that is generally understood by all reflecting men, and that is, no matter how wicked a man may be, how far he may have departed from the right, such a man will generally admire and respect a good man, an honorable man, and a virtuous man; and such a man will frequently say; "I wish I could do as that man does, but I cannot: I wish I could pursue a correct course, but I am overcome of evil." They cannot help respecting the good and the honorable, although they may not be governed by principles of honor and virtue themselves. This same spirit which is given to every man outside of the gospel has been manifested in the different ages of the world. . . .

But there is a very great difference between this spirit and feeling that leads men to do right, which is emphatically denominated a portion of the Spirit of God, which is given to every man to profit withal, and what is termed in the scriptures the gift of the Holy Ghost.[4]

There is and always has been a spirit abroad in the world which is really a portion of the Spirit of God, which leads mankind, in many instances, to discriminate between good and evil, and between right and wrong. They have a conscience that accuses or excuses them for their acts; and although the world of mankind is very wicked and very corrupt, yet it will be found that almost all men, though they may not do good themselves, appreciate good actions in others.

The scriptures say that God "hath made of one blood all nations of men for to dwell on all the face of the earth, and hath determined the times before appointed, and the bounds of their habitation; that they should seek the Lord, if haply they might feel after him, and find him, though he be not far from every one of us." (Acts 17:26–27.) The scripture further says, he has given unto them a portion of his spirit to profit withal [see 1 Corinthians 12:7]. But there is quite a distinction between the position that these people occupy and the one which we occupy. We have something more than that portion of the Spirit of God which is given to every man, and it is called the gift of the Holy Ghost, which is received through obedience to the first principles of the gospel of Christ, by the laying on of hands of the servants of God.[5]

Through the gift of the Holy Ghost, we can know the things of God.

When the Gospel was preached in former times among the people they were told to repent of their sins; to be baptized in the name of Jesus for the remission of their sins, and then to have hands laid upon them for the reception of the Holy Ghost [see Acts 2:37–38]. They were told, moreover, what this Holy Ghost would do; that it would take of the things of God and shew them unto them; that it would cause their old men to dream dreams and their young men to see visions; and that it would rest upon the servants and handmaids of God and they should prophesy [see Acts 2:16–18; see also Joel 2:28–29].

These are the operations of that Spirit which dwells with God, the Father, and God, the Son, namely the Holy Ghost. It is this Spirit that brings us into relationship with God, and it differs very materially from the portion of spirit that is given to all men to profit withal. . . .

Its province is to lead us into all truth, and to bring to our remembrance things past, present and to come. It contemplates the future and unfolds things we had not thought of heretofore, and these things are very distinctly described in the Bible, in the Book of Mormon, and in the Book of Doctrine and Covenants. Herein lies the difference between us and others, and it was so in former times.[6]

We believe that it is necessary for man to be placed in communication with God; that he should have revelation from him, and that unless he is placed under the influences of the inspiration of the Holy Spirit, he can know nothing about the things of God. I do not care how learned a man may be, or how extensively he may have traveled. I do not care what his talent, intellect, or genius may be, at what college he may have studied, how comprehensive his views or what his judgment may be on other matters, he cannot understand certain things without the Spirit of God, and that necessarily introduces the principle I before referred to—the necessity of revelation. Not revelation in former times, but present and immediate revelation, which shall lead and guide those who possess it in all the paths of life here, and to eternal life hereafter.[7]

Continuing revelation is the foundation of our religion.

We did not receive our ideas from any theologian, from any scientist, from any man of renown, or of position in the world, or from any body or conclave of religionists, but from the Almighty, and to Him we are indebted for all life, all truth, and all intelligence pertaining to the past, pertaining to the present, or pertaining to the future. Therefore we feel our dependence upon Him. . . .

No man knows the things of God but by the Spirit of God [see 1 Corinthians 2:11]; and if the Father did not reveal them we should be very ignorant indeed. . . . Having revealed His will to man, to Joseph Smith, as He had done to other men in former ages, it was necessary that that will should be made known to all nations, kindreds, tongues and people, that men might be informed of the things that He revealed for the salvation and exaltation of humanity. Hence the Twelve were set apart. For what purpose? That they might introduce the Gospel to the nations of the earth and preach the principles of life as they emanate from God. . . .

Their testimony to the people is that God has spoken, that the Gospel has been restored; they explain what the Gospel is; they call upon the people to repent and to be baptised in the name of Jesus for the remission of sins, promising that the obedient shall receive the Holy Ghost. . . . And being partakers of that spirit, there is a communication opened between them and their Heavenly Father through our Lord Jesus Christ, and being inspired by that spirit, their prayers ascend unto the God of the whole earth; they learn to place their confidence in Him and to obey His laws.[8]

The Bible is good. . . . The Book of Mormon is good, and the Doctrine and Covenants, as land-marks. But a mariner who launches into the ocean requires a more certain criterion. He must be acquainted with heavenly bodies, and take his observations from them, in order to steer his barque [or ship] aright. Those books are good for example, precedent, and investigation, and for developing certain laws and principles. But they do not, they cannot, touch every case required to be adjudicated and set in order.

We require a living tree—a living fountain—living intelligence, proceeding from the living priesthood in heaven, through the living priesthood on earth. . . . And from the time that Adam first received a communication from God, to the time that John, on the Isle of Patmos, received his communication, or Joseph Smith had the heavens opened to him, it always required new revelations, adapted to the peculiar circumstances in which the churches or individuals were placed.

Adam's revelation did not instruct Noah to build his ark; nor did Noah's revelation tell Lot to forsake Sodom; nor did either of these speak of the departure of the children of Israel from Egypt. These all had revelations for themselves, and so had Isaiah, Jeremiah, Ezekiel, Jesus, Peter, Paul, John, and Joseph. And so must we, or we shall make shipwreck.[9]

A good many people, and those professing Christians, will sneer a good deal at the idea of present revelation. Whoever heard of true religion without communication with God? To me the thing is the most absurd that the human mind could conceive. I do not wonder, when the people generally reject the principle of present revelation, that skepticism and infidelity prevail to such an alarming extent. I do not wonder that so many men treat religion with contempt, and regard it as something not worth the attention of intelligent beings, for without revelation religion is a mockery and a farce. If I can not have a religion that will lead me to God, and place me *en rapport* with him, and unfold to my mind the principles of immortality and eternal life, I want nothing to do with it.

The principle of present revelation, then, is the very foundation of our religion. . . . I would not only search the scriptures that we now have, but I would search also every revelation that God has given, does give, or will give for the guidance and direction of his people, and then I would reverence the Giver, and those also whom he makes use of as his honored instruments to promulgate and make known those principles; and I would seek to be governed by the principles that are contained in that sacred word.[10]

Each of us needs revelation to understand and fulfil our responsibilities.

There is not a position that we can occupy in life, either as fathers, mothers, children, masters, servants, or as elders of Israel holding the holy priesthood in all its ramifications, but what we need continually is wisdom flowing from the Lord and intelligence communicated by him, that we may know how to perform correctly the various duties and avocations of life, and to fulfil the various responsibilities that rest upon us. And hence the necessity all the day long, and every day and every week, month, and year, and under all circumstances, of men leaning upon the Lord and being guided by that Spirit that flows from him, that we may not fall into error—that we may neither do anything wrong, say anything wrong, nor think anything wrong, and all the time retain that Spirit, which can only be kept by observing purity, holiness, and virtue, and living continually in obedience to the laws and commandments of God.[11]

Now ask yourselves, when you have been living up to your privileges, and the Spirit of God has beamed upon your minds, and your souls have been enlightened with the candle of the Lord, with the intelligence of heaven, and you have walked according to the light of eternal truth, if in these moments you have not always felt ready to fulfill any obligations that were required of you, and whether you have not always performed your duties with pleasantness and satisfaction to yourselves. But when our minds are carried away with the things of this world, when we lose sight of the kingdom of God and its interests, its glory, the happiness and well being of the human family, and the events that we are expecting to transpire on the earth, and the part that we are to take in them; when we lose sight of our various duties as fathers, mothers, husbands, wives, children . . . , and get carried away with our own notions, ideas and selfishness, and we become involved in evil, it is then that it is difficult for us to comprehend the things of God.[12]

The Lord has given us revelations concerning both our temporal and spiritual affairs. He has commenced to build up Zion, and to establish his kingdom, and he will roll on his purposes, and fulfil the words of the prophets, and his work will roll forth until the designs of God shall be accomplished.[13]

Suggestions for Study and Discussion

- What is the difference between the Spirit of God that leads us to do right and the gift of the Holy Ghost? (See also D&C 93:2; John 14:26.)
- What experiences have you had in which revelation by the Spirit helped you understand the things of God? How can we recognize personal revelation from the Lord?
- How does focusing on worldly matters interfere with receiving revelation? What can we do to prepare ourselves to receive revelation?
- How can revelation given to us through our living prophet be more helpful than even the scriptures? Why is it important that we have both the scriptures and continuing revelation?
- What examples can you think of when the Holy Ghost helped you in your family, at work or school, or in the Church?

- Why do we sometimes fail to make full use of the gift of the Holy Ghost? How can we more fully benefit from this gift?
- Why is the gift of the Holy Ghost such a marvelous blessing to us in today's world? What can you do to show gratitude for this gift? How can we teach children and youth about the gift of the Holy Ghost?

Related Scriptures: 1 Corinthians 12:3; Jacob 4:8; Alma 5:46–48; D&C 45:56–57; 76:5–10; Articles of Faith 1:9

Notes

1. *The Gospel Kingdom,* sel. G. Homer Durham (1943), 35.
2. *Deseret News: Semi-Weekly,* 15 Jan. 1878, 1.
3. *Gospel Standards,* comp. G. Homer Durham (1941), 19–20.
4. *The Gospel Kingdom,* 41–42.
5. *The Gospel Kingdom,* 43; paragraphing altered.
6. *Deseret News: Semi-Weekly,* 9 Jan. 1883, 1; paragraphing altered.
7. *The Gospel Kingdom,* 35.
8. *Deseret News: Semi-Weekly,* 7 Mar. 1882, 1; paragraphing altered.
9. *The Gospel Kingdom,* 34; paragraphing altered.
10. *The Gospel Kingdom,* 35–36.
11. *The Gospel Kingdom,* 44–45.
12. *Deseret News* (Weekly), 22 Apr. 1863, 338.
13. *Millennial Star,* 15 Aug. 1851, 243.

President Taylor compared our individual membership and service to the parts of a tree, teaching that "we are cemented together, united in the bonds of one common covenant."

CHAPTER 18

Service in the Church

We are all interested in the great latter-day work of God, and we all ought to be co-workers therein.[1]

From the Life of John Taylor

From the moment of his conversion, John Taylor was committed to giving his all to the Lord's work. Reflecting on his call in 1837 to be an Apostle, he shared these thoughts: "The work seemed great, the duties arduous and responsible. I felt my own weakness and littleness; but I felt determined, the Lord being my helper, to endeavor to magnify it. When I first entered upon Mormonism, I did it with my eyes open. I counted the cost. I looked upon it as a life-long labor, and considered that I was not only enlisted for time, but for eternity also, and did not wish to shrink now, although I felt my incompetency."[2]

This "life-long labor" that he anticipated became a reality. Through his decades of service, John Taylor placed his trust in the Lord, knowing that if he served faithfully, the Lord would sustain him and enable him to accomplish His will. One example of how the Lord sustains those who serve Him occurred when Elder Taylor was preaching the gospel on the Isle of Man, an island near England. He had arranged for the printing of some tracts he had written in response to the false accusations against the Church and the Prophet Joseph Smith. However, the printer refused to deliver the tracts until he was paid in full. Anxious to distribute the tracts as soon as possible, Elder Taylor prayed to the Lord for help, which was soon given.

"[A] few minutes after his prayer was offered a young man came to the door, and upon being invited to enter handed Elder Taylor an envelope and walked out. The young man was unknown to him. The envelope contained some money and a little note which read: 'The laborer is worthy of his hire,' and no signature was placed thereon. [A] few minutes later a poor woman engaged as a fish vendor came to the house and offered a little money to assist him in his ministerial labors. He told her there was plenty of money in the world and he did not wish to take her money. She insisted that the Lord would bless her the more and she would be happier if he would accept it, whereupon he received the offering, and to his surprise the poor woman's mite, added to what the young man had given him, made exactly the amount sufficient to pay the printer the balance due him."[3]

Teachings of John Taylor

Each of us has a duty to serve in the Church and to magnify our calling.

It is not correct to suppose that the whole duty of carrying this kingdom devolves upon the twelve or the First Presidency, as the case may be, or upon the presidents of the stakes, or upon the high priests, or upon the seventies, or upon the bishops, or upon any other officer in the church and kingdom of God; that to the contrary, all of us have our several duties to perform. And I may go farther in regard to the duties of men, and also in regard to those of women; all have their duties to perform before God. The organization of this church and kingdom is for the express purpose of putting every man in his place, and it is then expected that every man in that place will magnify his office and calling.[4]

If you do not magnify your callings, God will hold you responsible for those whom you might have saved had you done your duty.[5]

What is it to be a Saint? And how far am I, and how far are you fulfilling the obligations that devolve upon us as Saints of God, as Elders in Israel, as fathers of families and mothers of families? Let us ask ourselves these questions. Are we performing our various duties in building up the kingdom of God, in rolling forth his work upon the earth? And what are we doing to bring about the latter day glory? Which of our acts tends to this? Do any of them, or do all of them? And what is really our position? These are things that it is well for us to weigh, consider and find out the real responsibilities that are resting upon us.[6]

It is not enough . . . that we are baptized and have hands laid upon us for the gift of the Holy Ghost. It is not enough even that we go further than this and receive our [temple ordinances], but that we daily and hourly and all the time live up to our religion, cultivate the Spirit of God and have it continually within us 'as a well of water springing up to everlasting life,' [see John 4:14] unfolding, developing, making manifest the purposes and the designs of God unto us, that we may be enabled to walk worthy of the high vocation whereunto we are called, as sons and daughters of God. . . . It would be found very difficult for any individual left to himself to do right, to think right, to speak right, and to fulfil the will and law of God upon the earth, and hence the necessity of the organization of the church and kingdom of God upon the earth, of the properly organized priesthood, of the legitimate channel, check, bounds, laws and governments that the Almighty has introduced into his church and kingdom, for the guidance, instruction, protection, welfare, upbuilding and further progress of his church and kingdom upon the earth. . . .

. . . It is like the branches of a tree, and the root and stock of a tree. The branches flourish on a healthy stock, and one little twig on the outside, with a few green leaves upon it and a little fruit, is very productive, beautiful and pleasant to look upon, but it is no more than a portion of the tree, it is not the tree. Where does it get its nourishment from? From the root and the stock or stem, and through the various branches that exist on the tree. . . .

As a Saint you say, "I think I understand my duty and I am doing very well." That may be so. You see the little twig; it is green, it flourishes and is the very picture of life, it bears its part and proportion in the tree, and is connected with the stem, branches and root; but could the tree live without it? Yes, it could. It need not boast itself and get uplifted, and say "how green I am and how I flourish, and what a healthy position I am in, how well I am doing and I am in my proper place and am doing right." But could you do without the root? No; you bear your proper part and position in the tree. Just so is this people. . . .

This is a fit similitude of the church and kingdom of God. We are cemented together, united in the bonds of one common covenant. We are part and parcel of the church and kingdom of God which the Lord has planted on the earth in the last days for the accomplishment of his purposes and the establishment of his kingdom, and the bringing to pass all those things which have been spoken of by all the holy prophets since the world was. We all stand in our proper place.

While we magnify our callings we honor our God. While we magnify our calling we possess a portion of the Spirit of God; while we magnify our calling we altogether comprise the tree; while we magnify our calling the Spirit of God flows through the proper channels by which and through which we receive our proper nourishment, and are instructed in things pertaining to our welfare, happiness and interest pertaining to this world and the world to come.[7]

The work of God is growing and increasing, and it will continue to do so until the words of the prophet will be fulfilled who said, "A little one shall become a thousand, and a small one a strong nation: I the Lord will hasten it in his time" [Isaiah 60:22] but He expects every man in his place to magnify his calling and to honor his God. And while there are evils . . . , there is a great amount of good, of virtue, of self-abnegation [or self-denial], and a great desire to do the will of God and carry out His purposes. And it is for every man and every woman to do his and her part.[8]

As we serve in the Church, we ought to conform to the word, the will, and the law of God.

We are here as Jesus was here, not to do our own will, but the will of our Father who sent us [see John 5:30]. He has placed us here; we have a work to do in our day and generation; and there is nothing of importance connected with any of us only as we are associated with God and His work, whether it be the President of the Church, the Twelve Apostles, the Presidents of Stakes, the Bishops, or anybody else, and we can only thus be of any service by placing ourselves in a position to act as God dictates us; as He regulates and manipulates the affairs of His Church in the interests of humanity, in behalf of the living and of the dead, in behalf of the world in which we live, and in behalf of those who have lived before us and who will live after us. We can none of us do anything only as we are assisted, guided and directed by the Lord. . . .

. . . We ought to wake up and put our houses in order and our hearts in order; we ought to conform to the word, the will, and the law of God; we ought to let God rule in Zion, to let His law be written upon our hearts, and to feel the responsibility of the great work we are called upon to perform. We should see that our bodies and our spirits are pure, and that they are free from contamination of every kind. We are here to build up the Zion of God, and to this end we must subject our bodies and our spirits to the law, to the word, and to the will of God. Being here in Zion we want to see that thing that Jesus told His disciples to pray for take place. "Thy kingdom come. Thy will be done on earth, as it is in heaven." [See Matthew 6:10.] How was it done in heaven? God spake and the worlds were formed according to His word. God said let us do this, and that and the other, and it was so. Was there anybody in heaven to object and say, "Don't you think you had better put it off a little. Would not this be a better way?" Yes, the devil said so, and he says so yet, and he is listened to sometimes by sinners and sometimes by Saints; for we become the servants of those whom we list to obey [see D&C 29:45]. . . .

. . . The law of God is perfect converting the soul [see Psalm 19:7], and we must be governed by that law and carry it out, or be made amenable unto the Lord our God for the course we pursue, or for neglecting to perform our duties. That is the way I look at these things, and if that is not the case, why are these laws given to us. Are they the laws of God? We so understand them. Then let us perform our duties and seek to magnify our callings that we may stand approved and acknowledged of the Lord. . . .

Arise! therefore, ye Elders of Israel—ye Priests, Teachers and Deacons, ye Presidents of Stakes, Bishops and High Counselors, ye Apostles and First Presidency, and all of us—Arise! and let us go to work with a will to do the will of God on earth as it is done in heaven; for if ever that is done, where is it to start, do you

"We hold up our right hand when voting in token before God that we will sustain those for whom we vote."

think, if it does not begin here among us? God expects it at our hands. We are full of weaknesses and imperfections, every one of us; but we want to learn the word, the will, and law of God, and to conform to that word and will and law. Let that law be written upon our hearts. Let us seek to magnify our callings and honor our God, and the Lord will take care of the balance. . . . We will . . . put our trust in the living God, and pursue a course that is wise, prudent and intelligent. We will glory not in ourselves, but in the Lord of Hosts.[9]

We need the sustaining hand of the Almighty as we serve.

God does not see as man; he reasons not as man. Although we may partially comprehend our individual duties, we do not understand how to regulate the church of God. It needs the regular organization and the Spirit to direct through the proper channels.[10]

We are acting in conjunction with the Almighty, with apostles and prophets and men of God who have lived in the various ages of the world, to accomplish the great programme that God had in his mind in relation to the human family before the world existed, and which will as assuredly come to pass as God lives. We feel, at the same time, that we are encompassed with the infirmities, weaknesses, imperfections and frailties of human nature, and in many instances we err in judgment, and we always need the sustaining hand of the Almighty; the guidance and direction of His Holy Spirit, and the counsel of his priesthood that we may be led and preserved in the path that leads to life eternal.[11]

We say that we are the Saints of God, so we are. . . . We have believed and do believe that God has spoken, that angels have appeared and that God has opened a communication between the heavens and the earth. This is a part of our faith and creed. We believe that God is going to revolutionize the earth, to purge it from iniquity of every kind and to introduce righteousness of every kind, until the great millennium is fully introduced. We believe moreover, that God having commenced his work, he will continue to reveal and make manifest his will to his priesthood, to his church and kingdom on the earth, and that among this people there will be an embodiment of virtue, of truth, of holiness, of integrity, of fidelity, of wisdom and of the knowledge of God.[12]

I feel I am enlisted for the war, and it is going to last for time, and throughout all eternity; and if I am a servant of God, I am under the direction of those servants of God, whom he has appointed to guide and counsel me by revelation from him, it is their right to dictate and control me amid all the affairs of those associated with the kingdom of God; and I feel moreover that everything whether spiritual or temporal, relating to time, or to eternity is associated with the kingdom of God. Feeling in that way it makes very little difference to me which way things go; it is not a matter of great moment whether they take that side, this side, or the other side, whether the path is rough or smooth, it will only last a certain time, and I can only last a certain time; but the chief thing with me is, how to hold on to my faith, and maintain my integrity, and honor my calling, and see to it, that I am found faithful at the latter end not only of this life, but in worlds without end; and continue to grow in all intelligence, knowledge, faith, perseverance, power, and exaltation.[13]

We should sustain other Church members in their callings.

All officers in the Church are first called by revelation, or those having authority, according to the nature of the case, and then are voted for by the people over whom they are to preside. Each person possesses power according to the position he occupies; and it is expected that all persons concerned will respect his judgement and decisions.[14]

We hold up our right hand when voting in token before God that we will sustain those for whom we vote. And if we cannot feel to sustain them, we ought not to hold up our hands, because to do this would be to act the part of hypocrites. . . .

What is meant by sustaining a person? Do we understand it? It is a very simple thing to me, I do not know how it is with you. For instance, if a man be a teacher, and I vote that I will sustain him in his position, when he visits me in an official capacity I will welcome him and treat him with consideration, kindness, and respect. If I need counsel, I will ask it at his hand, and I will do everything I can to sustain him. That would be proper and a principle of righteousness. I would not say anything derogatory to his character. If that is not correct, I have it yet to learn. And then if anybody in my presence were to whisper something about him, disparaging to his reputation, I would say, look here! are you a Saint? Yes. Did you not hold up your hand to sustain him? Yes. Then why do you not do it? Now, I would call an action of that kind sustaining him. If any man makes an attack upon his reputation—for all men's reputations are of importance to them—I would defend him in some such way.

When we vote for men in the solemn way in which we do, shall we abide by our covenants? or shall we violate them? If we violate them, we become covenant-breakers. We break our faith before God and our brethren, in regard to the acts of men whom we have covenanted to sustain.

But supposing he should do something wrong, supposing he should be found lying or cheating, or defrauding somebody, or stealing or anything else, or even become impure in his habits? Would you still sustain him? It would be my duty then to talk with him as I would with anybody else, and tell him that I had understood that things were thus and so, and that under these circumstances I could not sustain him. If I found that I had been misinformed, I would withdraw the charge; but if not, it would then be my duty to see that justice was administered to him, that he was brought before the proper tribunal to answer for the things he had done; and in the absence of that I would have no business to talk about him.[15]

Pray for those that God has placed in the different offices of this church that they may be enabled to perform their several duties. The Lord will sustain his servants and give them his Holy Spirit and the light of revelation, if they seek him in the way that he has appointed, and he will lead them and lead you in the right path. This is the order of the kingdom of God, as I understand it. . . . And it is for us to learn that order and be obedient to it.[16]

Suggestions for Study and Discussion

- Have you ever received a calling for which you did not feel prepared? How did you respond to the challenge? (See also 1 Nephi 17:50.) How can we prepare ourselves to serve the Lord in any capacity?
- President Taylor stressed that all of us have duties to perform in the Church. Why is it important for each of us to serve?

- In what ways have your Church callings benefited your life? In what ways can you serve more fully?
- How have you or your family been blessed by a Church member who magnified his or her calling? What feelings come into your heart for those who diligently serve you and your family?
- What experiences have you had when the Lord has helped you as you served? What can you do to receive His guidance more consistently as you serve? Why is it important, as we serve, to glory not in ourselves, but in the Lord?
- How can we actively sustain others in their callings? How does it strengthen the Church when we demonstrate our support for each other? What can we do within our homes to help our families sustain our Church leaders?

Related Scriptures: Proverbs 3:5–6; Mosiah 2:17; D&C 4:2–7; 24:7; 64:33–34; 76:5

Notes

1. *The Gospel Kingdom,* sel. G. Homer Durham (1943), 222.
2. B. H. Roberts, *The Life of John Taylor* (1963), 48.
3. Andrew Jenson, *Latter-day Saint Biographical Encyclopedia,* 4 vols. (1901–36), 1:16.
4. *The Gospel Kingdom,* 209.
5. *Deseret News: Semi-Weekly,* 6 Aug. 1878, 1.
6. *Deseret News* (Weekly), 11 Apr. 1860, 41.
7. *Deseret News* (Weekly), 16 Dec. 1857, 323.
8. *Deseret News: Semi-Weekly,* 5 Sept. 1882, 1.
9. *Deseret News: Semi-Weekly,* 24 Mar. 1885, 1.
10. *The Gospel Kingdom,* 381.
11. *Deseret News: Semi-Weekly,* 26 Jan. 1875, 1.
12. *Deseret News* (Weekly), 22 Apr. 1863, 338.
13. *Deseret News* (Weekly), 25 May 1854, 2.
14. "Organization of the Church," *Millennial Star,* 15 Nov. 1851, 339; paragraphing altered.
15. *The Gospel Kingdom,* 174–75.
16. *The Gospel Kingdom,* 167.

CHAPTER 19

Temporal Blessings and the Law of Tithing

We have been taught to pay our tithing, that we might acknowledge to God that we are his people, and that if he gave us all we ask, we might give one-tenth back to him, and by that act acknowledge his hand.[1]

From the Life of John Taylor

John Taylor believed that God provides for our temporal needs in addition to our spiritual blessings. He therefore encouraged the Saints to seek and acknowledge the hand of God in temporal affairs, teaching that "we have got to put ourselves in a position to be guided and directed of the Lord in temporal as well as spiritual things, or we will never obtain that glory for which many of us are looking."[2]

While recognizing the importance of temporal matters for the sustenance of life, President Taylor also maintained a proper perspective regarding the things of the world. Concerning President Taylor's view of temporal wealth, Elder B. H. Roberts of the Seventy wrote: "He never devoted himself to money getting. . . . Yet the amount of property he accumulated at Nauvoo, and which he sacrificed in order to flee into the wilderness with the Church of Christ, is sufficient to prove that he was not without financial ability. But he had his eyes and heart fixed upon the better riches, those which moth and rust could not corrupt, neither mobs break through nor steal [see Matthew 6:19–20]. These things filled his soul, engrossed his attention and left but a small margin of time to him in which to fall in love with the wealth of this world. His motto was—'Money is of little importance where truth is concerned.' "[3]

The Deseret Store, adjacent to the General Tithing Storehouse. President Taylor taught that "all things temporal and all things spiritual . . . are associated with the Gospel."

To President Taylor, observing the law of tithing was an important part of fulfilling his temporal responsibilities and acknowledging God's hand in all blessings. In a time when most tithing was paid in kind rather than with money, he taught his children the importance of giving only the best to the Lord in appreciation for all that they had received. "When gathering the fruit in the fall," his son Moses W. Taylor wrote, "father would come and inspect the baskets and selecting the largest and best fruit would say: 'Take the tithing out of this and be sure and pay it in full.' "[4]

Teachings of John Taylor

We are indebted to God for all that we have.

Who made us? Who organized us, and the elements with which we are surrounded and that we inhale? Who organized the planetary system that we see around us? Who provides breakfast, dinner and supper for the millions that dwell on the face of the earth? Who clothes them, as he does the lilies of the field? Who imparts unto man his breath, life, health, his powers of locomotion, thought, and all the godlike attributes with which he is endowed? Where did they come from? Who has controlled and managed the affairs of the world from its creation until the present time? The Great I Am, the Great Eloheim, the Great God who is our Father.[5]

[Jesus said], "Consider the lilies of the field, they toil not, neither do they spin, and yet Solomon in all his glory was not arrayed like one of these." [See Matthew 6:28–29.] Again, says he, reflect upon the fowls of the air, they do not sow, nor reap, nor gather into barns, yet your Heavenly Father takes care of them, and will he not also take care of you, O ye of little faith? [See Matthew 6:26.] . . .

If we have life, or health, or possessions; if we have children, and friends and homes, if we have the light of truth, the blessings of the everlasting gospel, the revelations of God, the holy priesthood, with all its blessings and government and rule, all these and every true enjoyment that we possess come from God. We do not always realize this, but it is nevertheless true that to God we are indebted for every good and perfect gift [see James

1:17]. He organized our bodies as they exist in all their perfection, symmetry and beauty. He, as the poet has expressed it,

"Makes the grass the hills adorn,
And clothes the smiling fields with corn.
The beasts with food his hands supply,
And the young ravens when they cry."

He is merciful and kind and benevolent towards all his creatures, and it is well for us to reflect upon these things sometimes, for we thus realize our dependence upon the Almighty.

In speaking of the affairs of this world, it is often asked by many—"Why, should we not attend to them?" Of course we should. Do we not talk of building up Zion? Of course we do. Do we not talk of building cities and of making beautiful habitations, gardens and orchards, and placing ourselves in such a position that we and our families can enjoy the blessings of life? Of course we do. God has given us the land and all the necessary elements for this purpose, and he has given us intelligence to use them. But the great thing he has had in view is, that whilst we use the intelligence that he gives us for the accomplishment of the various objects that are desirable for our well being and happiness, we should not forget him who is the source of all our blessings, whether pertaining to the present or the future.[6]

God is our God in whom we put our trust; we have nothing ourselves to boast of. Have we wealth? Who gave it to us? The Lord. Have we property? Who put us in possession of it? The Lord. Our horses, cattle and sheep, our flocks, herds and possessions, are his gifts. The gold and the silver and the precious things of earth, and also the cattle upon a thousand hills, are his, and we are his, and in his hands, and all nations are in his hands, and he will do with us and with them as seemeth him good. And as a kind, wise Father, he will watch over their interests; and when the time of judgment comes, it will not be withheld. We ought always to remember that our strength is in God; we have nothing to boast of ourselves, we have no intelligence that God has not given unto us; we have nothing in life, or property, but what has been given unto us of the Lord. Everything we possess pertaining to time and eternity has been imparted to us by him.[7]

All that we possess is the gift of God. We should acknowledge him in all things. We sometimes talk about men having this right and the other right. We have no rights, only such as God gives us. And I will tell you what he will show to the Latter-day Saints. He will yet prove to them that the gold and the silver are his, and the cattle upon a thousand hills, and that he gives to whom he will, and withholds from whom he pleases. He will yet show you this is a matter of fact. Our safety and happiness and our wealth depend upon our obedience to God and his laws, and our exaltation in time and eternity depends upon the same thing.[8]

Understanding our temporal blessings and responsibilities is part of the gospel.

I am pleased to talk about the things pertaining to the Kingdom of God, and also about other matters that some think are not so directly associated with the Kingdom of God, and yet they are; for all things temporal and all things spiritual, all things that are associated with our bodies and with our spirits, everything that is calculated to promote our happiness and well-being on the earth and to procure for us an exaltation in the kingdom of heaven, are things that are associated with the Gospel and that belong to us as Latter-day Saints.[9]

The object of our meeting is not altogether for religious purposes, but to consult upon all matters for the interest of the church and kingdom of God upon the earth. . . . We meet also to consult upon the best course for us to pursue with regard to temporal things as well as spiritual things; for as we possess bodies as well as spirits, and have to live by eating, drinking, and wearing, it becomes necessary that temporal matters should be considered and discussed in our conferences, and that we should deliberate upon all things that are calculated to benefit, bless, and exalt the Saints of God, whether they refer to our spiritual affairs or to our avocations and duties in life as husbands and wives, as parents and children, as masters and servants. . . . The idea of strictly religious feelings with us, and nothing else, is out of the question; yet we do everything in the fear of God. Our religion is more comprehensive than that of the world; it does not prompt its [members] with the desire to "sit and sing themselves away to everlasting bliss," but it embraces all the interests of humanity in every conceivable phase, and every truth in the world comes within its scope.[10]

The Lord is anxious to do us good, to enlighten our minds, to inform our judgment, to unfold unto us His will, and to strengthen us and prepare us for the great events that must transpire in these last days. He is desirous to show us how to save ourselves, how to bless ourselves temporally and spiritually, intellectually, morally, physically, politically and in every possible way that He is capable of bestowing His blessings upon fallen humanity.[11]

Through tithing, we acknowledge God, show our faithfulness, and prepare for greater blessings.

We as a people acknowledge that the law of tithing emanates from the Lord; then how is it that we need talking to so much in relation to it. If we are not honest with ourselves, and honest with our God, of what good to us are all our professions of being representatives of God, of being elders in Israel, of being clothed with the holy priesthood, of being teachers of the ways of life. The ancient Jews, the old Pharisees with all their wickedness and corruption, could boast of paying tithes of all they possessed. We profess to be better than the old Pharisees, and yet it seems that it is very difficult for men among us to be honest with themselves and with their God in relation to so simple a principle as this is. . . .

[The Lord] wants in the first place to get men to acknowledge God [in] one little earthly principle, he wants to get them to acknowledge him, by giving him a certain little part, or one-tenth of what he gives to them to see whether they will be honest in this trifle, to see whether they will act as honorable high-minded men or not, or whether they will try to cheat him out of it. If we do this honestly and conscientiously until we have fulfilled our duty, we are then prepared for anything else. It is the principle

When we pay tithing, we acknowledge the Lord's blessings to us and show our willingness to keep His commandments.

and not the tithing we pay that is esteemed of the Lord; he cares not for our tithing, but he cares about our doing right. If we cannot be faithful in a few things, we cannot expect to be made rulers over many things [see Matthew 25:21].[12]

[The law of tithing] is a test to the people of God, or for us who profess to be, that we may know whether people will observe a certain specific law given by the Almighty or not, and thus have a proof of their fidelity and obedience. Now, if we abide this, all well and good; if not, it is written, "They shall not be found worthy to abide among you." [D&C 119:5.] . . .

We are talking about building up Zion. Here is where the thing applies itself with great force to me as well as to you, when you comprehend it as it exists and see it by the light of the Spirit of Truth. For it is written: "And I say unto you, if my people observe not this law, to keep it holy, and by this law sanctify the land of Zion unto me, that my statutes and my judgments may be kept thereon, that it may be most holy, behold, verily I say unto you, it shall not be a land of Zion unto you." [D&C 119:6.] Well, we are talking about building up the land of Zion, which is one of the things we are here for. And God has said that if we do not obey this law, it shall not be a land of Zion unto us. . . .

[Tithing] is a principle we are to be governed by. I am not here, you are not here, to carry out our own designs, and feelings, and purposes. Why, Jesus himself did not come to do that. According to His own words, He came not to do his own will, but the will of His Father who sent Him [see John 5:30]. And we are here not to do our own will, but the will of the Father who also sent us, and who has called us to our holy and exalted calling. . . .

These temporal matters [some] assume are of very little importance, they are of very little importance judging from the way that many of us labor; but they are of very great importance when weighed in the balances of truth, the principles of eternal life which God has revealed are of the utmost importance to the Saints, both to the living and the dead, to the myriads of men that have lived and that may live, these things are of vast importance. . . .

I am desirous to see the people observe this law of tithing because it is a plain and direct command to us. Not that I care anything personally whether people pay their tithing or not, and I do not think the Lord cares much Himself. The gold and the silver are His, and so are the cattle upon a thousand hills; and to him belongs power to command all things. And what we do possess of this world's goods is given unto us to make a wise use of, because we cannot take them with us when we shall be called hence. It is for us, as Saints of the Most High, to be honest and upright and take a correct course, to be full of integrity and maintain correct principles everywhere and at all times.[13]

Suggestions for Study and Discussion

- What are some of the temporal blessings that God has given to us? Why is it important to recognize that all these blessings come as gifts from God? What causes some people to forget that God is the source of these blessings?
- What is the relationship between our use of earthly possessions and our spiritual well-being? (See also D&C 104:13–18.) How can we make better use of the blessings that God has given us?
- How does paying tithing show our love and gratitude to the Lord? How can we cultivate a feeling of thanksgiving when we give tithes and offerings?
- What can you do to teach your children and grandchildren to pay an honest tithing?
- Why is it sometimes a challenge to pay tithing? What can we do to overcome that challenge?
- Why is it important to pay tithing even though we may still struggle financially all our lives? What spiritual or temporal blessings have you received from being obedient to the law of tithing?

Related Scriptures: Leviticus 27:30; Isaiah 45:12; Malachi 3:8–12; Mosiah 2:20–22; D&C 59:21; 104:13–18; 119:1–7; 120

Notes

1. *The Gospel Kingdom,* sel. G. Homer Durham (1943), 265.
2. *Deseret News: Semi-Weekly,* 11 Feb. 1879, 1.
3. B. H. Roberts, *The Life of John Taylor* (1963), 424–25.
4. "Stories and Counsel of Prest. Taylor," *Young Woman's Journal,* May 1905, 218; paragraphing altered.
5. *Deseret News* (Weekly), 1 Jan. 1873, 728.
6. *Deseret News* (Weekly), 15 Jan. 1873, 760.
7. In Conference Report, Apr. 1880, 103.
8. *The Gospel Kingdom,* 248.
9. *Deseret News: Semi-Weekly,* 21 Aug. 1883, 1.
10. *The Gospel Kingdom,* 168.
11. *Deseret News: Semi-Weekly,* 19 Nov. 1865, 2.
12. *The Gospel Kingdom,* 264–65; paragraphing altered.
13. *Deseret News* (Weekly), 8 Mar. 1881, 1; paragraphing altered.

The Logan Utah Temple, dedicated by President Taylor in 1884. In temples, "the most sacred ordinances of God are to be performed, which are associated with the interest and happiness of the human family."

CHAPTER 20

The Temple, the Gateway to Exaltation

We are here to cooperate with God in the salvation of the living [and] in the redemption of the dead.[1]

From the Life of John Taylor

Because of increasing persecution in Nauvoo, the Prophet Joseph Smith feared that he might not live to see the Nauvoo Temple completed. Wanting to be sure that he conferred the needed keys and knowledge upon others, he prepared a room above a store in Nauvoo where he could administer temple ordinances to a select few.[2] Among those chosen was John Taylor, who had been particularly interested in temple ordinances from the time those principles were first revealed to the Church. From this and other experiences, President Taylor developed an understanding of and appreciation for the temple and the ordinances performed there.

While speaking at the dedication of the Logan Utah Temple site, President Taylor shared with the congregation the feelings he experienced when he visited the St. George Utah Temple, the first temple completed in the Utah Territory:

"When I visited that holy Temple, accompanied by my brethren who were with me, we experienced a sacred thrill of joy and a solemn, reverential sensation. As we entered its sacred portals, we felt that we were standing on holy ground, and experienced, with one of old, 'Surely this is the house of God, and the gate of heaven.' [See Genesis 28:17.] That is not simply a metaphorical expression, but a reality, for it is in that House, and it will be in the House to be built on this ground, that the most sacred ordinances of God are to be performed, which are associated with the interest and happiness of the human family, living and dead. I felt to rejoice in my heart that we had been thus far successful in the building of one temple to the name of our Father and God."[3]

In addition to understanding the importance of the temple, President Taylor knew that the number of temples and those who administered in them would continue to grow as God's plan was carried out. While showing the Salt Lake Temple construction site to a visitor from another country, President Taylor prophesied of the great increase in the number of temples in the world: "We expect to build hundreds of them yet, and to administer in them in carrying out the work of God."[4]

Teachings of John Taylor

God is interested in the exaltation of the dead as well as the living.

There was a great and comprehensive plan designed by the Almighty in his economy connected with the salvation of the human family who are his children, for he is the God and the Father of the spirits of all flesh. It means that He is interested in their welfare, in their prosperity, in their happiness, and in all that pertains to their exaltation in time and throughout the eternities that are to come. Being thus interested, and so little of the gospel having been revealed in the different ages, and so much of the power of darkness and iniquity having prevailed among men, it was necessary that something should be done for the dead as well as the living. God is interested in the dead as well as the living.[5]

We are here to cooperate with God in the salvation of the living, in the redemption of the dead, in the blessings of our ancestors, in the pouring out of blessings upon our children; we are here for the purpose of redeeming and regenerating the earth on which we live, and God has placed his authority and his counsels here upon the earth for that purpose, that men may learn to do the will of God on the earth as it is done in heaven. This is the object of our existence; and it is for us to comprehend the position.[6]

We are living, as I have said, in an important day and age of the world. . . . [God] has reserved us for the latter days, that we may perform that work which He decreed from before the foundation of the world. If there have been any blessings enjoyed by men in former dispensations of the world, they will also be given to you, ye Latter-day Saints, if you will live your religion and be obedient to the laws of God. There is nothing hidden but what shall be revealed, says the Lord. He is prepared to unfold all things; all things pertaining to the heavens and the earth, all things pertaining to the peoples who have existed, who now exist or will exist, that we may be instructed and taught in every principle of intelligence associated with the world in which we live or with the Gods in the eternal worlds.[7]

We build temples for the exaltation of all mankind.

When Elijah the prophet appeared to Joseph Smith, he committed to him the keys of this dispensation; and hence we are at work building temples. . . . There are ordinances associated behind these things that go back into eternity; and forward unto eternity; . . . that are intended for the welfare, the happiness, and exaltation of mankind; for those who are living and those that are dead and for those that will live hereafter, pertaining both to our progenitors and our posterity. And that is one of those keys that have been turned.[8]

Why do we build temples? Because Elijah conferred certain keys which he held upon Joseph Smith. And when he laid his hands upon elders conferring on them the holy priesthood, they carried the principles imparted by Elijah to Joseph to you and to others. . . . And by and by as the church began to gather together, we began to talk about building temples in which to receive and to administer ordinances which had been revealed unto Joseph Smith, pertaining to the interest of the living and the dead and necessary to our salvation and exaltation in the kingdom of our God, as well as for those for whom we administer. And we have not only talked about it but have done considerable in that direction.[9]

We have now finished this [the Logan Utah] temple, and some people inquire, what is it for? For many things: that our sealings and ordinances may be performed in a manner that will be acceptable before God and the holy angels; that whatsoever is bound on the earth according to the laws of the eternal priesthood shall be bound in the heavens; that there may be a connecting link between the living and the dead, between those who have lived, all those ancient fathers of which I have spoken who are interested in the welfare of their posterity; that there may be a royal priesthood, a holy people, a pure people, a virtuous people on the earth to officiate and operate in the interests of the living and the dead; not looking so much after themselves, but after God, after the work of God, and after the accomplishment of those things which God has designed to be carried out in the dispensation of the fulness of times [see D&C 128:18] when all things are to be united in one, and that they may be prepared to operate with the priesthood in the heavens in the redemption of the inhabitants of this world from the days of Adam unto the present time.[10]

We must be worthy to enter the holy temple of God.

People desirous to go and attend to ordinances in these houses, must have a recommendation from their bishop. . . . Then when they have obtained this recommendation from the bishop, it must be endorsed by the president of the stake. . . . This is quite an ordeal for many men to go through. For men and women who are upright, virtuous, and honorable, it is [a] very simple matter; there is no difficulty in their way at any time. But to those who have been careless of their duties, who have departed from the laws of God, and who have tampered with, or violated the ordinances of the gospel—to such people it is a critical time.

However, there is something far more difficult than that yet to come. That is only a starting point in these matters. The things that are ahead are a great deal more difficult to accomplish. What are they? The time will come when we shall not only have to pass by those officers whom I have referred to—say, to have the sanction and approval of our bishop [and] of the president of the stake . . . , but we are told in this book (The Doctrine and Covenants) that we shall have to pass by the angels and the Gods. We may have squeezed through the other; we may have got along tolerably well, and been passed and acted upon, and sometimes a "tight squeeze" at that. But how will it be when we get on the other side, and we have the angels and the Gods to pass by before we can enter into our exaltation? If we cannot pass, what then? Well, we cannot, that is all. And if we cannot, shall we be able to enter into our exaltation? I think not.[11]

You may deceive the Bishop and you may deceive the President of the Stake, and you may deceive the General authorities of the Church, but you cannot deceive the Lord Jesus Christ nor the Holy Ghost. You know yourselves better than anybody else and if there is anything wrong in you, now is the time to repent and make yourselves square with the Lord; and if you do not repent, the time will come when you will be humbled, and the higher up you get the greater will be your fall.[12]

We have a responsibility to be saviors on Mount Zion.

We are here to prepare to live, and to teach our children how to live after us; and to teach the world the same lesson if they will only receive it. We know that our spirits existed with the Father before we came here. We know that we are immortal as well as mortal beings, and that we have had to do with another world as well as this. We know that the world abounds with corruption; but it is our business to keep ourselves from it, and to progress in virtue, truth, integrity and holiness.

We came here to be saviors. "What, saviors?" "Yes." "Why, we thought there was only one Savior." "Oh, yes, there are a great many. What do the scriptures say about it?" One of the old prophets, in speaking of these things, says that saviors shall come up upon Mount Zion [see Obadiah 1:21]. Saviors? Yes. Whom shall they save? In the first place themselves, then their families, then their neighbors, friends and associations, then their forefathers, then pour blessings on their posterity. Is that so? Yes. . . .

We are desirous of blessing our posterity. We read of Abraham, Isaac and Jacob, before they left the world, calling their families together, and under the inspiration of the spirit of prophecy and revelation putting their hands upon their heads and pronouncing certain blessings upon them, which should rest upon their posterity through every subsequent period of time. We have the same gospel and priesthood, and the same light and intelligence, and we are after the salvation and exaltation of our families that shall come after us, as they were, and we are seeking for God's blessings to be poured upon their heads as they were. And if our fathers have died in ignorance of the gospel, not having had an opportunity to listen to it, we feel after them, and we go forth and are baptized for them, that they may be saved and exalted in the kingdom of God with us.[13]

When Jesus came, He came to do a work in many particulars similar to that in which we are engaged, and when He got through with His work here, He stood as the Savior of the world, and of the human family. He came to preach the Gospel to the poor, to open the prison doors to those that were imprisoned, to set them at liberty, and to proclaim the acceptable hour of the Lord, etc. This was a work connected with the people who lived at the time of the flood and were destroyed and kept in prison until the Lord should see proper to extend manifestations of His mercy to them. Hence, as we read, "Christ hath once suffered for sins, the just for the unjust, that He might bring us to God, being put to death in the flesh, but quickened by the spirit; by which also he went and preached to the spirits in prison: which sometime were disobedient when once the long suffering of God waited in the days of Noah." [See 1 Peter 3:18–20.] He having finished His work upon earth for the living, went and performed a work for the dead; as we are informed, "He went and preached to spirits in prison that had sometime been disobedient in the days of Noah."

It is reserved for us to do a work for those who have passed away who have not obeyed or had the Gospel in their lifetime. We are here to do a work connected with the redemption of the dead. When the Temple was commanded to be built in Nauvoo, after the Temple had been built in Kirtland, and after so many keys had been turned, and after so many manifestations, visions and ministrations had been had, yet it was said then that there was not a place upon the earth in which to perform the ordinance of baptism for the dead, and Joseph was commanded to build a house for that purpose.[14]

Many who have gone behind the veil are waiting for us to fulfill our duties.

The work we are engaged in is greater than we can generally conceive of. Our actions and operations now are connected with the past, with the present and with the future. Napoleon, on a certain occasion, told his army when in Egypt, that there were forty generations looking down upon them. But the heavenly hosts are looking down upon us. The Priesthood which has administered in the various generations and under the various dispensations, from the commencement of the world, have their eyes upon us; our brethren, with whom we have been associated here upon the earth and who are now behind the veil, have their eyes upon us. The myriads of dead that have slept in the silent tomb without a knowledge of the gospel have their eyes upon us, and they are expecting us to fulfil the duties and responsibilities that devolve upon us to attend to, in which they are interested.

All the holy priesthood—the ancient patriarchs, prophets and apostles and men of God who have lived in the different generations are looking upon us and expecting us to fulfill the great and important requirements of Jehovah in regard to the welfare and the redemption of the world: the salvation of the living and dead. God, our Heavenly Father, and his son Jesus Christ, our Redeemer, are also looking down upon us, and expect us to be faithful to our covenants.[15]

Suggestions for Study and Discussion

- What does it mean to you to be able to "cooperate with God in the salvation of the living [and] in the redemption of the dead"? How do you feel as you take the opportunity to bless your own ancestors through temple work?

- What was Elijah's purpose when he appeared to the Prophet Joseph Smith in the Kirtland Temple? (See also D&C 110:13–16.) What blessings are now available to us because of the keys that Elijah restored?
- Why is it important to be honest in our temple recommend interviews? What blessings are promised to us when we go worthily to the temple? (See also D&C 97:15–17.) How have you experienced these blessings? What can we do to prepare children and youth to be worthy to enter the temple?
- In what ways can we be "saviors on Mount Zion"? Why is our service critical to the salvation of those who have died?
- How do you feel when you consider that "the heavenly host are looking down upon us . . . expecting us to fulfill [our] duties and responsibilities"? What are our duties and responsibilities regarding temple and family history work? How can you improve in your temple and family history work?
- Read D&C 135:3. How does the Prophet Joseph's role in restoring temple work increase your understanding of this verse?
- Why do we need to go to the temple often? What does the temple mean to you personally? How can we increase the influence of the temple in our own lives and in the lives of our families?

Related Scriptures: D&C 109; 124:39–41; 128:15–25; 138

Notes

1. *The Gospel Kingdom,* sel. G. Homer Durham (1943), 286.
2. See *The Gospel Kingdom,* 286–87.
3. *Deseret News: Semi-Weekly,* 19 June 1877, 1.
4. *The Gospel Kingdom,* 294.
5. *The Gospel Kingdom,* 286.
6. *The Gospel Kingdom,* 286.
7. *Deseret News: Semi-Weekly,* 10 June 1884, 1.
8. *The Gospel Kingdom,* 292.
9. *The Gospel Kingdom,* 288.
10. *The Gospel Kingdom,* 290.
11. *The Gospel Kingdom,* 290–91.
12. Quoted in Matthias F. Cowley, "The Spirit of Discernment Manifested," in N. B. Lundwall, comp., *Temples of the Most High* (1941), 104.
13. *Deseret News: Semi-Weekly,* 11 Feb. 1873, 2; paragraphing altered.
14. *Deseret News: Semi-Weekly,* 10 June 1884, 1.
15. *Deseret News* (Weekly), 7 May 1879, 211; paragraphing altered.

CHAPTER 21

Strengthening Families

Look well to yourselves and to your families, to your sons and to your daughters; and let us seek to do right.[1]

From the Life of John Taylor

On 1 February 1885, John Taylor went into voluntary hiding to avoid persecution by federal authorities. Although he hoped that this exile would limit the oppression that the Church was experiencing at that time, he also knew that his hiding would likely separate him from most of his family for the remainder of his earthly life. Nonetheless, throughout this time, he remained ever concerned for their well-being. "Say unto them I remember them always," he told his nephew Angus M. Cannon just prior to his death. "I love them individually, and never cease to plead with God for them."[2]

President Taylor was a loving and devoted husband and father. Of him, his son Moses W. Taylor wrote the following: "He had a strong desire to keep his children under the family influence and provided play grounds for us. Even when he was past seventy years of age he would join us in our games. He provided a large sand pile for the little ones and if I have ever had any better time in my life than I did digging in the sand, I have failed to recognize it. . . .

"I have never heard him enter into any argument with any of his family; I have never heard him and my mother contend or disagree in the presence of the children. When talking about our duties in the church, it was always in the spirit of counsel and he would frequently say, 'It would please me if you are a faithful Latter-day Saint.' He was held in such high esteem by his children that to please him seemed to be their greatest desire."[3]

"Let us as parents train up our children in the fear of God and teach them the laws of life. If you do, we will have peace in our bosoms, peace in our families, and peace in our surroundings."

President Taylor taught the Saints the importance of parents setting a good example for their children. His son Frank Y. Taylor once spoke of the great influence for good that the example of his father had been in his life: "When I think of the careful training that I had, of the wonderful example that was set before me, in my youth, I feel that it would be inexcusable for me to do that which was not right in my life, because I feel that I had a perfect example to follow. As a boy, however, I have been tempted like other boys; but my father's life was so free and pure and clean that whenever temptation was presented to me, it seemed like my father rose up before me in majesty, like a monument, and I could not do the wrong which I was tempted to do. I felt that I would bring displeasure upon him, and I know there was nothing in his life that would warrant me in taking a course that would not be acceptable before our Father in heaven. I felt, as I thought of his life, O, I would like to live that kind of a life myself, so that I would be a light in the darkness to my boys and girls."[4]

Teachings of John Taylor

Marriage and family relations are eternal.

The gospel that we preach is the everlasting gospel; it reaches back into the eternities that are past; it exists in time and it stretches forward into the eternities to come, and everything connected with it is eternal. Our marriage relations, for instance, are eternal. Go to the sects of the day and you will find that time ends their marriage covenants; they have no idea of continuing their relations hereafter; they do not believe in anything of the kind. It is true there is a kind of natural principle in men that leads them to hope it may be so; but they know nothing about it. Our religion binds men and women for time and all eternity. This is the religion that Jesus taught—it had power to bind on earth and to bind in heaven, and it had power to loose on earth and to loose in heaven [see Matthew 16:19]. We believe in the same principles, and we expect, in the resurrection, that we shall associate with our wives and have our children sealed to us by the power of the holy priesthood, that they may be united with us worlds without end.[5]

The gospel, when introduced and preached to Adam after the fall, through the atonement of Jesus Christ, placed him in a position not only to have victory over death, but to have within his reach and to possess the perpetuity, not only of earthly, but of heavenly life; not only of earthly, but also of heavenly dominion; and through the law of that gospel enabled him (and not him alone, but all his posterity) to obtain, not only his first estate, but a higher exaltation on earth and in the heavens, than he could have enjoyed if he had not fallen; the powers and blessings associated with the atonement being altogether in advance of and superior to any enjoyment or privileges that he could have had in his first estate. Hence, he and his partner became the father and mother of lives—lives temporal, lives spiritual, and lives eternal, and were placed in the position to become Gods, yea, the sons and daughters of God, and to the increase and extent of their dominion there was to be no limit; worlds without end.[6]

What is more amiable and pleasant than those pure, innocent, endearing affections which God has placed in the hearts of the male and female, who are united in lawful matrimony, with a love and affection, pure as the love of God, because it springs from him, and is his gift: with bodies chaste and virtuous, and an offspring, lovely, healthy, pure, innocent, and uncontaminated: confiding in each other, they live together in the fear of God, enjoying nature's gifts uncorrupted, and undefiled as the driven snow, or the crystal stream. But how would this enjoyment be enhanced if they understood their destiny, could unravel the designs of God, and contemplate an eternal union in another state of existence, a connection with this offspring, commenced here, to endure for ever, and all their ties, relationships, and affections strengthened.

A mother feels great delight in beholding her child, and gazing on its lovely infant form; how would her bosom swell with delight at the contemplation of that child being with her for ever. And if we only understood our position, this was the object for which we came into the world. And the object of the kingdom of God, on which I have written at length, is to reestablish all these holy principles.[7]

Parents' influence extends to future generations.

The life of a saint is not simply a personal perfecting, it is also a factor in the entire scheme of earth's redemption. No one can be saved alone, by himself or herself, unassisted by or unassisting others. The weight of our influence must be either for good or harm, be an aid or an injury to the work of human regeneration, and as we assume responsibilities, form ties, enter into covenants, beget children, accumulate families, so does the weight of our influence increase, so does its extent broaden and deepen.[8]

The first commandment given to man was to "Be fruitful, and multiply, and replenish the earth." [Genesis 1:28.] And as man is an eternal being, and all his actions have a relevancy to eternity, it is necessary that he understand his position well, and thus fulfil the measure of his creation: for as he and his offspring are destined to live eternally, he is not only responsible for his own acts, but, in a great measure, for those of his children; in training their minds, regulating their morals, setting them a correct example, and teaching them correct principles, but more especially in preserving the purity of his own body.

And why? Because if he abuses his body and corrupts himself he not only injures himself but his partner or associates, and entails misery incalculable upon his posterity, . . . and this not only in time, but in eternity. Hence the Lord has given laws regulating marriage, and chastity, of the strictest kind, and entailed the severest punishment upon those who in different ages have abused this sacred ordinance. . . . And why? because man being made a free agent over his own body, that he might exalt himself and his posterity, both in time and eternity, if he abuses that power, he not only affects himself, but unborn bodies and spirits; corrupting the world, and opening the flood-gates of vice, immorality, and estrangement from God. . . . But when the order of God is carried out, it places things in a lovely position.[9]

If I . . . was the head of a family, I would want to teach my family right and teach them the principles of virtue, holiness, purity, honor and integrity, that they might be worthy citizens, and that they might be able to stand before God, that when they and I get through this world, we might be worthy to meet the elect of

God (those whom he has selected from the nations of the earth), and the Gods in the eternal world. Therefore, every morning, as head of my family, I should dedicate myself and my family to God.[10]

We should avoid unkind or harsh words and actions in our families.

You should never say a word or do an act which you would not want your children to copy after. The idea of men who profess to fear God, and some of them Elders in Israel, being addicted to swearing, . . . is a shame and a disgrace to high heaven, and this is sometimes done before their families; it is a shame. And then some men give way and say they have a bad temper: I would sell it for nothing, and give something to boot to get rid of it. I would be careful that all my acts and doings were right. . . .

We will treat our wives right. He is a mean man who would abuse a woman. . . . Have you not made covenants with your wives for time and eternity? Yes, you have. Would you not like, when you get through, to be able to say, Mary, Jane, Ann, or whatever the name may be, I never injured you in my life. And if you are wives, would you not like to be able to say, Thomas, or William, I never injured you in all my life. And, then, to spend an eternity together hereafter.[11]

Husbands, do you love your wives and treat them right, or do you think that you yourselves are some great moguls who have a right to crowd upon them? . . . You ought to treat them with all kindness, with mercy and long suffering, and not be harsh and bitter, or in any way desirous to display your authority. Then, you wives, treat your husbands right, and try to make them happy and comfortable. Endeavor to make your homes a little heaven, and try to cherish the good Spirit of God. Then let us as parents train up our children in the fear of God and teach them the laws of life. If you do, we will have peace in our bosoms, peace in our families, and peace in our surroundings.[12]

Do away with unkind or harsh words, and do not allow hard feelings to exist in your hearts, or find place in your habitations. Love one another, and by each trying to enhance the welfare of the other, that element will characterize the family circle, and your children will partake of the same feeling, and they in turn will imitate your good example, and perpetuate the things they learn at home.[13]

We should teach and practice principles of godliness in our families.

Parents, be truthful; let your children have confidence in your word, so that if father or mother says anything, they might say, "if father or mother says such and such a thing, I know it is right, because father or mother said it, and they never prevaricate or tell a falsehood." That is the kind of feeling we want to cultivate among ourselves and with our families.

And again we want to be cleanly in our persons, in our houses and in everything. And mothers, you ought to cultivate in your hearts the spirit of peace; you ought to be like angels of God, full of every virtue. And the father ought to treat the mother right. Has she her infirmities? Yes. And so has he. . . . Make your homes joyous. And let your children see that you love one another, that they may grow up with the same feeling, and be led from principle to honor their father and mother. These are the kind of feelings that will elevate us.[14]

Do you have prayers in your family? . . . And when you do, do you go through the operation like the grinding of a piece of machinery, or do you bow in meekness and with a sincere desire to seek the blessing of God upon you and your household? That is the way that we ought to do, and cultivate a spirit of devotion and trust in God, dedicating ourselves to him, and seeking his blessings.[15]

We have been commanded of the Lord to set our households in order. Apostles, Presidents of Stakes and Bishops, have you done this with your own households? Have you also seen that the Saints have done the same? Have you impressed upon the people under your charge the absolute necessity of purity if they desire the blessing and protection of the Most High? Wolves never watched with greater cunning and more ravenous hunger a flock of sheep and lambs than the people of your wards and stakes are now being watched by those who are ready to devour them. Are you awake to this danger, and do you take every precaution against it?

Parents, are you full of fidelity yourselves to every principle of godliness, and do you surround your sons and daughters with every safeguard to shield them from the arts of the vile? Do you teach them that chastity in both man and woman should be more highly esteemed than life itself? Or do you leave them in their ignorance and inexperience to mix with any society they may choose, at any hour that may be convenient to them, and to be exposed to the wiles of the seducer and the corrupt? These are questions you will all have to answer either to your shame and condemnation or to your joy and eternal happiness. Know this, that God, in giving us the precious blessings we possess, demands from us a suitable return. By receiving them we are placed under obligations. If these are not discharged, condemnation inevitably follows.[16]

Parents, treat your children aright; train them up in the fear of the Lord; they are of more importance to you than many things that you give your attention to.

And you, children, obey your parents; respect your fathers and mothers. Your mothers have watched over you, and your fathers are desirous for your welfare, and their hearts and feelings and affections are drawn out towards you. Do not give them pain by departing from correct principles; but walk in the paths of life. And parents, and children, husbands and wives and all people, fear God and put your trust in him and carry out the principles of your holy religion which God has revealed to us.[17]

Suggestions for Study and Discussion

- How does a knowledge of the eternal nature of marriage and family relations influence the feelings in your home? How does this knowledge help you to be a better spouse or family member?
- What specifically can husbands and wives do to help them keep their marriage covenants?
- In what ways can parents teach their children the principles that are necessary for their salvation? How can parents help their children who may be rebellious or have made serious mistakes?

- Read Proverbs 3:5–6. How can parents and grandparents prepare themselves to hear the Spirit so they can counsel their children and grandchildren correctly? In what ways has the Holy Ghost helped you make decisions that have influenced your children or grandchildren for good?
- What have you learned from the example of your parents?
- Read or sing the hymn "I Am a Child of God" (*Hymns,* no. 301). How should knowing that we are all the spirit children of our Father in Heaven affect the way we treat our children? our spouse?
- John Taylor warned against harsh words or actions within our families. How can we guard against these things in our homes?
- Why is emotional or physical abuse of a spouse or child a serious sin in the eyes of God? How can abusive situations be resolved?
- How can we cultivate a feeling of love and peace in our homes? What blessings have come into your home when the Spirit of God was present? How can those who do not live in a peaceful home find peace in their own life?

Related Scriptures: Psalm 127:3–5; Matthew 18:1–6; 3 Nephi 18:21; D&C 68:25–28; 93:40–43; 132:19–20

Notes

1. *Deseret News: Semi-Weekly,* 23 Feb. 1883, 1.
2. B. H. Roberts, *The Life of John Taylor* (1963), 459.
3. "Stories and Counsel of Prest. Taylor," *Young Woman's Journal,* May 1905, 219; paragraphing altered.
4. In Conference Report, Oct. 1919, 156.
5. *Deseret News: Semi-Weekly,* 30 Mar. 1869, 3.
6. *The Gospel Kingdom,* sel. G. Homer Durham (1943), 278–79.
7. "Extract from a Work by John Taylor about to Be Published in France," *Millennial Star,* 15 Mar. 1851, 82; paragraphing altered.
8. In James R. Clark, comp., *Messages of the First Presidency of The Church of Jesus Christ of Latter-day Saints,* 6 vols. (1965–75), 3:87.
9. "Extract from a Work by John Taylor," *Millennial Star,* 15 Mar. 1851, 81–82; paragraphing altered.
10. *Deseret News: Semi-Weekly,* 18 Oct. 1881, 1.
11. *Deseret News: Semi-Weekly,* 10 Mar. 1885, 1; paragraphing altered.
12. *The Gospel Kingdom,* 284.
13. *Deseret News: Semi-Weekly,* 16 Apr. 1878, 1.
14. *Deseret News: Semi-Weekly,* 3 Jan 1882, 1; paragraphing altered.
15. *The Gospel Kingdom,* 284.
16. *The Gospel Kingdom,* 282–83.
17. *Deseret News: Semi-Weekly,* 1 June 1880, 1; paragraphing altered.

The Saints leaving Nauvoo in February 1846.
President Taylor taught that "trials have the effect to prove the Saints and those who are only Saints in name."

CHAPTER 22

Being Perfected through Trials

If we have to pass through a few trials, a few difficulties, and a few afflictions and to meet with a few privations, they have a tendency to purify the metal, purge it from the dross, and prepare it for the Master's use.[1]

From the Life of John Taylor

John Taylor passed through many trials in his life. Perhaps one of the greatest trials was his experience in Carthage Jail. During the attack in which the Prophet Joseph and his brother Hyrum were martyred, Elder Taylor was shot several times. Severely wounded and unable to travel to Nauvoo, he remained in Carthage for a few days. During this time a local doctor came to remove a bullet from his leg. Elder Taylor's wounds were of such a serious nature that his wife, who had just arrived, "retired to another room to pray for him that he might have strength to endure it and be restored to her and her family." When the doctor asked Elder Taylor if he wanted to be tied during the operation, Elder Taylor said no. The surgery took place without any restraints on him and without anesthesia.[2]

When several members of the Church arrived in Carthage to return Elder Taylor to Nauvoo, he was so weak from the loss of blood that he could barely whisper. Being unable to ride in a wagon, he was carried on a stretcher toward Nauvoo. However, "the tramping of those who carried him at last produced violent pain. A sleigh was therefore obtained and hitched to the back of [a] wagon. A bed was made on the sleigh, and with Sister Taylor by his side to bathe his wounds with ice-water," the sleigh slid gently over the thick prairie grass to Nauvoo.[3]

Tribulations continued in Nauvoo as Elder Taylor and hundreds of the Saints began leaving the city during February 1846 to escape increasing persecution. A historical account describes their suffering as they camped across the river from Nauvoo: "There they lay, exposed to the inclement season, while only a short distance away—almost in view—were their comfortable houses, their beautiful city and magnificent temple! These homes which they had left, and that city were still theirs, for so hurried had been their departure that they had no time to dispose of property."[4]

Many years later, in 1885, when the Saints were well established in the Salt Lake Valley, President Taylor faced the trial of loneliness and isolation. While in hiding to help ease the persecution of the Church by federal authorities, he was unable to see his loved ones, who were themselves under surveillance. His seclusion became especially difficult during the illness and eventual death of his wife Sophia. Because of safety concerns, he was not able to visit her or even attend her funeral. Though heartbroken, President Taylor "bowed to the hard conditions with that Christian fortitude which had been characteristic of him all his life."[5] His attitude toward trials was perhaps best expressed in an excerpt of a letter he wrote to his family while he was in hiding: "Some people suppose that persecutions and trials are afflictions; but sometimes, and generally, if we are doing the will of the Lord and keeping His commandments, they may be truly said to be blessings in disguise."[6]

In spite of a life marked with trials, John Taylor remained a valiant servant of the Lord and leader among the Saints, always an example of faith and endurance amid affliction.

Teachings of John Taylor

Trials are necessary for our perfection.

It is necessary men should be tried and purged and purified and made perfect through suffering. And hence we find men in the different ages that have passed through trials and afflictions of every kind, and they had to learn to put their faith in God, and in God alone.[7]

We have learned many things through suffering. We call it suffering. I call it a school of experience. I never did bother my head much about these things. I do not today. What are these things for? Why is it that good men should be tried? . . . I have never looked at these things in any other light than trials for the purpose of purifying the Saints of God that they may be, as the scriptures say, as gold that has been seven times purified by the fire.[8]

We complain sometimes about our trials. We need not do that. These are things that are necessary for our perfection. We think sometimes that we are not rightly treated, and I think we think correctly about some of these things. We think there are plots set on foot to entrap us; and I think we think so very correctly. At the same time we need not be astonished at these things. We need not be amazed at a feeling of hatred and animosity. Why? Because we are living in a peculiar day and age of the world; which is distinctively called the latter days.[9]

I know that as other men we have our trials, afflictions, sorrows, and privations. We meet with difficulties; we have to contend with the world, with the powers of darkness, with the corruptions of men, and a variety of evils; yet at the same time through these things we have to be made perfect. It is necessary that we should have a knowledge of ourselves, of our true position and standing before God, and comprehend our strength and weakness; our ignorance and intelligence, our wisdom and our folly, that we may know how to appreciate true principles, and comprehend and put a proper value upon all things as they present themselves before our minds.

It is necessary that we should know our own weaknesses, and the weaknesses of our fellow men; our own strength as well as the strength of others; and comprehend our true position before God, angels, and men; that we may be inclined to treat all with due respect, and not to over value our own wisdom or strength, nor depreciate it, nor that of others; but put our trust in the living God, and follow after him, and realise that we are his children, and that he is our Father, and that our dependence is upon him, and that every blessing we receive flows from his beneficent hand.[10]

Peter in speaking of [trials], said: "Beloved, think it not strange concerning the fiery trial which is to try you, as though some strange thing happened unto you: But rejoice, inasmuch as ye are partakers of Christ's sufferings; that, when his glory shall be revealed, ye may be glad also with exceeding joy." [1 Peter 4:12–13.] He might just as well have told them that it would be so, so long as there was a God in heaven, and a devil in hell; and it is absolutely necessary that it should be so. Concerning these matters I do not have any trouble. What if we have to suffer affliction! We came here for that purpose; we came in order that we might be purified; and this is intended to give us a knowledge of God, of our weakness and strength; of our corruptions, . . . to give us a knowledge of eternal life, that we may be enabled to overcome all evil and be exalted to thrones of power and glory.[11]

The Savior fully comprehends our trials.

It was necessary that he [Christ] should have a body like ours, and be made subject to all the weaknesses of the flesh, that the devil should be let loose upon him, and that he should be tried like other men. Then again, in Gethsemane, he was left alone, and so great was the struggle that, we are told, he sweat, as it were, great drops of blood [see Luke 22:44]. In the great day when he was about to sacrifice his life, he said, "My God, my God, why hast thou forsaken me?" [Matthew 27:46.] He has passed through all this, and when he sees you passing through these trials and afflictions, he knows how to feel towards you—how to sympathize with you.[12]

It was necessary when the Savior was upon the earth, that he "should be tempted in all points like unto us," and "be touched with the feelings of our infirmities," [see Hebrews 4:15] to comprehend the weaknesses and strength; the perfections and imperfections of poor fallen human nature; and having accomplished the thing he came into the world to do, having had to grapple with the hypocrisy, corruption, weakness, and imbecility of man—having met with temptation and trial in all its various forms, and overcome, he has become "A faithful high priest" [see Hebrews 2:17] to intercede for us in the everlasting kingdom of his Father. He knows how to estimate, and put a proper value upon human nature, for he, having been placed in the same position as we were, knows how to bear with our weaknesses and infirmities, and can fully comprehend the depth, power, and strength of the afflictions and trials that men have to cope with in this world, and thus understandingly and by experience, he can bear with them as a father and an elder brother.[13]

We will be blessed if we endure our trials with patience and obedience.

In all these events which are now taking place we recognize and acknowledge the hand of God. There is a wise purpose in it all, which He will yet more fully make plain to us. One thing is clear, the Saints are being tried in a manner never before known among us. The faithful rejoice and are steadfast; the unfaithful fear and tremble. Those who have oil in their lamps and have kept them trimmed and burning now have a light for their feet and they do not stumble or fall; those who have neither light nor oil are in perplexity and doubt; they know not what to do. Is not this the fulfillment of the word of God and the teachings of His servants? Have not the Latter-day Saints been taught all the day long that, if they would remain faithful and endure to the end, they must live their religion by keeping every commandment of God? Have they not been continually warned of the fate which awaited them if they committed sin? Can adulterers, fornicators, liars, thieves, drunkards, Sabbath breakers, blasphemers, or sinners of any kind endure the trials, which Saints must pass through and expect to stand? . . .

If all who call themselves Latter-day Saints were true and faithful to their God, to His holy covenants and laws, and were living as Saints should, persecution would roll off from us without disturbing us in the least. But it is painful to know that this is not their condition. . . . He has also said that if His people will obey His laws and keep His commandments, to do them, not in name only, but in reality, He will be their shield and protector and strong tower, and no man will be able to hurt them, for He will be their defense. These trials of our faith and constancy which we are now passing through will be overruled for our good and future prosperity. In days to come we shall be able to look back

Saved by his pocket watch from a bullet in 1844, President Taylor lived several more decades and taught the Saints much about the purpose of trials.

and perceive with clearness how visibly God's providence is in all that we now witness. Let us do all in our power to so live before the Lord that if we are persecuted, it shall not be for wrong-doing, but for righteousness.[14]

Do you not see the necessity of these trials and afflictions and scenes we have to pass through? It is the Lord who puts us in positions that are the most calculated to promote the best interest of his people. My opinion is that, far from these things that now surround us being an injury to us and the kingdom of God, they will give it one of the greatest hoists [or lifts] that it has ever had yet, and all is right and all will be right if we keep the commandments of God. What is the position, then, that we ought to occupy—every man, woman and child? Do our duty before God, honor him, and all is right. And concerning events yet to transpire, we must trust them in the hands of God and feel that whatever is, is right, and that God will control all things for our best good and the interest of his church and kingdom on the earth. . . .

If we have to pass through affliction, all right. By and bye, when we come to gaze on the fitness of things that are now obscure to us, we shall find that God, although he has moved in a mysterious way to accomplish his purposes on the earth and his purposes relative to us as individuals and as families, all things are governed by that wisdom which flows from God and all things are right and calculated to promote every person's eternal welfare before God.[15]

We say to all the Latter-day Saints, these trials through which we are now passing will have the effect to prove the Saints and those who are only Saints in name. Those who have been careful to keep oil in their lamps, now have the needed light to guide them; and those who have been living in borrowed light, or in that furnished by others, may find themselves in perplexity and uncertain as to the path to pursue. For all these circumstances the Saints should be prepared. They have been faithfully taught and warned to not depend upon man or upon his strength to enable them to stand the trying day. They have been told, "Love not the world, neither the things that are in the world. If any man love the world, the love of the Father is not in him." [1 John 2:15.] They have been told that no man can serve two masters; that we cannot serve God and mammon [see Luke 16:13]. Those who have observed these teachings, and have diligently kept the other commandments of the Lord, will find themselves in the possession of the needed strength and faith to enable them to bear every trial.[16]

I rejoice in afflictions, for they are necessary to humble and prove us, that we may comprehend ourselves, become acquainted with our weakness and infirmities; and I rejoice when I triumph over them, because God answers my prayers; therefore I feel to rejoice all the day long.[17]

Suggestions for Study and Discussion

- What are some of the purposes of trials? Why is adversity not withheld from the righteous?

- How would your life be different if you had no trials or hardships? What have you learned about yourself and about God from the things that you have suffered?
- Reflect on your current trials. How can your attitude about your trials change the way you endure or overcome them? How might you improve the way you face your trials?
- Why does the Savior fully understand our suffering? (See also Alma 7:11–12; D&C 19:16–19; 122:8.) How can a knowledge of the Savior's suffering help us be faithful in our trials?
- What can we do to more fully partake of the comfort and strength that Jesus offers? (See also Hebrews 4:16; 1 Peter 5:6–11.) How have you been strengthened by the Savior's comfort during times of trial?
- Why is it sometimes difficult to remain patient and obedient when we experience adversity? How can we come to see adversity from the Lord's eternal perspective?
- What have others done to help you through your trials? How can you help others during their trials? What have you learned from President Taylor's teachings that you could share with someone who is experiencing trials?

Related Scriptures: Psalm 34:19; 2 Corinthians 4:8–18; 1 Peter 4:12–13; Alma 36:3; Ether 12:6; D&C 121:7–8

Notes

1. *Deseret News: Semi-Weekly,* 9 Aug. 1857, 1.
2. See B. H. Roberts, *The Life of John Taylor* (1963), 146.
3. See *The Life of John Taylor,* 148–49.
4. *The Life of John Taylor,* 169.
5. See *The Life of John Taylor,* 389–91, 400.
6. *The Life of John Taylor,* 391–92.
7. *Deseret News: Semi-Weekly,* 14 Oct. 1879, 1.
8. *Deseret News: Semi-Weekly,* 28 Oct. 1884, 1.
9. *Deseret News: Semi-Weekly,* 28 Oct. 1884, 1.
10. *Deseret News* (Weekly), 26 Jan. 1854, 1.
11. *Deseret News* (Weekly), 11 Apr. 1860, 41.
12. *Deseret News* (Weekly), 11 Apr. 1860, 41–42.
13. *Deseret News* (Weekly), 26 Jan. 1854, 1–2.
14. In James R. Clark, comp., *Messages of the First Presidency of The Church of Jesus Christ of Latter-day Saints,* 6 vols. [1965–75], 3:36–37; paragraphing altered.
15. *Deseret News* (Weekly), 16 Dec. 1857, 324; paragraphing altered.
16. In *Messages of the First Presidency,* 3:17.
17. *The Gospel Kingdom,* sel. G. Homer Durham (1943), 234.

CHAPTER 23

Eternal Truth

There is nothing of more value to me than the principles of eternal truth.[1]

From the Life of John Taylor

One of John Taylor's most admirable qualities was his devotion to the truth, no matter what opinion others held. "The praise or censure of the world had little influence over the mind of John Taylor where truth was concerned," wrote Elder B. H. Roberts. "The more men despised [truth], the more intense seemed his devotion."[2] The events surrounding John Taylor's conversion to the gospel provide one of the earliest examples of his love of truth.

John Taylor was introduced to the gospel by Parley P. Pratt in Canada. Elder Pratt's teachings delighted John Taylor and his religious friends, who had similar beliefs concerning such ordinances as baptism by immersion and the laying on of hands for the gift of the Holy Ghost. However, when Elder Pratt told them about Joseph Smith and the Book of Mormon, many of John Taylor's friends hesitated to learn more, and some even refused to investigate the Book of Mormon and its teachings. With boldness, John Taylor addressed the group as follows:

"We are here, ostensibly in search of truth. Hitherto we have fully investigated other creeds and doctrines and proven them false. Why should we fear to investigate Mormonism? This gentleman, Mr. Pratt, has brought to us many doctrines that correspond with our own views. . . . We have prayed to God to send us a messenger, if He has a true Church on earth. Mr. Pratt has come to us . . . without purse or scrip, as the ancient apostles traveled; and none of us are able to refute his doctrine by scripture or logic. I desire to investigate his doctrines and claims to

"While others are content with chaff and husks, . . . [the man of God] seizes on the kernel, substance, [and] the gist of all that's good."

authority. . . . If I find his religion true, I shall accept it, no matter what the consequences may be." John Taylor's thorough investigation resulted in his baptism on 9 May 1836. He later stated, "I have never doubted any principle of Mormonism since."[3]

As a member and leader in the Church, John Taylor could always be relied on to teach and defend the truth. "He proclaimed the gospel in many lands; and as the champion of truth, stood ready to meet all who assailed it; and whether he met his opponents in the forum, before a multitude steeped full of prejudice against him, or in the columns of the public press, he was equally successful in vanquishing them by his powerful statement of the truth."[4]

Teachings of John Taylor

Those who love truth are blessed with knowledge and power.

Standing upon its broad platform, encircled by the mantle of truth, the man of God, by faith, peers into the future, withdraws the curtains of eternity, unveils the mystery of the heavens, and through the dark vista of unnumbered years, beholds the purposes of the great Elohim, as they roll forth in all their majesty and power and glory. Thus standing upon a narrow neck of space, and beholding the past, present, and the future, he sees himself an eternal being claiming an affinity with God, a son of God, a spark of Deity struck from the fire of his eternal blaze. He looks upon the world and man, in all their various phases, knows his true interests, and with intelligence imparted by his Father Celestial, he comprehends their origin and destiny. . . .

His intelligence, lit up by God and followed out, will be expansive as the world and spread through space; his law is the law of love; his rule, the rule of right to all. He loves his neighbor, and he does him good; he loves his God and therefore worships him; he sees the power of truth, which, like the light of God, spreads through all space, illuminates all worlds, and penetrates where men or angels, God or spheres are known; he clings to it. Truth is his helmet, buckler, shield, his rock, defense; his all in time and in eternity. Men call him a fool because he cannot be directed by their folly, nor follow in their erratic, truculent wake. But while they are grasping at shadows, he lays hold of the substance. While they are content with a rickety, sprawling religion, fashionable for a time, but having nothing to do with eternity, and smother the highest, noblest principles of man, he dare acknowledge God; and acknowledging him, he dare obey him and confess that faith which God has given to him. He grasps at all truths, human and divine. He has no darling dogma to sustain or favorite creed to uphold. He has nothing to lose but error, and nothing to gain but truth. He digs, labors, and searches for it as for hidden treasure; and while others are content with chaff and husks of straw, he seizes on the kernel, substance, the gist of all that's good, and clings to all that will ennoble and exalt the human family. . . .

Did ancient men of God revel in the truth? So do we. Did they have revelations and visions? So do we. Did they prophesy? So do we. Did God communicate with them? He does with us. Did they prophesy of "the restitution of all things?" [See Acts 3:21.] We say it is at our doors. Did they prophesy of a kingdom of God? We are helping to build it up. Had they the ministering of angels? So have we. Had they prophets, apostles, pastors, teachers, and evangelists? So have we. Had they the spirit of prophecy and revelation? So have we. Did they look for the second advent and glorious appearance of our Lord and Savior Jesus Christ? So do we. Did they expect that God would purge the wicked out of the earth and introduce a reign of righteousness? So do we. Did they look for Jesus and the saints to reign on the earth? So do we. We are, in fact, looking for all things that they did; seeking to know all things that they knew, and to bring to pass all things that they prophesied of, the great consummation of which is the restitution of all things; and men may lie and rant and rave; they cannot frustrate the designs of God, nor stop the progress of eternal truth one moment—its course is *onward,* ONWARD, ONWARD, and it defies opposition. . . .

The omnipotent power of eternal truth will stand unscathed in the view of gathering hosts, and the nations will know that God rules in the heavens.[5]

Truth, eternal truth, is the groundwork of the Christian's hope: it is the only sure rock on which he can build. Forsaking that to support some favourite dogma, he falls into the mazes of infidelity, scepticism, error, and delusion, and is on the highway to destruction. The power of God will always attend those who love the truth and keep it.[6]

The gospel will lead us from truth to truth.

The gospel is calculated to lead us on from truth to truth and from intelligence to intelligence, until that scripture will be fulfilled which declares that we shall see as we are seen and know as we are known [see D&C 76:94], until one will not have to say to another, know ye the Lord, but all shall know Him from the least unto the greatest [see Jeremiah 31:34], until the light and intelligence of God shall beam forth upon all, and all shall bask in the sunlight of eternal truth.[7]

In regard to our religion, I will say that it embraces every principle of truth and intelligence pertaining to us as moral, intellectual, mortal and immortal beings, pertaining to this world and the world that is to come. We are open to truth of every kind, no matter whence it comes, where it originates, or who believes in it. Truth, when preceded by the little word "all," comprises everything that has ever existed or that ever will exist and be known by and among men in time and through the endless ages of eternity. And it is the duty of all intelligent beings who are responsible and amenable to God for their acts, to search after truth, and to permit it to influence them and their acts and general course in life, independent of all bias or preconceived notions, however specious and plausible they may be.

We, as Latter-day Saints, believe, first, in the gospel, and that is a great deal to say, for the gospel embraces principles that dive deeper, spread wider, and extend further than anything else that we can conceive. The gospel teaches us in regard to the being and attributes of God. It also teaches us our relationship to that God and the various responsibilities we are under to him as his offspring. It teaches us the various duties and responsibilities that we are under to our families and friends, to the community, to the living and the dead. It unfolds to us principles pertaining to futurity. In fact, according to the saying of one of the old disciples, it "brings life and immortality to light" [see 2 Timothy 1:10], brings us into relationship with God, and prepares us for an exaltation in the eternal world.[8]

God has revealed unto us great and glorious truths, and He is prepared to reveal more if we will only place ourselves under His guidance and His direction. Let us seek to follow the principle that Jesus inculcated—to do the will of our Father who is in heaven, who said, "I seek not mine own will, but the will of the Father which hath sent me." [John 5:30.] We are here as much as He was here, and under obligations as He was to do the will of our Heavenly Father. We should subject ourselves to the law of God, the word of God, and the will of God.[9]

We must not be afraid to sacrifice for the sake of truth.

Truth has always been opposed by the children of men, it comes in contact with the corrupt hearts and wicked practices. The Prophets have always been persecuted; and why? because they dared to tell the word of the Lord to the people. Stephen, in speaking on the same subjects, says, "Which of the Prophets have not your forefathers killed who testified before of the coming of the Just One, of whom ye have been the betrayers and murderers?" [See Acts 7:52.] "But in this age," say the people, "we know they were wicked and we would not have done that." So said the Jews to Jesus, and yet they crucified him. . . .

The Lord has restored the Gospel as it existed in the Apostle's days. This Gospel does not agree with the systems of men, which are conflicting and various; and instead of acknowledging, as honest men, the truths contained in the Bible, which they profess to believe, but, in reality do not, they try to cover over their tottering systems and unscriptural theories, to wrap themselves in their cloak of self-righteousness. . . . But truth will roll forth; the honest in heart will be aroused from their slumber; the purposes of God will roll forth; the kingdom of God will be established, and . . . truth will stand proud and erect, . . . and no power can stay its progress.[10]

I will now tell you about some of my feelings when I first came into this church. It is a long while ago. When I first heard the gospel, I was compelled to admit there was something reasonable about it. I almost hoped it was not true. "If it is true," said I, "as an honest man I shall be obliged to obey it, or else I cannot have any confidence in myself." When I had investigated the subject, and became convinced that it was true, I said, "I am in for it; I must embrace it; I cannot reject the principles of eternal truth." And I will say, moreover, I don't know of a time in my life when, if anybody presented a truth that could not be controverted, but I was ready to obey it and I am today.

If any person in the religious world, or the political world, or the scientific world, will present to me a principle that is true, I am prepared to receive it, no matter where it comes from. Well, says one, you believe the Bible? Yes. You believe in the Book of Mormon? Yes. You believe the Book of Doctrine and Covenants? Yes. I believe all that God has ever written or spoken, everything that we have on record, and I am prepared to believe everything that he will communicate to the human family. We profess to believe in all truth, and to be governed by all truth.[11]

I expected when I came into this church, that I should be persecuted and proscribed. I expected that the people would be persecuted. But I believed that God had spoken, that the eternal principles of truth had been revealed, and that God had a work to accomplish which was in opposition to the ideas, views, and notions of men, and I did not know but it would cost me my life before I got through. . . . If they killed Jesus in former times, would not the same feeling and influence bring about the same results in these times? I had counted the cost when I first started out, and stood prepared to meet it.[12]

The Lord, through simple means, is able to take care of and deliver his people, but they must put implicit faith and confidence in him; and when they are crowded into a tight place they must not be afraid to make sacrifice for the sake of maintaining the truth, and all will be well with us whether living or dying, in time or in eternity.[13]

We must continue to search for and embrace truth.

We are after the truth. We commenced searching for it, and we are constantly in search of it, and so fast as we find any true principle revealed by any man, by God, or by holy angels, we embrace it and make it part of our religious creed.[14]

A man in search of truth has no peculiar system to sustain, no peculiar dogma to defend or theory to uphold. He embraces all truth, and that truth, like the sun in the firmament, shines forth and spreads its effulgent rays over all creation. If men will divest themselves of bias and prejudice, and prayerfully and conscientiously search after truth, they will find it wherever they turn their attention.[15]

One great reason why men have stumbled so frequently in many of their researches after philosophical truth is that they have sought them with their own wisdom, and gloried in their own intelligence, and have not sought unto God for that wisdom that fills and governs the universe and regulates all things. That is one great difficulty with the philosophers of the world, as it now exists, that man claims to himself to be the inventor of everything he discovers. Any new law and principle which he happens to discover he claims to himself instead of giving glory to God.[16]

There is nothing of more value to me than the principles of eternal truth; than the principles of eternal lives; eternal salvation, and eternal exaltations in the kingdom of God. But then it is for us to comprehend them, for if we do not comprehend them, no matter how great the truths, they cannot benefit us.[17]

We are open for the reception of all truth, of whatever nature it may be, and are desirous to obtain and possess it, to search after it as we would for hidden treasures; and to use all the knowledge God gives to us to possess ourselves of all the intelligence that he has given to others; and to ask at his hands to reveal unto us his will, in regard to things that are the best calculated to promote the happiness and well-being of human society.

If there are any good principles, any moral philosophy that we have not yet attained to, we are desirous to learn them. If there is anything in the scientific world that we do not yet comprehend, we desire to become acquainted with it. If there is any branch of philosophy calculated to promote the well-being of humanity, that we have not yet grasped, we wish to possess ourselves of it. If there is anything pertaining to the rule and government of nations, or politics, if you please, that we are not acquainted with, we desire to possess it. If there are any religious ideas, any theological truths, any principles pertaining to God, that we have not learned, we ask mankind, and we pray God, our Heavenly Father, to enlighten our minds that we may comprehend, realize, embrace, and live up to them as part of our religious faith. Thus our ideas and thoughts would extend as far as the wide world spreads, embracing everything pertaining to light, life, or existence pertaining to this world or the world that is to come. . . . They would soar after the intelligence of the Gods that dwell in the eternal worlds. They would grasp everything that is good and noble and excellent and happifying and calculated to promote the well-being of the human family.

There is no man nor set of men who have pointed out the pathway for our feet to travel in, in relation to these matters. There are no dogmas nor theories extant in the world that we profess to listen to, unless they can be verified by the principles of eternal truth. We carefully scan, investigate, criticize, and examine everything that presents itself to our view, and so far as we are enabled to comprehend any truths in existence, we gladly hail them as part and portion of the system with which we are associated.[18]

If there is any truth in heaven, earth, or hell, I want to embrace it; I care not what shape it comes in to me, who brings it, or who believes in it; whether it is popular or unpopular, truth, eternal truth, I wish to float in and enjoy.[19]

Suggestions for Study and Discussion

- What sources of eternal truth do we have? How can you improve the way you respond to these sources?
- How does the gospel lead us "from truth to truth"? What changes have you noticed in your life as you learn and accept new truths?

- What sacrifices have you or others you know made for the sake of truth? What blessings came because of this?
- Many of God's people have died for the truth. How can we *live* for the truth with the same dedication and devotion?
- Why do you think eternal truth is frequently opposed by the world in general? What can we do to help children recognize and accept eternal truth? What can we do as families to strengthen our commitment to the truth?
- Why is it important to continually increase our understanding of the truth? In what ways can we follow President Taylor's counsel to continue to search for truth? How can we discern truth from error?
- What are some gospel truths that you find especially inspiring and strengthening? How can you as a member of the Church help others understand and embrace truth?

Related Scriptures: Philippians 4:8; 1 Thessalonians 5:21; Alma 32:28–29; Moroni 10:4–5; D&C 45:57; 93:24; Articles of Faith 1:13

Notes

1. *The Gospel Kingdom,* sel. G. Homer Durham (1943), 48.
2. B. H. Roberts, *The Life of John Taylor* (1963), iv.
3. *The Life of John Taylor,* 37–38.
4. *The Life of John Taylor,* 20.
5. *The Gospel Kingdom,* 1–3.
6. K. Groves, *Three Nights' Public Discussion between the Revds. C. W. Cleeve, James Robertson, and Philip Later, and Elder John Taylor, of the Church of Jesus Christ of Latter-day Saints* (1850), 28.
7. *Deseret News: Semi-Weekly,* 16 May 1866, 2.
8. *The Gospel Kingdom,* 93.
9. *Deseret News: Semi-Weekly,* 10 June 1884, 1.
10. K. Groves, *Three Nights' Public Discussion,* 6–7.
11. *The Gospel Kingdom,* 369; paragraphing altered.
12. *The Gospel Kingdom,* 369–70.
13. *The Gospel Kingdom,* 355.
14. *The Gospel Kingdom,* 47.
15. *The Gospel Kingdom,* 94.
16. *The Gospel Kingdom,* 47.
17. *The Gospel Kingdom,* 48.
18. *The Gospel Kingdom,* 48–49; paragraphing altered.
19. *Deseret News* (Weekly), 26 Jan. 1854, 2.

CHAPTER 24

The Kingdom of God

We are laying the foundation of a kingdom that shall last forever;—that shall bloom in time and blossom in eternity. We are engaged in a greater work than ever occupied the attention of mortals.[1]

From the Life of John Taylor

John Taylor firmly believed that the kingdom of God would be established on earth. He understood that this effort was not dependent on the Prophet Joseph Smith or any other man, but that it was ultimately directed by the Lord. And he was ready to defend this effort with his life.

In 1838, soon after his call to the Quorum of the Twelve, John Taylor traveled toward Far West, Missouri, to join the Saints. Along the way, he was scheduled to speak to a group near Columbus, Ohio. A little before the appointed time, some brethren brought news that a number of men had gathered at the meeting place and were plotting to tar and feather Elder Taylor. The brethren advised him to cancel the meeting because they were outnumbered and would not be able to protect him. However, Elder Taylor insisted he would go and preach as planned and would do so even if he had to go by himself.

When he reached the large crowd assembled to hear him, he proceeded to speak first about his having recently come from countries ruled by monarchs. He told them about the honor he felt of standing on free soil. In reference to how that freedom was achieved, he said: "Gentlemen, I now stand among men whose fathers fought for and obtained one of the greatest blessings ever conferred upon the human family—the right to think, to speak, to write; the right to say who shall govern them, and

Even in the face of opposition, John Taylor testified boldly of the truth and worked tirelessly for the establishment of the kingdom of God.

the right to worship God according to the dictates of their own consciences—all of them sacred, human rights, and now guaranteed by the American Constitution. I see around me the sons of those noble sires, who, rather than bow to the behests of a tyrant, pledged their lives, fortunes and sacred honors to burst those fetters, enjoy freedom themselves, bequeath it to their posterity, or die in the attempt."

Elder Taylor then continued: "But, by the by, I have been informed that you purpose to tar and feather me, for my religious opinions. Is this the boon you have inherited from your fathers? Is this the blessing they purchased with their dearest hearts' blood—this your liberty? If so, you now have a victim, and we will have an offering to the goddess of liberty."

Having said that, he tore open his vest and exclaimed: "Gentlemen come on with your tar and feathers, your victim is ready; and ye shades of the venerable patriots, gaze upon the deeds of your degenerate sons! Come on, gentlemen! Come on, I say, I am ready!" Elder Taylor paused for a few minutes, but no one would move or speak. He then continued his remarks and preached to the crowd with boldness and power for three hours.[2]

As Elder Matthias F. Cowley of the Quorum of the Twelve said many years later after the death of President Taylor, "He lived, labored and died the perfect exemplification of his favored motto, 'The Kingdom of God or nothing.' "[3]

Teachings of John Taylor

The earth is the Lord's and He is its rightful ruler, judge, and king.

Who made this earth? The Lord. Who sustains it? The Lord. Who feeds and clothes the millions of the human family that exist upon it, both Saint and sinner? The Lord. Who upholds everything in the universe? The Lord. . . . Who has given to man understanding? The Lord. Who has given to the gentile philosopher, machinist, etc., every particle of intelligence they have with regard to the electric telegraph, the power and application of steam to the wants of the human family and every kind of invention that has been brought to light during the last century? The Lord. . . . Who has a right to rule the nations, to control kingdoms and govern all the people of the earth?[4]

This earth is properly the dwelling place, and rightful inheritance of the Saints. Inasmuch as it belongs to Jesus Christ, it also belongs to his servants and followers, for we are told, "The earth is the Lord's, and the fulness thereof," [Psalm 24:1] and that, when things are in their proper place, "the Saints of the Most High shall take the kingdom, and possess the kingdom, and the greatness of the kingdom under the whole heaven, shall be given to the saints of the Most High." [See Daniel 7:18, 27.] It is therefore their rightful inheritance.[5]

The Scriptures . . . represent Christ as being the rightful heir, and inheritor of this world; they represent him as having come once to atone for the sins of the world; but that he will afterwards come as its ruler, judge, and king.[6]

The Church represents the introduction of the kingdom of God on the earth.

The kingdom of God means the government of God. That means, power, authority, rule, dominion, and a people to rule over. But that principle will not be fulfilled, cannot be entirely fulfilled, until, as we are told in the scriptures, the kingdoms of this world are become the kingdoms of our Lord and his Christ, and he will rule over them [see Revelation 11:15], and when unto him every knee shall bow and every tongue confess that he is Christ [see D&C 88:104], to the glory of God, the Father. That time has not yet come, but there are certain principles associated therewith that have come; namely, the introduction of that kingdom, and the introduction of that kingdom could only be made by that Being who is the King and Ruler, and the Head of that government, first communicating his ideas, his principles, his laws, his government to the people. Otherwise we should not know what his laws were.[7]

What is the first thing necessary for the establishment of his kingdom? It is to raise up a prophet and have him declare the will of God; the next thing is to have a people yield obedience to the hand of the Lord through that prophet. If you cannot have these, you never can establish the kingdom of God upon the earth.[8]

God was desirous of introducing his kingdom upon the earth, and he had, in the first place, to organize his church, to organize the people that he had scattered among the nations and to bring them together, that there might be one fold and one shepherd [see John 10:16], and one Lord, one faith, and one baptism, and one God, who should be in all and through all [see Ephesians 4:5–6], and by which all should be governed. To facilitate this object, he organized his holy priesthood as it existed in the heavens.[9]

We talk sometimes about the church of God, and why? We talk about the kingdom of God, and why? Because, before there could be a kingdom of God, there must be a church of God, and hence the first principles of the gospel were needed to be preached to all nations, as they were formerly when the Lord Jesus Christ and others made their appearance on the earth. And why so? Because of the impossibility of introducing the law of God among a people who would not be subject to and be guided by the spirit of revelation.[10]

God could not build up a kingdom on the earth unless he had a church and a people who had submitted to his law and were willing to submit to it; and with an organization of such a people, gathered from among the nations of the earth under the direction of a man inspired of God, the mouthpiece of Jehovah to his people; I say that, with such an organization, there is a chance for the Lord God to be revealed, there is an opportunity for the laws of life to be made manifest, there is a chance for God to introduce the principles of heaven upon the earth and for the will of God to be done upon earth as it is done in heaven.[11]

Jesus Christ will yet fully establish His kingdom and reign on the earth.

"Thy kingdom come." [Matthew 6:10.] . . . This was taught by Jesus to his disciples when they came to him, saying, teach us to pray. . . . Thy kingdom come. What kingdom? What is the meaning

When Christ returns to establish His kingdom on earth, He will usher in "a kingdom of peace, righteousness, justice, happiness, and prosperity."

of "thy kingdom come"? It means the rule of God. It means the law of God. It means the government of God. It means the people who have listened to and who are willing to listen to and observe the commands of Jehovah. And it means that there is a God who is willing to guide and direct and sustain his people. Thy kingdom come, that thy government may be established, and the principles of eternal truth as they exist in the heavens may be imparted to men; and that, when they are imparted to men, those men may be in subjection to those laws and to that government, and live in the fear of God, keeping his commandments and being under his direction. Thy kingdom come, that the confusion, the evil, and wickedness, the murder and bloodshed that now exist among mankind may be done away, and the principles of truth and right, the principles of kindness, charity, and love as they dwell in the bosom of the Gods, may dwell with us.[12]

I have demonstrated . . . that the kingdom of God would be literally established on the earth. It will not be an aerial phantom, according to some visionaries, but a substantial reality. It will be established, as before said, on a literal earth, and will be composed of literal men, women, and children; of living saints who keep the commandments of God, and of resurrected bodies who shall actually come out of their graves, and live on the earth. The Lord will be king over all the earth, and all mankind literally under his sovereignty, and every nation under the heavens will have to acknowledge his authority, and bow to his scepter. Those who serve him in righteousness will have communications with God, and with Jesus; will have the ministering of angels, and will know the past, the present, and the future; and other people, who may not yield full obedience to his laws, nor be fully instructed in his covenants, will, nevertheless, have to yield full obedience to his government. For it will be the reign of God upon the earth, and he will enforce his laws, and command that obedience from the nations of the world which is legitimately his right. Satan will not then be permitted to control its inhabitants, for the Lord God will be king over all the earth, and the kingdom and greatness of the kingdom under the whole heaven will be given to the saints.[13]

What will be the effects of the establishment of Christ's kingdom, or the reign of God on the earth? . . . It is the doing away with war, bloodshed, misery, disease, and sin, and the ushering in of a kingdom of peace, righteousness, justice, happiness, and prosperity. It is the restoration of the earth and man to their primeval glory and pristine excellence; in fact, the restitution of all things spoken of by all the prophets since the world began [see Acts 3:21].[14]

The Lord has called His Saints to help establish His kingdom.

A gentleman in France commenced talking to me, and wished to know if we thought of accomplishing something great in the world? I told him we had come to preach the gospel to all the world; and that it had already reached the ends of the earth. It is not a work that will be done in a little corner, but it will reach throughout time into eternity. It will go back into eternity, and take hold of those who have died thousands of years ago, and bring them into the kingdom of God. It will pour blessings upon generations to come, and ultimately unite heaven and earth together, and this we will accomplish in the name of Israel's God. The powers of heaven lend us their aid, and our fathers in the eternal world are uniting with us; for we have the promise of the life which now is, and also that which is to come.

We have only just commenced in our glorious enterprise. By and bye we will accomplish all that the fathers have spoken. . . . We will go forth brethren, and not study our own ease, but how to bring about the accomplishment of the glorious purposes of God. . . . The power of truth has to go forth, the chains of darkness have to be severed, and the kingdom of God has to be built up, and no power can stay it.[15]

We have been talking for years about the rule and government of the kingdom of God and its final establishment upon the earth, in peace and righteousness; and also about the time when every creature which is in the heavens and on the earth, and under the earth, and such as are in the sea, and all that are in them will be heard saying, "Blessing, and honor, and glory, and power, be unto him that sitteth upon the throne, and unto the Lamb for ever and ever." (Revelation 5:13.) We have been talking about these things, but there is much to be done in the intermediate space between the present and that impenetrable period in the great future. It is not all a matter of faith, but there is some action required; it is a thing that we have got to engage in ourselves, individually and collectively as a people, and it is a matter of no small concern.[16]

We have a great mission to perform—we have to try to govern ourselves according to the laws of the kingdom of God, and we find it one of the most difficult tasks we ever undertook, to learn to govern ourselves, our appetites, our dispositions, our habits, our feelings, our lives, our spirits, our judgment, and to bring all our desires into subjection to the law of the kingdom of God and to the spirit of truth. It is a very critical thing to be engaged in the upbuilding of the kingdom of God—a nucleus of which we have here.[17]

Fear God; work the works of righteousness; live your religion; keep the commandments and humble yourselves before him; be one, and be united with the holy priesthood and with each other, and I will tell you in the name of God that Zion will arise and shine and the power of God will rest upon her; and her glory will be made manifest, and we will rejoice in the fulness of the blessings of the gospel of peace; and the work of God will go on and increase until the kingdoms of this world shall become the kingdoms of our God and his Christ [see Revelation 11:15], and every creature in the heaven and on the earth and under the earth will be heard to say, Blessing, and glory, and honor and praise and power, might and majesty and dominion be ascribed to him that sits upon the throne and to the Lamb for ever and ever [see Revelation 5:13].[18]

Suggestions for Study and Discussion

- Why is Jesus Christ the rightful heir and ruler of the earth? How should this knowledge influence your relationship with Him?
- Why was the Restoration of the Church necessary to establish the Lord's kingdom on earth? What have you learned as a member of the Church about preparing to live with the Lord? In what ways can our service in the Church contribute to establishing the Lord's kingdom?
- How have you observed the Church growing and developing to more fully establish God's kingdom on earth? What can you do individually and with your family to help establish God's kingdom on earth?
- President Taylor spoke of the great blessings we will enjoy when the Savior returns to reign over His kingdom in the Millennium. What will life on earth be like during the Millennium? (See also D&C 29:11; 43:29–32; 101:22–35; Articles of Faith 1:10.)
- President Taylor's personal motto was "The kingdom of God or nothing!" What examples have you seen of people who have this same conviction? What does this motto mean to you? What do you think would be the results if we as Church members adopted this motto as our own?

Related Scriptures: Daniel 2:26–45; Matthew 6:33; D&C 45:1; 65; 104:58–59

Notes

1. *Times and Seasons,* 15 July 1844, 578.
2. See B. H. Roberts, *The Life of John Taylor* (1963), 47, 53–55.
3. In Kate B. Carter, comp., *Our Pioneer Heritage,* 20 vols. (1958–77), 7:218.
4. *Deseret News* (Weekly), 11 Nov. 1857, 283; paragraphing altered.
5. *The Government of God* (1852), 72–73.
6. *The Government of God,* 74.
7. *The Gospel Kingdom,* sel. G. Homer Durham (1943), 205.
8. *The Gospel Kingdom,* 214.
9. *The Gospel Kingdom,* 208–9.
10. *The Gospel Kingdom,* 210.
11. *The Gospel Kingdom,* 210.
12. *The Gospel Kingdom,* 205–6.
13. *The Gospel Kingdom,* 207–8.
14. *The Gospel Kingdom,* 216; paragraphing altered.
15. *Millennial Star,* 1 Dec. 1850, 361–62; paragraphing altered.
16. *The Gospel Kingdom,* 211.
17. *The Gospel Kingdom,* 214.
18. *Deseret News: Semi-Weekly,* 27 Jan. 1880, 1.

List of Paintings

Index

I

J

K

L